Why Does College Cost So Much?

Why Does College Cost So Much?

ROBERT B. ARCHIBALD

DAVID H. FELDMAN

OXFORD
UNIVERSITY PRESS

2011

OXFORD
UNIVERSITY PRESS

Oxford University Press, Inc., publishes works that further
Oxford University's objective of excellence
in research, scholarship, and education.

Oxford   New York
Auckland   Cape Town   Dar es Salaam   Hong Kong   Karachi
Kuala Lumpur   Madrid   Melbourne   Mexico City   Nairobi
New Delhi   Shanghai   Taipei   Toronto

With offices in
Argentina   Austria   Brazil   Chile   Czech Republic   France   Greece
Guatemala   Hungary   Italy   Japan   Poland   Portugal   Singapore
South Korea   Switzerland   Thailand   Turkey   Ukraine   Vietnam

Published by Oxford University Press, Inc.
198 Madison Avenue, New York, New York 10016

www.oup.com

Oxford is a registered trademark of Oxford University Press

Library of Congress Cataloging-in-Publication Data
Archibald, Robert B., 1946–
Why does college cost so much? /
Robert B. Archibald, David H. Feldman.
p. cm.
Includes bibliographical references and index.
ISBN 978-0-19-974450-3
1. College costs—United States.   2. Education, Higher—United
States—Finance.   I. Feldman, David Henry.   II. Title.
LB2342.A685 2011
378.3'80973—dc22   2010007925

9 8 7
Printed in the United States of America
on acid-free paper

To our families:
Nancy Vincent, Brian Archibald, Emily Archibald,
and Ben Paradise
Susan Lontkowski, Anthony Feldman, and Aidan Feldman

Preface

This book is the result of ten years of active collaboration and perhaps
twenty years of ruminations. We both teach in the economics department
of the College of William and Mary. While it may be a surprise to some
readers, William and Mary is a state-supported institution. Over the
years we have watched the economic fortunes of the Commonwealth of
Virginia ebb and flow. The fortunes of the college followed a similar
pattern with one glaring exception. Dips in the Virginia economy were
always followed by recoveries taking the state to new economic highs.
On the other hand, the share of the cost of running William and Mary
covered by the commonwealth would shrink when the economy dipped,
but with the recoveries the state's share of the bill did not return to its old
levels. The finances of the college were slowly and somewhat erratically
being privatized. Wags started to say that we used to be "state supported" but now we are "state assisted," and visibly on the horizon we
can see the outlines of a time when we will be only "state located." Such
talk annoys governors and state legislators. They counter that with
economic recovery the actual dollar contributions of the commonwealth
did return to and then surpass old levels. They argue that the share of the
budget covered by the commonwealth only shrank because the costs of
running William and Mary had grown so rapidly.

The College of William and Mary may be special in many ways, but
this story is not an example of one of them. Most state universities are
slowly being privatized as their costs grow more rapidly than state
support. And the rapid growth in costs is not a public-institution

phenomenon. Private institutions also regularly experience increases in costs that outstrip the inflation rate.

Our ruminations about the economic condition of the college and about higher education in general eventually launched us on a serious collaborative research program. This program has led to a series of research papers, policy analyses, and opinion articles on the economics of higher education broadly construed. The big question about higher education cost was in the back of our minds all the time. Some of our work looked at costs directly, but other articles were more tangential (on college graduation rates, for instance). As we continued our research, the big picture became clearer to us, and we decided to take on a larger project. Writing this book has allowed us to bring together a decade's worth of reading, thinking, and writing about why college costs rise so rapidly.

In many ways, our work reflects who we are, so it is important to explain our viewpoint. Our first premise is that the study of higher education cost does not require us to park what we know about economics at the door. We study colleges and universities as economic entities, and we think of higher education as an industry. Incentives are very important shapers of behavior and the structure and workings of markets exert an important influence on incentives. Experience tells us that some readers are quite uncomfortable with this approach. They often recoil at the idea that higher education is a mere industry. To them, higher education serves a higher purpose, so it shouldn't be compared directly to other earthier industries that fulfill baser needs. Alternatively, we hear that adopting an economic approach requires one to consider professors as laborers and students as customers in some oversimplified way. Both of these views reflect preconceived notions of how economists operate and of what the discipline of economics studies. We think that the viewpoint provided by the economics discipline is useful, and we hope those who read this book will agree.

A second strongly held belief of ours is that evidence is very important. The question on which we focus is why higher education costs consistently rise faster than the inflation rate. No answer to this question is possible without a cogent story, but no story about a question as complex as ours can be compelling without rigorous evidence. Anecdotes are a time-honored way to bolster an argument, and the higher education literature is full of anecdotal evidence. To a certain extent, this is the use of particular stories in support of more general stories. While we are not shy about using a few anecdotes ourselves, a meaningful look at the college-cost question requires that we examine real data, and as it turns out, lots of data. Also, the question of why college costs rise more rapidly than prices in general is inherently comparative. We cannot answer it simply by looking at the higher education industry in splendid isolation. We must situate higher education within the overall economy. This is why we must bring our tools of economic analysis to the party.

We recognize that many people will think that a book by economists featuring lots of data has the curb appeal of a broken-down tricycle. These are the people we tried to keep in mind as we wrote the book. Colleges and universities have professional leaders: presidents, provosts, and deans, and they have lay leaders: members of college governing boards, state commissions, and state legislators. And college leaders are not the only ones interested in higher education finance. Students and their parents have a big stake in the outcomes of decisions about how to finance a college education. We want our book to appeal to this broad audience. The issues we talk about are too important to hide behind economic jargon and complicated statistics. We are teachers, so when we need to use some economics, we teach it. Readers should walk away knowing a little more about economics and a lot more about why higher education costs rise so rapidly.

Many people helped us along the way. First, we make no claims to theoretical innovation. We do string some theories together differently than others have done, and we are a bit creative about the data we use, but we are inventing no new theories. In the text and in the notes, we have made every effort to indicate our intellectual debts. We have leaned particularly heavily on the work of William Baumol of Princeton University and New York University. Also, a recent book by Claudia Goldin and Lawrence Katz of Harvard University helped us immensely. Second, our colleagues at William and Mary have been very helpful. Students in Professor Archibald's "Seminar on the Economics of Higher Education" have read and commented on various portions of the manuscript. We would like to particularly thank Caitlin Coffey, Hans Leonard, and Maxim Lott who gave us detailed comments on early versions of the manuscript. W. Taylor Reveley, president of the college; Michael Halleran, provost; Davison Douglas, dean of the law school; and Eric Jensen, director of the Thomas Jefferson Program in Public Policy, all provided useful comments. Others outside the college also were very helpful. We would like to particularly thank Sandy Baum, professor emeriti of economics at Skidmore College and senior policy analyst at the College Board, for her many useful comments. Edward Tower of Duke University also was kind enough to read a portion of the manuscript, and Isaac Yates helped us with the cover design.

Contents

PART I
Introduction

1

The Landscape of the College Cost Debate

The ongoing college cost explosion is a disturbing trend, and one that cannot be allowed to continue. After all, education is the great equalizer in our nation. It can bridge social, economic, racial, and geographic divides like no other force. It can mean the difference between an open door and a dead end. And nowhere is this truer than in higher education.
— *John A. Boehner and Howard P. "Buck" McKeon (2003)*

Early in September of 1960, two tired-looking parents from northern Ohio rolled into Williamsburg, Virginia, ready to move their son into the assigned dorm for his freshman year at the College of William and Mary. The family passed by the Sir Christopher Wren Building, the oldest academic building still in use in the United States. They glanced across the street at Colonial Williamsburg. They had visited the restored colonial town three years earlier during the 350th anniversary of the English settlement at Jamestown, and the visit had sparked a family interest in William and Mary. The drive from Ohio had been long and taxing. Good roads ran out well before they reached Williamsburg. Even though it was a public university, the year at William and Mary was going to be expensive. Tuition and fees were $722 for an out-of-state student. Room and board would cost even more, $782 for the full year.[1] The total bill of $1,504 would stretch the family finances.

Twenty-one years later, another set of parents from Ohio brought their child, this time a daughter, on a similar trip. The son from the first trip was a family friend, and he had raved about his William and Mary education. William and Mary became the daughter's first-choice school. Since William and Mary had moved up its starting date, her trip was in late August instead of September. This family passed the Wren Building and Colonial Williamsburg just as the other family had done years earlier. Because it was August, the air was even hotter and muggier than what the first family had experienced, yet the second family wasn't as tired. By 1981 an interstate highway ran right by Williamsburg, so the drive was shorter and less taxing. William and Mary was still pricy for an out-of-state student, but not as pricy as many private colleges they had investigated. Tuition and fees amounted to $3,368 for an out-of-state student while room and board added another $2,384. The total bill was $5,752. This was 3.8 times as much as the son in the first story had paid in 1960. This did not seem too far out of line. There had been a lot of inflation in the intervening years. The Consumer Price Index (CPI) had increased 3.1 times from 1960 to 1981. And in any case, the family's earnings were sufficient to ensure that important things did not have to be sacrificed in order to put the daughter through college, even a pricy out-of-state college.

Now fast-forward to the next generation student from Ohio arriving in Williamsburg in late August of 2006. The Wren Building and Colonial Williamsburg were still there, and again the weather was stifling. Some things don't change. The parents had taken a big gulp when their daughter had been admitted to William and Mary. As an out-of-state student she would face a daunting bill. What was wrong with Ohio State, Miami of Ohio, or Bowling Green? Still, William and Mary was where she wanted to go, so they would find a way to pay. She would likely have to take out some loans before all was said and done. Tuition and fees for an out-of-state student had climbed to $25,048 and room and board to $7,385. The total bill of $32,433 was still below the charges at many fine private schools they had considered, but it was way above those good state schools back home. This time appealing to the rise in the Consumer Price Index did not bring much relief. The average price level measured by the Consumer Price Index was 2.2 times higher in 2006 than in 1981, but tuition, fees, room, and board for an out-of-state student at William and Mary had increased 5.9 times.

Variants of these same three stories could be told about students starting college at almost any institution in the United States. Between the 1987–88 academic year and the 2007–8 academic year, tuition and fees rose on average by 7.4 percent per year at public four-year schools and by 6.3 percent per year at private four-year schools.[2] Over that same time frame, William and Mary's out-of-state tuition and fees rose 6.8 percent per year and our in-state residents had to come up with an extra

6.2 percent. The inflation rate over this period averaged a mere 3.1 percent per year.

These numbers are important. As the quotation from Representatives Boehner and McKeon's *The College Cost Crisis* indicates, education is a critical component of the American dream of rising living standards from one generation to the next, and of social mobility based on hard work and achievement. Public opinion surveys consistently find that how much one has to pay for a college education is a serious national concern.[3] Presidential candidates always mention "fears that they can't afford a college education for their children" in a listing of the concerns of the middle class. Newspapers fan the flames with headlines such as "College May Become Unaffordable for Most in U.S." (*New York Times*, December 3, 2008). The survey numbers and the headlines then fuel congressional commissions like the one that produced *The College Cost Crisis*. These numbers also motivated us to write this book, and we expect that they are part of the reason you decided to pick it up. And these numbers explain the black humor in the *Close to Home* cartoon at the beginning of the chapter.

Where You Sit Affects What You See

Before we start to answer the question posed in our title, we need to walk through the set of issues and perspectives that collectively define the landscape of higher education. Like any landscape, what you see tends to reflect where you sit. The world of higher education looks very different from the president of Swarthmore's window than it does from the office of a member of Congress who chairs a House subcommittee and who hears from an angry slice of the electorate each summer after tuition increases are announced. The world also looks different from the perspective of a small private liberal arts college that lives year-to-year largely on current tuition, a public university facing sudden state budget cuts that throw its planning process out the window several times each decade, or a prestigious and well-endowed private research university whose spending per student largely is independent of tuition revenue. This divided world of higher education defies easy generalizations.

For starters, the sticker-price explosion that generated the numbers of popular concern, and which energizes our politics as a result, masks important underlying differences in the economic environment faced by different types of schools and in how these different types respond to changes in that environment. The reasons for sticker-price *tuition* inflation, for instance, often are quite different at public universities and at private universities even though the basic forces that push up their *costs* over time are quite similar. Public universities are subject to swings in state funding that can affect tuition, independent of any changes in the university's costs. Private universities are more subject to the vagaries of financial markets that affect their endowment portfolios. Yet private and public universities alike are subject to a similar set of cost drivers they share in common with many other industries. Exploring this commonality between higher education and a set of important and related industries will be a major focus of our understanding of the real college cost problem.

We will start with a simple example to show that where you sit does indeed influence what you see. Figure 1.1 gives the time path from 1965 to 2006 of two important variables.[4] The first is the growth rate of real Gross Domestic Product (GDP). This is a measure of the nation's output as a whole in a given year, and the data series in the figure shows by how much the nation's output grew, expressed as a percentage, relative to last

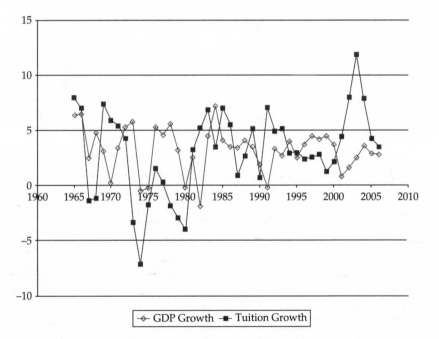

Figure 1.1 Growth Rate of Real GDP and Growth Rate of Real Tuition and Required Fees, Public Universities, 1965–2006

year's output. The second data series is the growth rate of the real value of tuition and required fees at public universities from 1965 to 2006. The term "real" just means that we have corrected for the effects of inflation. At first glance the diagram seems messy, but there are many stories lurking in there.

Suppose we asked the president of a public university to explain what he or she sees. Very likely that president would point out the fact that tuition and fees tend to rise very rapidly after decreases in growth in the overall economy. Your attention would be drawn to the rapid tuition increases following the episodes of negative GDP growth in 1982 and 1991 and the very slow GDP growth in 2001. Even the decade of falling tuition in the 1970s was interrupted by the oil shock years around 1974. The university president would say something like this: "When the overall economy slows down, state tax collections fall, and states cut appropriations for universities. As a result public universities have to resort to large tuition increases to make up for lost public funding."

If we asked Representatives Boehner and McKeon to comment on the data, they would focus on an entirely different phenomenon. In *The College Cost Crisis* they say "the facts show tuition increases have persisted regardless of the circumstances such as the economy or state funding, and have far outpaced inflation year after year, regardless of whether the economy has been stumbling or thriving." Essentially, they are looking at the fact that after 1980 the "real" growth in college tuition and fees always has been positive. This means that tuition and fees always have grown more rapidly than the CPI. Representatives Boehner and McKeon also claim they know why this has happened. They place the blame squarely on "wasteful spending by college and university management."[5]

Clearly, where you sit affects what you see and the factors you choose to highlight. Yet there is one critically important difference between these two accounts of what the data tell us. Our hypothetical university president's discussion focused on the *price* charged by public universities. On the other hand, the congressmen focused on wasteful spending by university management. This is an assertion about *cost*. Higher education is one place where we need to be very careful with the distinction between cost and price. As economists we have a clear idea of what we mean when we say cost. We use the word cost to refer to the value of the resources used to produce a good or service. Yet people usually have something different in mind when they ask, "Hey, how much does that car cost?" When people ask about the cost of a car, they are not interested in the value of the resources Ford or Toyota used to make the car. They want to know the price they must pay to get the car.

For the vast majority of college students, the largest cost of higher education is the opportunity costs of their time. Each year a student spends fully enrolled in classes, that person gives up the income that could have been earned had he or she been gainfully employed. There are two reasons this cost will not play an important role in our analysis. First, changes in the opportunity cost faced by students do not directly affect the tuition set by colleges and universities. Second, while these costs are large, they have been decreasing over time, not increasing. The lost value of work time is not part of the "cost problem." Over the last thirty years, the wages earned by workers in the kind of low-skilled jobs students could get if they forego college have not risen as rapidly as the inflation rate. While the explanation for this fact will play an important role in the analysis to come, its effect on the opportunity cost of college attendance is not important to the story we will tell.

For many industries, the distinction between cost and price is of little consequence. In most cases, a firm charges a price that is a bit higher than the cost of labor and other resources, and earns a profit as a result. This profit may ebb and flow, but over a many-year horizon it is fairly stable. In these situations, the factors explaining costs are very similar to the factors explaining prices. Higher education is different. Colleges and universities receive substantial subsidies, from state appropriations for state-supported institutions and from gifts and endowment income for private institutions. These subsidies allow the institution to charge prices (tuition and fees) that are often quite a bit less than costs. There is great variation in these subsidies, so there is great variation in how dependent institutions are on tuition revenue. In some instances tuition covers as little as 10 percent of costs and in other instances it can cover as much as 90 percent. Price and cost are very different in higher education. The university president in our example was saying that when subsidies go down the price charged by institutions has to go up or the value of what students get from their school will fall in other ways as the quantity, quality, and variety of offerings declines. He or she was not making any claim about cost. The congressmen, on the other hand, were making a claim about cost, and they were pointing a finger directly at the college president.

At this point, we will forgive you if you are wondering about our book's title. Do we mean cost, or do we really mean price? Actually, the book you are reading is about both. Frankly, we thought you would pick up the book with its current title more readily than one with the longer title, *Why Does College Cost So Much, and Why Is Its Price So High?* The more accurate but longer title might well be off-putting. But now that you have picked up the book, we admit that the title is ambiguous. In what follows, we will get into the details of what drives cost, of how tuition and fees are set, and of what links them together.

Choosing a Vantage Point

If where you sit determines what you see, we should explain where we want to sit as we do our analysis. Choosing a framework for thinking about an industry as large and complex as the higher education system is a matter of some importance, so how does one go about choosing a framework? Suppose you are a student of urban environments. If you walk the streets of a major city, your attention naturally will be drawn to certain themes and not to others. Gritty detail is a lot easier to see at street level. By contrast, an aerial view will make you think about an entirely different set of issues. Some details may get blurred, but a broader perspective becomes easier. The same is true in the study of higher education. Poring over the details of a school's budget may incline a researcher to think about problems in a particular way. Placing higher education squarely within the broader context of the national and global economy leads down a very different analytical path.

Much of the contemporary writing on college cost puts a magnifying glass up to the higher education industry, or places individual schools under a microscope for an even more detailed view. We have two major objections to this approach. First, in many important respects taking an up-close look often does not help you truly understand what is going on inside an organization as complex as a college or university. Second, the close-up look tends to focus attention almost exclusively on the university itself or on the policies that affect schools directly, The environment the industry operates in often is ignored or downplayed as just another factor. To put it differently, an analyst who takes a close-up look at a college or university in order to answer a particular question, like why does cost always seem to rise, will naturally tend to find the answers within the college or university. We are tempted to call this the "industry-analyst trap," and both of these objections deserve an extended discussion.

Our first objection is that looking at a blizzard of detail is not always conducive to sorting out "big pictures." In its attention to fine detail, the magnifying glass can be quite misleading. The modern university is a multi-product firm. It "produces" many things, including undergraduate teaching, graduate training, individual mentoring, basic and applied research, policy analysis, and public service. Attributing cost increases to each of these activities individually is not possible. As good as detailed data may be, trying to find the "cause" of rising cost in examining the books of a modern university is akin to finding the Holy Grail without the help of Harrison Ford.

In 2001, David Breneman, who was then dean of the School of Education at the University of Virginia, argued forcefully that separating out the individual strands of cost in a multi-product university is fundamentally impossible. Breneman put it this way:

> How one chooses to allocate costs among these joint products was essentially arbitrary, and one could generate wildly different cost estimates for the parts, based on that allocation. The profundity of this problem was sufficiently persuasive that I ceased to view internal cost analysis as a worthy economic topic, although its application often served internal political purposes.[6]

Here is a simple example of the problem. How do you measure the cost of teaching? Do you allocate some, all, or none of the central administration's time and salary to this? Might some faculty research also contribute to teaching? Should some of the equipment cost then be placed as a teaching cost? Do you split library expenditures somehow? Where do you place career services for students or IT support of academic computing? More generally, if one wanted to allocate costs to teaching and to research separately, one would have to split faculty salary into shares devoted to each. This is a fool's errand.

Our second objection centers on the fact that a close-up view is likely to inflate the relative importance of what is going on in the view provided by the magnifying glass or the microscope. The view through the magnifying glass or microscope tends to see certain things more clearly than others. This close perspective reveals warts and blemishes in clear detail. The magnifying glass to the industry reveals potentially unsettling things. Some universities seem engaged in prestige games with each other, driven in part by an obsession with the annual *U.S. News and World Report* rankings. Some faculty members seem disconnected from the teaching mission of the university and focused instead on individual achievement and personal recognition. Line items for things as diverse as central administration, psychological counseling, and equipment for laboratories or for student recreation centers may seem to have grown "disproportionately." Thus the glass and the microscope together may suggest a shift in mission toward research and student services, seemingly without offering a substantial payoff to families, taxpayers, and university-endowment donors.

The close-up view seems to suggest more than a whiff of inefficiency and dysfunction in our colleges and universities. This is also the perspective that forms much of the expert opinion that fuels both the popular perception of the college-cost problem and the public policy response to it. In chapter 7, we elaborate on this micro view in greater detail, and we argue that the pattern of cost increase seen in higher education over the past sixty years probably does not conform to a narrative based on stories of increasing dysfunction in the higher education industry as a whole or in the institutions that comprise the industry.

Still, we recognize the power of the close-up view. Paying careful attention to the details of university spending leads to many pertinent questions about how universities allocate their resources. In other words, it helps us to think about evolving university priorities. The close-up view also is instrumental in building up reliable data about what is going on financially inside of the ivory tower. On some occasions, we too will use these micro data to help us sort out differences between types of institution—public versus private four-year research universities, for instance—which is another feature of the landscape of higher education.

Instead of the magnifying glass and the microscope, in our search for the bigger picture we will survey the landscape from a higher altitude. We will place the higher education industry in the context of broader economic forces that have shaped the whole American economy, and indeed the world economy, over the course of the past century. So instead of looking at the exceptionalism of colleges and universities, we will be examining the connections between higher education and industries to which it is similar, seeking the commonalities that explain the evolution of higher education costs and pricing over the past century.

The view from ten thousand feet reveals that the question: "Why do higher education costs rise more rapidly than other costs?" could just as easily be phrased as, "Why do the costs of other goods and services rise more slowly than the costs of higher education?" Both are questions about the same comparison, but the second question frames things quite differently. As we will demonstrate, exploring this second question leads to interesting findings. In fact, there are some industries whose costs rise even more rapidly than the costs of higher education as well as industries whose costs rise more slowly than the costs of higher education. Sorting out which industries are which will tell us quite a bit about what drives cost increases in those industries as well as in higher education.

Placing ourselves above the flurry of detail included in the accounts of a college or university has its dangers, too. As we look across time, we have to be acutely aware of the differences between the economic environment of the 1950s and 1960s and the economic environment of the early twenty-first century. The three vignettes that began the chapter did account for one small aspect of change over time, namely the tendency for the overall price level to move upward almost every year. Most analyses of college cost and price recognize this, which is why things like tuition and fees are adjusted (deflated) to reflect "real" values that account for ongoing inflation. But the impact of time on how we should think about higher education is far more subtle, and interesting, than dealing with simple inflation.

The average standard of living is much higher today than it was in 1960, and this affects what students and their families expect a university to provide. This standard-of-living effect influences many aspects of university life (and cost), including room and board, medical care, career services, and counseling. Accounts of college cost that uncritically presume that upgraded services are mere gold plating or fluff are subjecting higher education to the kind of scrutiny that they might not apply to housing or cars. The concept of value cannot be divorced easily from conditions in the rest of the market.

In addition, the distribution of income in the United States today is quite different than it was in 1960. The middle-class society of 1960 has morphed into a world of greater inequality, so the impact of rising college cost varies by where one sits in the American income distribution. And where one sits in the income distribution is determined in large part by one's prior education and by the educational level of one's parents. This is one reason why the question of higher education affordability is complex, certainly more complex than watching how any one measure of cost has risen over time. Colleges and universities individually have no direct control over the broad shape of the U.S. income distribution, but as we will show, the broad social and economic changes that have raised inequality have had a significant effect on higher education costs and on the extent to which people face affordability problems in acquiring a higher education for their children. The question of college affordability will occupy a significant place in our narrative, but only after we have told our story of college cost.

The multi-generational saga that introduced this chapter offers us a simple road map to the landscape of college cost. The most basic feature of the map is that the price of a year in college always seems to go up faster than inflation. In certain eras, the price pressure seems livable while at other times the problem acquires a marked virulence, but over the long haul college price increases tend to outstrip our broad measures of price inflation in the economy as a whole. The multi-family narrative also makes plain that the rate of price climb has accelerated in recent years. This is the second big feature of the road map we will follow. Any comprehensive overview of college cost has to explain these two basic facts, and we will indeed work very hard to demystify the process behind these stories.

Preview of the Argument

The book is divided into four parts. We will complete part I by taking an aerial view of the data on costs and prices in higher education and in a wide set of other industries as they have evolved since the 1940s. This allows us to situate colleges and universities within the broader economic history of the U.S. economy as a whole, and it lays out a set of facts that any narrative should explain. Higher education costs and prices follow a time path that is by no means unique. Several other industries have experienced a rather similar trajectory. These industries include things like the services of physicians, dentists, and lawyers, as well as bank service charges and the expenses associated with providing life insurance. This similarity could just be a coincidence, or it could reflect commonalities that lead these industries to react to changes in the economic environment in broadly similar ways.

Part II of the book makes the case that the similarity is not a mere coincidence. We identify three major forces operating in the broader economy whose combined effects explain the evolution of cost in higher education and in a set of kindred industries. These three forces are like a strong tripod or three-legged stool that firmly supports our story. Each of these forces is a component of the technological progress that has occurred in the United States since the end of World War II, and each is independent of the others. The three legs each require a chapter to fully explain. We will provide a short introduction here.

First, technological progress is not evenly distributed across industries. It is quite rapid in some industries and much slower in others. Rapid technological progress generally holds down costs because it allows a firm to use less input, especially labor input, to make its products. Economists have long known that technological progress tends to lag in most service-providing industries such as higher education, and costs thus rise rapidly compared to industries with significant growth in labor productivity. All of the industries whose costs behave similarly to higher education are service industries. This is no coincidence.

The second leg of our stool is based on the kind of technological progress the U.S. economy has experienced. For quite some time, technological progress has favored workers with ever-higher levels of education. For the first three quarters of the twentieth century, the educational system was able to meet the increasing demand for skilled workers by producing more graduates. Over the last thirty years, however, the growth of educational attainment has not kept pace with the demand. As a result, the wages offered to highly educated workers have increased. The data for wage differentials across education levels are very clear. The monetary payoff to getting additional years of schooling started to grow rapidly starting in the late 1970s. As a result, all industries that use highly educated labor have had to pay more for their major service providers: college professors, physicians, dentists, lawyers, bank loan officers, and accountants and actuaries.

The third leg of our stool explores how technological advancements in higher education can raise costs instead of lowering them. Technological change always has two possible effects on an industry. New techniques can reduce the cost of making the same old thing. Alternatively, new ways can improve the quality of what we do or they can make the product or service we provide different from the older version in ways that benefit the buyer. Technology has transformed many important services in recent years, including higher education and medicine. We argue that the changes in higher education have been largely cost increasing, and that they have been driven by the needs of students and employers in the contemporary labor market. In plain language, our product is different today in important ways, and being up-to-date has raised cost.

Putting all three legs of the stool together, the unifying theme is that technological change and innovation itself are major forces behind rising higher education costs. Costs rise rapidly in higher education and in other related industries because of the kinds of industries they are and because of the economic environment in which they operate. If our story is true, rapidly rising costs need not reflect bad behavior or the wrong incentives. Many people who study higher education have taken a very different approach, one that takes a close-up view of colleges and universities. What they see is not very pretty. They see dysfunctional decision making at the institutional level and a dysfunctional market for higher education as a whole. This view also shapes much of the current political landscape of higher education. After presenting our full explanation, we spend a chapter exploring this alternative view. This chapter ends with a set of examples drawn from well-used data that we think show that our aerial view provides a much more compelling explanation of the overall evolution of cost and price in higher education.

In part III, our focus shifts from costs to prices. Higher education is a highly subsidized industry. Colleges and universities receive subsidies from state governments if they are public, and all institutions receive subsidies from gifts and endowment earnings. These subsidies allow institutions to charge the average student much less than the actual cost of providing an education. There are also student-specific subsidies through grants and scholarships that change the price that individual students pay. Some grants and scholarships are offered by institutions, while others are awarded by governments and private entities. In this part of the book, we explore how list-price tuition is set and what determines the average tuition that students actually pay. We end this part of the book with a look at the charged question of affordability in higher education. Changes in affordability depend on changes in family incomes, changes in college costs, and changes in the subsidies available to college students. Perhaps surprisingly, our analysis suggests that college has become more affordable over time except for families at the lower end of the income distribution.

In part IV, we turn our attention to higher education policy. Our aerial view of the higher education industry suggests that many of the cost and price drivers in higher education defy easy fixes, but one area where policy can make a real difference is in helping to create access. The word "education" does not appear in the U.S. Constitution; nevertheless, and particularly in the second half of the twentieth century, the federal government has played a significant role in higher education. Starting in 1965, the federal government became a provider of financial aid. More recently, the federal government has started monitoring college tuition. There is a growing body of evidence that the complexity of our financial aid system is a real barrier to many students who could otherwise succeed in college. Most reform proposals highlight simplifying this process and making it more transparent to students and their families. In addition to laying out the costs and benefits of simplifying the current system, we advance an immodest proposal that would radically simplify and universalize how the federal government supports students.

Lastly, state governments have been involved in education for much longer than the federal government. The vast majority of college students attend state-supported colleges and universities. The last thirty years have seen a significant decline in the share of the average state's budget allocated to higher education, despite a substantial increase in the student population being served. The states now cover a much smaller fraction of the cost of providing college training than in the past. This retreat of the state has left public higher education leaders in a difficult economic and political position, pushing simultaneously for more state support and for substantial tuition increases in order to maintain the integrity of their programs. We do not think a return to the high state appropriation and low-tuition model is a reasonable hope for restoring quality and access to state institutions. Our political and educational leadership needs to recognize the permanence of this new world of different state priorities, and they need to find ways to enable more of their citizens to take advantage of high-quality programming. We offer a reform idea that would change the fundamental relationship between states and their public higher education institutions. States should stop funding schools. They should fund students instead. Likewise, public universities need decision-making independence so they can plan effectively like other forward-thinking institutions. We show how these twin pillars of a *New Compact* would change incentives in public higher education for the better. Our proposal is not a privatization plan, but it recognizes the permanently reduced role of the state.

2

Is Higher Education All That Unusual?

This chapter explains why higher education costs and prices almost always rise more rapidly than the inflation rate. Our aerial view of the higher education landscape emphasizes the importance of economy-wide changes that influence higher education. Higher education does not operate in a vacuum. Just like every other industry, colleges and universities are part of the larger economy. They have to compete with other firms for workers. They have to purchase equipment just like other firms do. Technological progress affects higher education even if that progress occurs in other sectors of the economy. And importantly, what is going on in other parts of the national and global economy affects the kind of education that is demanded.

In this chapter, we take a broad look at the data. Our review of the evidence is motivated by two questions. First, are there other industries whose costs and prices behave similarly to higher education? Second, if there are such industries, is their common behavior driven by the same factors?

As we will show in some detail, there are a number of important industries whose costs and prices broadly track costs and prices in higher education. Of course, finding these similarities does not completely or automatically make our case. The similarity could simply be a coincidence. There might be industry-specific factors at work in industry X that fully explain costs and prices in industry X, and a completely separate set of industry-specific factors that fully explain costs and prices in higher education. This is why our second question is so important. If we can show that the common behavior is explained by the *same* broad economic factors, we can eliminate the possibility that what we are seeing is merely a coincidence.

This chapter is devoted to the first question: are there other industries whose costs and prices behave similarly to higher education? Getting at this question requires a detailed look at how costs have evolved in lots of industries. As is often the case, the available data are not perfect. Ideally, we would have data on costs in a large number of industries that we could compare with data on costs in higher education. Unfortunately, comparable cost data are not available, so we will have to content ourselves with looking at data on prices. Appendix 1 explains our choice of data in more detail and compares the price data we use for higher education with available data on higher education costs. We think the price data are a close enough approximation to ideal data, and we encourage interested readers to see the appendix for our complete argument.

Industries with Similar Price Behavior

Are there other industries whose price behavior is very similar to the price behavior we observe in higher education? We could approach the question in a highly technical statistical fashion, but little would be gained. Instead, we will present several diagrams comparing the time series of prices in higher education with time series for the prices of other types of goods and/or services. These diagrams will reveal differences and similarities in sufficient detail for us to make our points without relying on statistical wizardry. We start by comparing the higher education price series with a sample of prices of durable goods.

The data displayed in figures to come are the "real price" for each industry over time. There are several things going on here. First, the price in any given year for a particular industry is an average of the prices of the products produced by all the firms in that industry. Second, the term "real price" is economic jargon telling us that the prices have been corrected for inflation. To correct prices for inflation, we have to choose a base year against which everything is compared. In this figure and the figures to follow, we have used 1970 as the base year. All of the prices are equal to 1.0 in 1970. If the time path of prices in an industry is upward sloping, as it is for higher education, this indicates that prices in that industry have increased more rapidly than prices in general. If the time path of prices is downward sloping, that means that prices have increased less rapidly than prices in general.

Our data come from the National Income and Product Accounts. These accounts give the detail from the Department of Commerce's

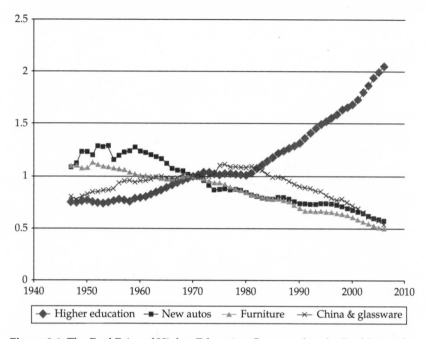

Figure 2.1 The Real Price of Higher Education Compared to the Real Price of Selected Durable Goods, (1970=1)

quarterly calculations of Gross Domestic Product, which help people understand how the economy is growing over time.[1] Figure 2.1 provides our first look at these data. It compares higher education prices with the prices of a sample of durable goods industries. Durable goods are defined as products that are expected to provide services for longer than a year. We have selected new autos, furniture (technically, furniture, including mattresses and bedsprings) and china and glassware (technically, china, glassware, tableware, and utensils) as examples of durable goods. A sample of three product categories does not capture everything that is happening to durable goods, but this small sample is broadly representative. The real price of all durable goods decreased 67.3 percent from 1947 to 2006. The average decrease for the three goods in figure 2.1 is 44.6 percent, so our three goods did not fall quite as much as all durable goods, but they definitely fell.

Figure 2.1 clearly shows that the time path of prices for durable goods has little in common with the time path of prices charged by colleges and universities. Real prices of higher education are rising for most of the 1947–2006 time period. In contrast, the real prices of autos and furniture are falling for most of the time period. The real price of china

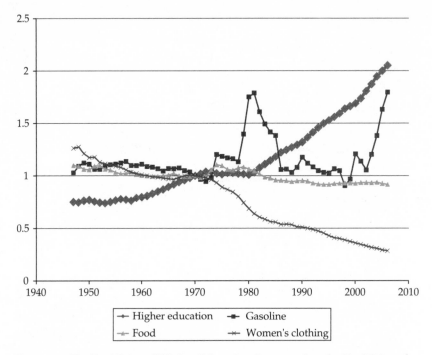

Figure 2.2 The Real Price of Higher Education Compared to the Real Price of Selected Non-Durable Goods, (1970=1)

and glassware rises in the first portion of the data, but it falls thereafter. We can conclude that prices in higher education do not behave like the prices of durable goods, no matter what representative subset of durable goods one chooses.

Figure 2.2 repeats the exercise for a sample of non-durable goods. Non-durable goods are products that are expected to provide services for less than a year. We have selected gasoline (technically, gasoline and oil), food (technically, food for off-premises consumption) and women's clothing (technically, women's and children's clothing and accessories except shoes). Again, our sample of three does not exactly mirror what is going on with all non-durable goods, but it is close. The real prices of the three goods have an average decrease of 6.6 percent over the 1947 to 2006 time period compared to a 16.9 percent decrease for the real prices of all non-durable goods. Our choice to include gasoline and oil, which have increased in price significantly over the entire time span, is largely responsible for the difference.

As with durable goods, the time series behavior of non-durable goods prices is not very similar to the time series behavior of higher education prices. Food prices have trended down slightly compared to the overall price index, while women's clothing has become substantially less expensive. In contrast, the price of higher education rises for most of the time period. The price of gasoline is interesting. It shows decided upticks in 1974, in 1979 and 1980, in 2000, and starting in 2003. If our data continued, we would have picked up another surge in gasoline prices in 2008 and a subsequent drop in 2009. Despite the fact that the price of gasoline and oil and the price of higher education both rise, the two price paths are not very similar. Gasoline prices are much more erratic.

Figure 2.3 repeats our exercise for three services. Services are defined in the National Income and Product Accounts as transactions in which no tangible product is traded. We have selected rent (technically, owner-occupied nonfarm dwellings—space rent), dentists, and barbershops (technically, barbershops, beauty parlors, and health clubs) as our representative services. Again, these three product categories do not exactly mirror the overall category of services, but they are close. The real price for all services rose 59.6 percent from 1947 to 2006. This is less than the

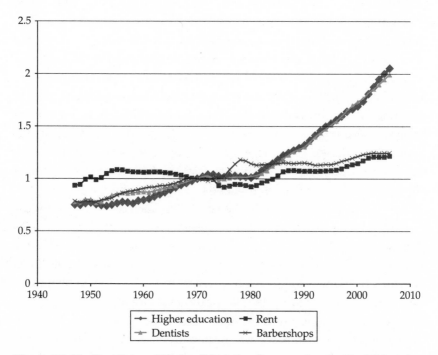

Figure 2.3 The Real Price of Higher Education Compared to the Real Price of Selected Services, (1970=1)

average real price increase over the same time period for our three services of 81.9 percent.

This diagram is the first instance in which we have found a product category whose prices behave similarly to higher education prices. The time series of the price of dentist services is almost identical to the time series of the price of higher education. The prices of other services also share some similarities with the price of higher education. In the first half of the time period, the behavior of the price of barbershops is quite similar to the behavior of the price of higher education and the prices of dentists. The series for the price of barbershops diverges from the other two prices in the mid-1970s, and it is very different after 1980. After 1980, the real price of higher education and dentists rises quite rapidly, but the price of barbershops only rises slightly during the 1980s and 1990s.

The similarity of the real price of dentists' services and the real price of higher education suggests a hypothesis—the price of higher education will behave similarly to the prices of personal services offered by highly educated service providers. Dentists are highly educated and so are college professors. Dentists are not the only ones who work in dentist offices, and professors are not the only ones who work at colleges and universities. Still, this similarity might be important. As a first step to test this hypothesis, we added the prices of the services of physicians and the services of lawyers (technically, legal services) to our diagram containing the prices of dentists and the prices of higher education.[2]

Figure 2.4 suggests that we are on to something. The four series are not identical, but they are quite similar. All four price series rise most of the time. All four price series flatten out in the 1970s, though the series for physicians is not as flat as the others during this period. Also, all four series start a decided upward march in roughly 1980. We can spot some differences, of course. Overall, the price of legal services rises more than the others (it starts out lower and ends up higher), and the price of physicians' services stops rising in the late 1990s. Each of these four industries does face some market challenges or government policy changes that are specific to them, and these industry-specific features most likely have some effect on the time path of prices in that industry. All things considered, though, the prices of these personal services delivered by highly educated service providers (physicians, dentists, lawyers, and college professors) are quite similar. And after a quick review of the other diagrams, we think we are on solid ground in saying that the evolution of prices for these services are much closer to what higher education has experienced than are the prices of goods, both durable and

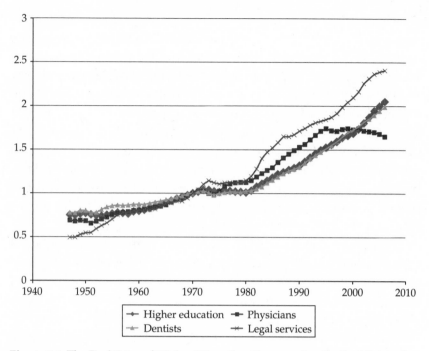

Figure 2.4 The Real Price of Higher Education Compared to the Real Price of the Services of Physicians, Dentists, and Lawyers, (1970=1)

non-durable, and the prices of services provided by buildings (rent) and the prices of services offered by less-well-educated service providers (barbers).

Before we pat ourselves on the back too prematurely, we need to check on the time series behavior of a few more personal services produced by highly educated service providers. Figure 2.5 shows the time series behavior of three other services whose main providers generally are quite well educated. We have included brokerage charges (technically, brokerage charges and investment counseling), life insurance (technically, expenses of handling life insurance and pension plans), and bank service charges (technically, bank service charges, trust services, and safe-deposit-box rental). Brokers and investment counselors almost always have bachelor's degrees and often advanced degrees or advanced certificates or charters. The accountants and actuaries who work for life insurance companies and pension plans have similar educational backgrounds, as do bank loan and trust officers. Safe-deposit boxes do not belong, but the way the data are compiled does not allow us to eliminate them.

Figure 2.5 shows us something very interesting. There is an anomaly that doesn't fit the pattern. The behavior of life insurance expenses and of bank service charges is fairly similar to the time series behavior of higher education prices. Again we see a slowing of the price increases in the 1970s and an acceleration starting in 1980 matching the pattern for higher education. Now comes the interesting part. The time series pattern for the prices of brokerage charges is not at all similar to the time series pattern of any of the other personal services offered by highly educated service providers. From the beginning of the data until the early 1980s, brokerage charges rose more rapidly than the other prices. Thereafter, there was a decided downturn. Brokerage charges started to decline relative to the average price of goods and services.

Brokerages charges don't fit the pattern. Is there something about brokerage services, and potentially about some other personal services, that mark them as different from the clear pattern we have uncovered among personal services that rely on highly educated labor? Any story about higher education price increases that does not comprehend outliers like brokerage services is weakened by the lack of an explanation of

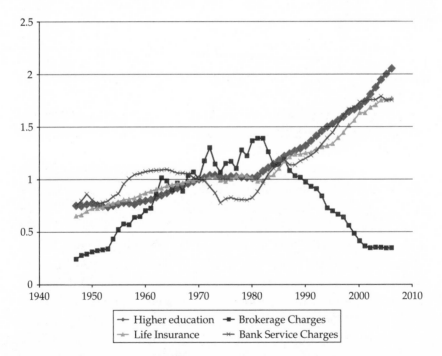

Figure 2.5 The Real Price of Higher Education Compared to the Real Price of the Services of Brokers, Life Insurance, and Banks, (1970=1)

something so fundamental. To foreshadow our story a bit, some service industries have been better at breaking the bonds of personal or face-to-face interaction than others. Simply put, some have figured out how to deliver the same or better quality service with less labor.

Before we summarize the facts we have uncovered, we want to make one important point. Our look at the data shows that the time series behavior of higher education prices is unusual. There are many goods and services whose prices do not behave at all like higher education prices. Still, while the behavior of higher education prices is unusual, it is not all that unusual. There *are* other services whose prices track higher education prices quite closely. The similarity of pricing behavior is important. If we could not find any other price series that were similar to higher education, it would have been time to fold up our tent and go home. If we could find no common behavior, we would have had nothing to explain.

A Listing of Some Important Facts

Here we lay out the facts our preliminary analysis of prices has uncovered. The task we set for ourselves in the next three chapters is to explain these facts.

> Fact 1—The price behavior of higher education is more similar to the price behavior of services than it is to the price behavior of goods.

Any broad price index, like the price index for personal consumption expenditures, is an average. It includes some sub-indexes that rise more rapidly than the overall index and other sub-indexes that rise less rapidly than the overall index. We constructed the data so that the overall index was flat. That allowed us to see which sub-indexes rose less than average and which sub-indexes rose more than average. The sub-index for durable goods and the sub-index for non-durable goods both rose less than average. In both cases, their real prices declined from 1947 to 2006. In contrast, the sub-index for service prices rose more than average. Real service prices increased between 1947 and 2006. The behavior of the real price of higher education is much more like the behavior of service prices than it is like the behavior of goods prices.

> Fact 2—Higher education prices behave very similarly to the prices of most personal services offered by highly educated service providers.

Figures 2.4 and 2.5 demonstrate that the time series behavior of prices in higher education was quite similar to the time series behavior of the prices charged by dentists, physicians, lawyers, bank trust officers, and by life insurance companies. A common feature of these services is that the main service providers are all highly educated: college professors, dentists, physicians, lawyers, loan officers, accountants, and actuaries. Also, for the most part the services are personal services. They rely on face-to-face interaction between you and the service providers. You have to go to your appointment at the doctor's office or your meeting with your lawyer, and you have to attend the classes offered by college professors. The exception is life insurance, which is partially based on face-to-face discussions with agents, but where much of the work of the highly educated workforce is out of contact with the buyer.

These personal services offered by highly educated service providers are quite distinct from the broader group of personal services. The time series for barbershops in figure 2.4 demonstrates this. Barbers and hair dressers provide a personal service. One has to have a face-to-face encounter with the barber, or at least be close enough to have a scissors-to-hair encounter. The data show that the prices of barbershop services closely tracked the price of higher education in early years, but not in the later years. Our story will have to explain the difference in the pricing behavior of services created by highly educated service providers and the services provided by less highly educated service providers in the two time periods.

Fact 3—The prices of some personal services produced by highly educated service providers behave quite differently than the prices of higher education.

The data for the prices of brokerage services in figure 2.5 illustrate this fact. Stockbrokers are highly educated, and they offer advice to clients either in face-to-face meetings or over the telephone. Brokers' services would seem to be very similar to the services of lawyers, doctors, and dentists, though it is difficult to get many dental services over the telephone. During the first portion of the post–World War II time period, the prices of brokerage services rose relative to the average price of all goods and services. Though more erratic than the prices of the services of similarly educated service providers, on net the prices of brokers flattened out during roughly the 1970s just like the prices of the other services. The big difference starts in the 1980s, when the real price of brokerage services started a precipitous decline. This is very different from what happened to the price of the other personal services provided by highly educated service providers. Any explanation of what has happened in higher education will have to account for this anomalous pricing behavior in a seemingly similar industry.

> Fact 4—From 1947 to 2006, the real price of higher education experienced two periods of growth separated by roughly a decade of almost no growth.

Explaining fact four is the bottom-line requirement for any explanation of college costs. In the twenty-three years from 1947 to 1970, the real price of higher education grew 33.0 percent. In the next ten years it only grew 1.1 percent, just over a tenth of a percent a year. In the twenty-six years from 1980 to 2006, the real price of higher education grew 102.9 percent. Any explanation of the experience in higher education has to be able to deal with the different rate of price change in these three periods.

So Is Higher Education All That Unusual?

The four facts will form the basis for the analysis to come. We have painted with a fairly broad brush, and this has been intentional. The explanation of the time series behavior of the prices for any good or service is a combination of factors, some of which are particular to that good or service while others are common economy-wide forces. Our emphasis will be on the economy-wide forces. We will grapple with how groups of industries have responded to changes that ripple through the entire economy. We will seek our explanations in broad similarities and differences between industries. And our working hypothesis will be that these economy-wide forces have important effects that explain the similarities and differences we have uncovered in this chapter.

We don't deny the impact of industry-specific changes. They are real. If you refer back to figure 2.4, you will see a tail-off in physicians' charges starting in the 1990s. There is clearly a story to be told about managed care, changes in Medicaid and Medicare, and changes in the relationship between physicians' offices, insurance companies, and regulators. But we do not think that industry-specific effects are the whole story, or even the most interesting part of the story. We recognize that there will be those who are more naturally drawn to the analysis of specific industries one by one. They will be very uncomfortable with our mode of analysis.

And we understand that in some cases, the industry behaves so distinctly that it is difficult to see the independent effect of economy-wide forces. Industries like this do have to be studied individually. The data for the prices of gasoline and oil suggest that it might be such an industry. Our claim is that higher education is not an industry that should be studied on its own. In other words, the answer to the question posed by the title to this chapter—is higher education all that unusual?—is NO.

A Note on Economic Modeling

In the process of completing this project, we test marketed several of the ideas in various venues. Usually our ideas have been politely received in academic circles, but often they encounter a more visceral reaction from nonacademic readers, who have very strong ideas about how markets work. Comments on an interview with Professor Feldman on the "Motley Fool" website in late November of 2009 included words like "poppy-cock" and the claim that we "can't understand the basic concepts of supply and demand." One responder to a short article in the Fall 2009 *William and Mary Alumni Magazine* told us that we had completely missed the major cause of rising college costs.[3] He and several of those who responded to the Motley Fool interview were sure that government sub-sidies, particularly student loans, were the cause of rising college costs. The argument seems to be that government subsidies drive up the demand for spots at colleges and universities, and this drives up the price—simple supply and demand analysis. We understand that anonymous critics often stake out extreme positions, but we have encountered this one frequently enough that it merits a preemptive counterstrike.

We do have a supply and demand framework lurking in the background and it helps motivate our story, but it differs from the text-book model underlying these comments. There are several reasons to be suspicious of the notion that changes in demand are an important part of the explanation for rising college costs. First, the evidence is not kind to this idea. Federal government subsidies started with the Higher Education Act of 1965 and they increased substantially in 1972 with the initiation of Pell Grants. A quick check of our diagrams shows that the time path of higher education prices does not take a jump upward around 1965 or 1972. Also, broad demographic forces such as the baby boom and its echoes surely changed the demand for higher education, but they don't seem to be strong influences on the cost of a college degree. For example, the baby boom generation was still pouring into college at the same time higher education costs were leveling off in the 1970s. Secondly, and perhaps more fundamentally, the thinking implicit in the claim that rising demand pushes up costs and price uses the wrong supply and demand model.

The appropriate supply and demand analysis of a multiple-decade-long increase in college costs and prices would have to use long-run demand and long-run supply curves that allow buyers and suppliers fully to adjust to changes in their economic environment. In the short run, people tend to be stuck doing what they are doing. They may have a gas-guzzling car that they cannot immediately sell, so the amount of gasoline they buy doesn't fall much immediately after the price goes up. But over time, they can find many ways to economize on fuel. Likewise, a family with a student in a particular college may not be as quick to switch to a less expensive alternative as someone who has more time to plan. Yet as in the short run, the long-run demand curve is downward sloping. Other things equal, higher prices lead people to demand less.

The slope of the long-run supply curve is more problematic and more interesting. It depends on the underlying production relationships. In the long run, institutions can adjust the entire scale of their operations. This means increasing the size of the faculty, the staff, and the physical plant along with increasing the number of students served. If raising the scale of operation leads to higher cost per student, the long-run supply curve for higher education as a whole is upward sloping. In this case, pushing a larger number of students through the system means higher cost per student. This is what many people seem to think when they claim that rising demand over time would push up cost. But if the scale can be increased without increasing cost per student, the long-run supply curve is flat. In this case, rising demand would have no impact on cost. The supply curve could even be downward sloping if increasing the scale of the operation lowers cost per student.

Our story is based on a flat long-run supply curve. For starters, this keeps things very simple, yet it is an assumption that makes a lot of sense. It is also an assumption with a great deal of support in the academic literature. Suppose a small college on the west side of the river could open an identical branch on the east side of the river. This new, bigger two-branch college would be twice as large, use twice as many resources, and have twice as many students. But the cost per student could easily be the same on both sides of the river. More generally, we are assuming that any percentage increase in the scale of operation will lead to equal percentage increases in total costs and the size of the student body. This leaves cost per student unchanged. In economic jargon, we are assuming "constant returns to scale." Many higher education researchers have investigated the question of returns to scale. Darrell R. Lewis and Halil Dundar (2001) summarize the findings as follows: "Evidence from economies of scale studies over the past sixty years indicates that, generally, unit costs for two-year and four-year institutions decline with an increase in the number of students, and after a certain size, become relatively constant."[4] These studies do not find decreasing returns to scale, so the notion of an upward sloping long-run supply curve is a complete non-starter.

If there are basically constant returns to scale in producing higher education (a flat long-run supply curve), then a change in demand has no effect on cost. In the long run, a college education will cost the same amount to produce if demand is large or if demand is small. Essentially, as more and more students are attracted to college, in the long run institutions are able to accommodate them without having to incur higher cost per student. The evidence even shows that increases in demand at small colleges might lead to lower cost per student if those schools move toward a somewhat larger scale of operation.

If the long-run supply curve is indeed flat, then an account of rising college costs has to explain why the flat supply curve has shifted upward over time. This is exactly what our metaphorical three-legged stool will do. Costs rise over time independent of any changes in demand, and they do so for the three basic reasons we introduced in the last chapter. All three reasons are related in some way to the kinds of technological progress we have experienced in higher education and to the pattern of productivity growth in the economy as a whole. Sometimes these shifts are gradual and continual, and sometimes they come in bursts, but over the past sixty years this technology-based story of rising college cost has a lot of explanatory power. As the data we have presented in this chapter suggests, our explanation has to fit several other industries as well as higher education. And it has to tell us why higher education is different from another set of industries. It is now time to start the analysis.

PART II
Costs

3

Higher Education Is a Service

We will start our explanation of the factors that cause higher education costs to increase rapidly by focusing on the first fact described in the last chapter. Economists have long known that the prices of services tend to behave differently than the prices of goods. In this chapter, we will explain why and tell the story of how higher education fits into the broader landscape of services.

Growth, in fact, is the essential element of our story. Technological progress is a major engine driving average living standards higher over time, but technological improvements that raise labor productivity have not been randomly sprinkled throughout the economy. Instead, productivity gains have tended to clump in certain sectors of the economy (like manufacturing) while skipping lightly over many others (such as many personal services). As we will show, sectors that have experienced slow productivity growth suffer rising costs compared to sectors blessed with technological gains.

David Ricardo

The first person to think rigorously about the difference between goods prices and service prices was the English financier and economist David Ricardo, who lived from 1772 to 1823. Ricardo was one of the most influential of the early economists who followed in the footsteps of Adam

Smith. One of the puzzles that interested him was his observation that the value of money did not seem to be the same everywhere. A gold sovereign had more purchasing power in some countries than in others, or even in some regions within Great Britain than in others. The reason, he noted, was that the cost of living was not the same everywhere. The average price level was higher in what today we would call more economically developed areas where the standard of living was higher, and this was true both within and between countries. In his well-known chapter on foreign trade, this is how Ricardo (1821) expressed the link between systematic differences in price levels and per capita income: "the prices of home commodities, and those of great bulk, though of comparatively small value, are independently of other causes higher in those countries where manufactures flourish."[1]

Ricardo's prose style may be unfamiliar, so it takes a bit of explanation. By "home commodities, and those of great bulk," Ricardo is referring to services provided directly to the buyer, on the one hand, and on the other, to physical commodities that are difficult and expensive to transport relative to their value. A haircut or many other personal services would be good examples of the former, and extremely heavy items or highly perishable ones would be fine examples of the latter. These are all examples of what today we call "non-tradables." Non-traded goods and services are ones that sell in a local market at a local price. Traded goods sell in broader, or world, markets at a largely uniform world price.

The language about "those countries where manufactures flourish" is his way of singling out the more economically developed countries, in which the average standard of living is higher. Ricardo's claim is therefore that non-traded goods and services will be more expensive in highly developed countries. Abstracting from the effects of tariffs and transportation costs, the prices of traded goods should be the same in all countries. But if the non-traded goods and services that people consume are systematically more expensive in richer countries, then the cost of living in those countries, measured by an index combining traded and non-traded goods and services, should be higher as well.

The mechanism behind Ricardo's claim is relatively easy to explain. Countries produce a wide variety of goods and services, some of which are traded and some of which are not. Imagine, for a moment, a hypothetical world of two countries. Economists are good at setting up this sort of hypothetical because it helps us see the essential logic behind otherwise speculative claims, and it tells us what we need to do in order to test that logic against the evidence. Now back to our hypothetical. Suppose one country's workers are simply better at producing tradable things than the other country's workers. In other words, one country's technology is superior, so labor productivity in the tradable goods industries is higher. One more supposition completes the picture. Lastly, let us suppose that the productivity of workers in the non-tradable services sector is the same in both countries. A hair cut takes a half hour in both, for instance.

The country with the higher labor productivity in the tradable goods industries is the richer, more developed country. Its people will have a higher average standard of living. Putting it another way, real wages are higher in the nation with higher labor productivity. What about prices in each nation? The tradable goods sell on a world market at a world price, so there is no fundamental difference in the cost of living that comes from these prices. On the other hand, services are sold in a local market, and the price will reflect local conditions. Here is the local condition that matters. Producers of services have to compete for labor with producers of tradable goods. Since real wages are higher in the more technologically advanced country, the service workers in that country are paid more than corresponding service workers in the less advanced country. This gives the result. As long as labor is somewhat mobile between the two sectors of the economy, the barber in a highly productive country will have to earn more than the barber in the less productive country. A barber in the "poor" country who is just as productive as a barber in the "rich" country thus will earn less than his or her rich-country counterpart because that barber's other options are not as attractive. This is the reason why the prices of "home commodities" are higher in those countries where manufactures flourish. In modern terms, a haircut in Detroit will cost you more than a haircut in Djakarta.

Without knowing it explicitly, most people are aware of Ricardo's result even if they have not priced haircuts in Detroit and Djakarta. Some people have lived in less developed economies in Africa, Asia, and Latin America, and most people know of someone who has or at least have heard of someone who has. People with experience living in the less developed parts of the world often tell a story about their staff. Westerners living in less developed countries very often have a maid, a cook, and a gardener. They could never afford to have these personal servants in the West, but because wages are so low where they were, they could have a household staff. The stories about living in the less developed world are not about how inexpensive automobiles were or how inexpensive clothing was. Automobiles and standardized clothing are traded goods. The stories are about how inexpensive Ricardo's home goods were.

We used the past tense (were) in the last sentence for a reason, because Ricardo's insight also tells us something about time. Technological improvement in poorer regions of a country, or in poorer countries, can lead to catch-up behavior in living standards. One of the things people notice about countries that are experiencing very rapid economic growth is that the price level seems to soar right along with the real living standards. What they are experiencing is this Ricardo effect pushing up the price of non-tradables, most of which are services in a modern economy.

There is another impact of technological change over time that has affected all of us. Technology has worked wonders to reduce the cost of transporting basic commodities throughout the world. This is a driving force in the emergence of a global economy over the past two hundred years. Goods that once were sold on a local market now have global reach. Even cement and fresh-cut flowers now are internationally traded. Yet the importance of Ricardo's hypothesis about home goods remains undiminished. The fraction of the labor force that works in the service sector has increased markedly over the last half century. Part of the reason is the remarkable increase in labor productivity in manufacturing that has so enriched us. We have gotten very good at producing more steel, for instance, with fewer hours of labor. Thus the jobs move to sectors of the economy, like personal services, where productivity growth is slower. And part of the reason is that many of the services that are increasingly in demand are ones that people purchase as their incomes rise. This includes everything from financial management and fancy restaurant meals, to higher quality postsecondary education for their children.

William Baumol and William Bowen

Ricardo's insight, extended to incorporate technological change over time, is behind the work of William Baumol and William Bowen in their well-known work on the economics of the performing arts. It is their work that gives us the economic growth story that ultimately explains our first fact about higher education. In their 1966 book, Baumol and Bowen argued that prices in the performing arts would have to rise more rapidly than prices in general. The key to their argument is that compared to other goods and services, labor productivity in the performing arts is much more difficult to increase. The oft-quoted and only partly tongue-in-cheek example Baumol gives us is the famous horn quintet story: "A half hour horn quintet calls for the expenditure of 2.5 man hours, and any attempt to increase productivity here is likely to be viewed with concern by critics and audiences alike."[2] Productivity improvement—more music per minute or the same music performed by fewer players—would not yield the same performance. Similarly, it takes a given amount of time and a given number of performers to stage *Oklahoma* or *Hamlet*. Reducing the time or reducing the number of performers would not yield the same theater-going experience.

To advance the argument, Baumol and Bowen took it as given that productivity growth is essentially stuck at zero in the performing arts. Productivity growth is not stuck at zero in other sectors. Thus workers in other sectors will be experiencing wage gains, and to hang on to their performers stage companies and orchestras will have to offer competitive wages. If Baumol and Bowen had then concluded that audiences would have to pay higher ticket prices to see actors and musicians in more productive countries than audiences will have to pay in less productive countries, they would have just been repeating Ricardo's insight.

Baumol and Bowen did not follow Ricardo and compare prices across countries. Rather, they focused on the time-series implications for prices in an industry like performing arts that had productivity growth stuck at zero. Consider what would happen to the ticket prices of a Shakespeare festival that staged *Hamlet* each year. Each year, it has to hire the same number of actors and the same staff. Also, assuming this Shakespeare festival is in a country that is experiencing productivity growth in other industries, each year the wages it has to pay will go up, or it will not be able to attract the same level of talent. When the Shakespeare festival sets its ticket prices, it will have to raise them to cover the higher wage bill it faces each year. The alternatives are to put on *Hamlet* with an inferior cast, get a subsidy from local government, or to close down the festival.

This is the insight behind our first fact. The process is usually called "cost disease." Rapidly rising service prices follow from the fact that service industries' costs are rising more rapidly than the costs of producing most goods. Higher education and many other service industries have considerable difficulty increasing the productivity of their workers. And as a result, their prices will be driven up over time by cost disease.

The horn quintet example often is attacked for being simplistic and unrepresentative. Indeed, this example is an extreme case, and one that is true by definition. You simply cannot increase the productivity of the five key workers in a live performance. Yet the presence of cost disease does not depend upon productivity being completely stagnant. The only requirement for an industry to experience cost disease is that its productivity growth over some specified time period has to be slower than the average level of productivity growth for the economy as a whole. This is why our search for commonalities among industries, begun in the last chapter, is an important component of any understanding of cost increases in higher education.

In the horn quintet example, low (or zero) labor productivity growth cannot be avoided. In other situations, slow productivity growth may be a choice. For example, mechanization of hair cutting can only proceed so far before many people would begin to consider the outcome a decrease in the quality of the experience. Put simply, people like their barber or hair dresser to fuss over them. Often in personal-service industries, quality is determined by the time and effort expended by the professional. If a physician's patients are given cursory examinations or are shunted off to nurses, costs will not rise as fast. But patients will be aware that the quality of care is not the same, and many will be unsatisfied. The same is true if the dentist only stops by your chair occasionally to check on the work of his or her assistants, or if legal clients are routinely turfed out to paralegals. Eventually, the clients will think the quality of the service has diminished.

But does higher education have to be like horn quintets, barbershops, or other similar personal-service industries? Productivity gains are indeed possible in higher education, and we will have more to say on the subject in chapter 8. Technological innovations like closed-circuit television in the 1960s or web-based distance learning today have the potential to increase productivity. Yet, at least to this point, the primary delivery vehicle remains the faculty member who interacts with students. An institution can increase class size to raise measured output (students taught per faculty year) or it can use an increasing number of less expensive adjunct teachers to deliver the service, but these examples of productivity gain are likely to be perceived as decreases in quality, both in the quality rankings and in the minds of the students. An institution can also increase the number of courses each faculty member teaches per year, but not without having an impact on other attributes of higher education output such as research or public service.[3]

Contrast the pricing of the Shakespeare festival or a higher education with the pricing of a basic manufactured good like steel. If the steel manufacturer can discover a better way of making steel, one that allows it to produce a ton of equal-quality steel with less labor, the steel maker will be able to hold down costs. The immediate effect of growth in labor productivity is higher profits, but those profits tend to be transitory. Competition in the labor markets and goods markets ultimately passes these productivity gains on to people in the form of higher wages and/or lower goods prices. One of the most stable numbers in economic history is labor's share of national income. Labor earns 70 cents of every dollar of GDP. This means that over time increases in labor productivity ultimately become increases in the standard of living for the broad mass of the population.

To summarize, often the slow productivity growth in personal-service industries is a choice, one that is driven by the desires of the service provider and his or her customers. The key consideration is the quality of the service. Productivity growth that would be accepted by both service providers and customers alike will have to be productivity growth that maintains the quality of the service. This does not distinguish the production of services from the production of goods. Productivity growth that is acceptable in the production of goods also has to be either quality preserving or quality enhancing. The difference is that it is often easier, particularly with the application of new machinery, to find ways of producing standardized commodities at lower costs or of producing higher quality manufactured goods at the same cost than it is to find ways of generating productivity improvements in personal services.

Cost disease thus is not dependent on the conditions of the horn-quintet example. Productivity growth does not have to be stuck on zero for technological reasons. Cost disease will be an important phenomenon as long as there are systematic differences in productivity growth between identifiable classes of industry. At least for our history to this point, productivity growth differentials have favored goods production instead of services, and in terms of labor productivity growth, personal services have brought up the rear. Higher education is a personal service that has experienced cost disease along with other similar service industries. This is the basic explanation of the second fact.

More Evidence on Cost Disease

Data presented in the previous chapter provided considerable support for the notion that higher education prices and service prices behave quite similarly. For example, the average prices of both durable goods and non-durable goods have risen less rapidly than the average price of the items included in personal-consumption expenditures. On the other hand, the average price of services has risen more rapidly than the average price of the items included in personal-consumption expenditures. Now we must probe deeper and present additional examples, including ones that seems inconsistent with cost disease.

First, we should check Baumol and Bowen's hypothesis about performing arts. The closest product category available is for the product category "legitimate theaters and opera, and entertainments of nonprofit institutions (except athletics)." Prices for this product category are only available starting in 1959. From 1959 to 2006, the price index for personal-consumption expenditures rose 5.61 times. In contrast, the price index for legitimate theater rose by a factor of 10. This is exactly the kind of difference that Baumol and Bowen's analysis of cost disease in the performing arts would predict.

The way the accounts deal with food provides a second example. The price index for the non-durable goods category "food for off-premises consumption" is the one we included in figure 2.3 in the last chapter. This product category captures the prices of food at grocery stores. To be clear, the food we buy in the grocery store is not just a commodity. You are not buying the stuff wholesale from a farm or dairy. The price you pay for groceries includes the cost of two embedded services, distribution and retailing. These two embedded services are not personal services, and the primary industry (groceries) is providing basic goods to consumers. So, how much has the price of groceries increased? The price of food for off-premises consumption rose 5.09 times from 1947 to 2006, just slightly less than the price of personal-consumption expenditures, which grew 6.30 times. There is another category of food prices that should be closely related to food for off-premises consumption, namely "purchased meals and beverages." Purchased meals and beverages are essentially restaurant meals. The basic difference between food at grocery stores and food in restaurants are the costs of preparing and serving the meals. This is a personal service. From 1947 to 2006, the average price of purchased meals and beverages rose 8.73 times, which is well above the increase in the average price for all personal-consumption expenditures (6.30). This comparison shows clearly that the costs of the services associated with preparing and serving food rose more rapidly than the cost of the food being prepared and served. This is just what the cost disease argument would predict.

Third, consider the difference in behavior between the price index for the purchase of new autos, which we displayed in the previous chapter, with the price index for auto repair (technically, repair, greasing, washing, parking, storage, rental, and leasing of automobiles). The average price of new autos increased 3.90 times from 1947 to 2006, which is considerably less than the average price of all items in personal-consumption expenditure (6.30 times). In contrast, the average price of auto repairs rose 11.26 times. This comparison shows that the charge for the services of auto mechanics rose much more than the price of the auto-mobiles they were servicing. Again, this is just what the cost disease argument would predict.

As the first fact emphasizes, while higher education prices generally behave similarly to service prices, there are clear exceptions. In our next example, we will highlight service industries that do not seem to fit the cost-disease model well. Figure 3.1 is similar to the diagrams in the previous chapter. It compares the real price of higher education with three other services. The first is the real price of brokerage charges and investment counseling, which was the anomaly we highlighted in the last chapter. The other two are telephone (technically, telephone and tele-graph) and electricity.

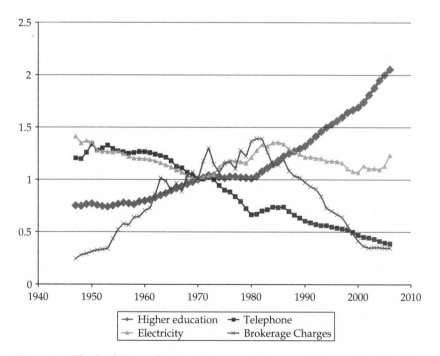

Figure 3.1 The Real Price of Higher Education Compared to the Real Price of Telephone, Electricity, and Brokers' Services, (1970=1)

The prices indexes for brokerage services, telephone, and electricity do not behave at all like the price index for higher education. Nor do they behave much like other services, personal or otherwise. As we saw before, in the years between 1947 and 1980 the real prices of brokerage charges grew much faster than the real price of higher education, but then in more recent years it fell very rapidly. The real price of telephone service shows an almost-steady decrease, very different from the steady increase we see in higher education prices. Finally, the real price of electricity decreases until the mid-1970s, then increases until the second half of the 1980s, and decreases thereafter. As in the other two product categories, the behavior of electricity prices is very different from the behavior of higher education prices.

All three of these industries fail to display the kind of behavior one might expect based on the cost-disease argument. Yet this does not turn out to be a fundamental challenge to the overarching cost-disease theory. One important reason is that these three industries have not suffered from lagging productivity growth. When we displayed a diagram like this and asked a group of undergraduate students what had happened to brokerage services, they all responded, "online trading." This is in fact the likely explanation for the behavior of the price for brokerage services. Prior to the advent of the Internet and the personal computer, it was very difficult to make a stock trade without having a phone conversation or a face-to-face meeting with a broker. After that a series of phone calls or wire messages would get a customer's order to the floor of the exchange. This is the same basic technology that had been used by brokers since the advent of the telephone. More recently, new technology has streamlined the business dramatically. There is no need for face-to-face meetings or even phone calls, if one is trading securities online.

The case of brokerage services is very important for our continued discussion. Stockbrokers and investment counselors are highly educated service providers who offer a personal service. The other product categories that fit that description, for instance those relying on the services of physicians, dentists, lawyers, college professors, and bank trust officers, exhibited very different time series behavior of their prices. The case of brokerage services indicates that personal services need not have stagnant productivity growth if a way can be found to make them *less personal* without diminishing quality.

The other two examples in figure 3.1 are also instances in which technology has advanced. First, consider telephones. The 1947 to 2006 time period includes transitions from telephones that you picked up and the operator asked "number please?" to dial phones, to push-button phones, to clumsy mobile phones, and now to sleek cell phones with free long distance and Internet access. All of this increase in the capability of our phones has happened as the same time that real price of telephone services has declined. Second, the situation for the real price of electricity is different in its own way. Real electricity prices vary in a fairly narrow range, declining slightly prior to 1970 and rising slightly thereafter. Overall, they end up roughly where they started out. Clearly, there have been advances in the technology of electricity production. But these increases in productivity have not been as fast as the increases involved in providing telephone services, and they are balanced on the other end by increases in the prices of the fuels that are used in the production of electricity. The net effect is that electricity prices do not behave at all like higher education prices.

Examples like brokerage services and the services of telephones represent an important new direction in the economy. Jack E. Triplett and Barry P. Bosworth wrote a book in 2004 titled *Productivity in the U.S. Services Sector: New Sources of Economic Growth*. They start the book with data comparing labor productivity growth in goods-producing industries and service-producing industries. From 1987 to 1995, labor productivity in goods-producing industries grew at an annual rate of 1.8 percent and labor productivity in service-producing industries grew at an annual rate of 0.7 percent. This is just what one would expect. Goods-producing industries experienced faster productivity growth than service-producing industries. Surprisingly, things change when they move forward in time to 1995 through 2001. For the later time period, labor productivity in goods-producing industries grew 2.3 percent, but labor productivity in service-producing industries grew 2.6 percent. In the more recent period, labor productivity growth in service-producing industries caught up to, and slightly passed, labor productivity growth in goods-producing industries.

One might interpret the Triplett and Bosworth finding as the death of cost disease. Cost disease in services is based on lower productivity growth rates in service-producing industries. Since that does not seem to be the case anymore, cost disease must be dead. Like Mark Twain, the cost disease argument could say of itself, "the report of my death was an exaggeration."[4] After presenting the aggregate data, Triplett and Bosworth then break it apart at the industry level. They say,

> In the services sector, the overall growth in labor productivity and MFP (multifactor productivity) camouflages a wide disparity

of trends within the individual two-digit industries. Advancing labor productivity in four large services industries—telephone, wholesale trade, retail trade, and finance (both brokerage and depository institutions)—drove the overall sector improvement.[5]

In their data, the two largest growth rates for labor productivity in the 1995 to 2001 period are for security and commodity brokers (10.3 percent) and telephone and telegraph (7.9 percent). Other services exhibit much more modest rates of labor productivity growth. In fact, from 1995–2001 a large majority of the services industries, twenty-one of the twenty-nine, have labor productivity growth rates that were less than the average labor productivity growth rate of goods-producing industries. As cost disease would predict, educational services, legal services, health services, and amusements and recreational services are among the industries whose labor productivity growth lagged behind the average labor productivity growth rate in goods-producing industries. In conclusion, there are some service industries that have escaped the grip of cost disease, but cost disease is by no means dead. Moreover, the fact that some service industries may have found ways to accelerate productivity growth does not invalidate the importance of cost disease for explaining the past. And a large number of service industries have not yet found a way to generate significant labor productivity growth and as a result still suffer from cost disease. This has been forgotten in some commentaries.

A Look Forward

As a way of introducing the next chapter, we will take a quick look at fact two again. Fact two says that higher education prices behave very similarly to the prices of services offered by *highly educated* service providers. Most of the evidence we presented in the previous chapter confirmed this, again with the striking exception of stockbrokers. We think we have offered an understanding of the curious case of the brokers. What we did not do was to compare the price path of services provided by highly educated workers to that of services provided by less highly educated workers.

Figure 3.2 compares the behavior of the real price of higher education with the real price of barbershops (which we included in the previous chapter), domestic service, and dry cleaning (technically, cleaning, storage, and repair of clothing and shoes). These three services generally rely on less-well-educated service providers, and their price series behave very similarly. For the first half of the time period, they mirror the behavior of higher education very closely. The price index for higher education levels off in the 1970s, and dry cleaning declines slightly but barbershops and domestic services increase during the early 1970s. The big difference between the prices of these services and the higher education price series emerges starting in the early the 1980s. Higher education prices start to increase very rapidly, and the other price indexes are almost flat thereafter.

This figure shows that higher education prices behave very differently in recent years than services that use less-well-educated labor. Contrast this diagram with figure 2.4, which includes the prices of lawyers, physicians, and dentists, along with higher education. The price series for lawyers, physicians, and dentists match higher education, and all of them accelerate starting in roughly 1980. We will have to find an explanation for the difference in the virulence of cost disease shown in figure 2.4 and figure 3.2. Why did cost disease become more aggressive

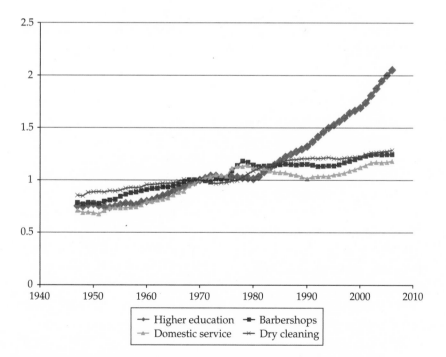

Figure 3.2 The Real Price of Higher Education Compared to the Real Price of the Barbershop Service, Domestic Service, and Dry Cleaning, (1970=1)

in service industries that use a lot of highly educated workers starting in 1980? This will be the subject matter of the next chapter.

Concluding Remarks

At this point, readers might wonder what they signed up for when they cracked the cover of this book. This is supposed to be a book about higher education, but this chapter includes as much discussion about Shakespeare festivals, lawyers, and restaurant meals as it does about the functioning of colleges and universities or about the market for higher education. This follows from our thesis that higher education is an industry that is similar to several others, and that the characteristics it shares with other industries explain a great deal about the experience of higher education costs. Although the way may seem roundabout, we have made considerable progress toward understanding what is going on in higher education.

Consider the question, "why do tuition and fees almost always increase more rapidly than prices in general?" The fact that higher education is a service is a very good start to an answer to that question. The prices of almost all services rise more rapidly than the average price of goods and services, and higher education is certainly a service. The cost-disease argument outlined in this chapter explains why the prices of services will tend to rise more rapidly than the prices of goods.

We are also interested in more nuanced questions than why tuition and fees rise more than prices in general. We want to know why during some time periods they rise much more rapidly than the prices of some other services, and why during other time periods they do not (we still have to explain fact number four). We want to explain why they behave very similarly to some services and very differently than other services (we have more to do on facts two and three). The answers to these questions are ahead of us, but it is important to not to undervalue what we have learned to this point. Any discussion of the evolution of prices in the higher education industry that does not lead with the recognition that higher education is a service, and which does not accord a central role to the fact that service prices have risen more rapidly than goods prices, is a discussion that ignores a very important part of the story.

4

The Costs of Employing Highly Educated Workers

If we had to summarize our story so far, we would say that a driving engine of rising cost in higher education is economic growth itself. Technical change has pushed up productivity in manufacturing dramatically more than in the service sector, and especially in the slower growing personal services. The cost of these services must rise as a result. This is the cost-disease process, and the evidence is broadly consistent with it. However, we have discovered some exceptions. There are service industries whose price behavior is not at all similar to the price behavior of higher education. Still, in general services prices clearly rise more rapidly than goods prices.

There are a lot of service industries that have experienced slow (or no) productivity growth over the last quarter century. Barbershops, domestic servants, and dry cleaners were not inoculated against cost disease, and their costs have increased relative to the general price level. The prices of these services tracked prices in higher education quite closely until around 1980. Then they began to diverge, with higher education prices rising very rapidly, and the prices of barbershops, domestic service, and dry cleaners rising much more slowly. Apparently the cost disease experienced by some slow-productivity-growth service industries became much more virulent after 1980. Legal services and the services of physicians and dentists experienced the same infection as higher education.

These differences in price behavior among important classes of services are large *and systematic*. In the decade of the '80s, an important set of service prices began to accelerate even faster than the others, and that pattern has persisted to the present day. This brings us back to the third fact, which we will explore in this chapter and the next. Higher education prices behave very similarly to the prices of most personal services offered by highly educated service providers. Why is it that cost disease has been more virulent in these cases than in others? And what is it about personal services, particularly personal services offered by highly educated service providers, that has made them behave so differently in recent years?

Employment and Education Levels

The workforce in higher education, legal services, and health care on average is more highly skilled than are the workers in industries such as barbershops, domestic service, and dry cleaning, and higher also than in the manufacturing industries that have experienced more-rapid productivity growth. This is not quite as obvious as it may seem at first glance. Industries like higher education and health care are large and complex. They employ millions of people with diverse skills. So a quick look at the data will help us understand the differences in skill levels across industries in the United States.

Table 4.1 gives a selected subset of the industry-level information available for the United States in 2005. The United States defines "highly skilled" workers as those with a college degree.[1] There are many more industries in the data. We selected just 12 out of 107. We highlighted

Table 4.1   The Percentage of High-Skill Workers by Industry, 2005

Industry	High-Skill
Research and Development	72.0
Education	68.3
Computer and Related Activities	65.7
Publishing	49.3
Aircraft and Spacecraft	43.7
Electrical and Optical Equipment	42.8
Post and Telecommunications	38.2
Motor Vehicles	22.1
Transport and Storage	18.1
Metals	14.3
Textiles	11.6
Construction	11.2

these to give a sense of the range of skilled labor use in the United States, and a flavor of the kinds of industries that appear in the top, middle, and bottom of the data. For all industries together, the high-skill percentage in the United States is 32 percent. The education sector is clearly among the most skill-intensive sectors of the economy.

Our interest is in *higher* education and not the entire education sector, so we need to look at finer industry classifications. Data from the National Industry-Specific Occupational Employment and Wage Estimates conducted by the Bureau of Labor Statistics allow us to focus more narrowly on the specific industries of interest. We were able to find information on five of the seven service industries we are comparing.[2] We use the personal-care-services industry as a stand-in for barbershops and beauty salons because it is dominated by occupations associated with barbershops and beauty shops. A quick look at table 4.2 shows how different these services are from one another in their use of highly educated labor and in how important highly educated labor is in determining cost in the industries.

The message of table 4.2 is very similar to the message of table 4.1. A high percentage of the workers in education in table 4.1 and higher education in table 4.2 are highly educated workers. Despite the different industry definitions, different years, and the different ways of measuring highly educated workers, the percentages of highly educated workers are surprisingly close. Table 4.2 also highlights the stark differences between the percentage of highly educated workers in the high-skill service industries (higher education and the offices of dentists, physicians, and lawyers) and in low-skill service industries (barbershops, beauty shops, and dry cleaners). If we want to understand why prices in these

Table 4.2   Percentage of Highly Educated Workers and Highly Educated Workers' Percentage of the Wage Bill in Various Industries—May 2007

Industry	Percent of Highly Educated Workers	Highly Educated Workers' Percentage of Wage Bill
Personal Care Services	1.87	4.28
Dry Cleaning and Laundry Services	2.24	7.25
Offices of Dentists	33.65	59.75
Offices of Physicians	45.89	73.79
Legal Services	55.49	76.53
Colleges, Universities and Professional Schools	67.87	81.18

industries have behaved so differently, the behavior of wages for highly educated people and less-well-educated workers is a great place to start looking for reasons.

Wage Differences and Education

We have shown that the time path of higher education prices diverges from the time path of prices for less-skill-intensive services like barber-shops, domestic service, and dry cleaning roughly around 1980. Other service industries that use highly educated labor intensively, such as health care and legal services, follow the pattern set by higher education. This would make sense if something happened in the late 1970s or early 1980s that started an ongoing process of pushing up the earnings of highly educated workers relative to the amounts paid to less highly educated workers. There is a lot of evidence that this is exactly what has taken place.

The first information to look at is the data on the rate of return to a college education. Figure 4.1 shows the rate of return to a year of college compared to high school for young men. The data come from a book by Claudia Goldin and Lawrence F. Katz (2008) and cover the years 1914 through 2005.[3] The returns to a year of college fell dramatically from 1914 to 1950 before beginning a slow turnaround. This increase was inter-rupted in the 1970s. Around 1980, the rate of return started to grow again, and the subsequent increase has been rapid and sustained. The increase in the rate of return to college over the last thirty years is consistent with the time paths of prices that we have observed for industries that rely on different amounts of highly educated labor.

The middle of these data, roughly 1940 to 1980, is a period that Claudia Goldin and Robert Margo (1992) have called "The Great Compression." In 1940, an American male at the 90th percentile of the income distribution (only 10 percent of working men earned more) earned five times as much as a man at the 10th percentile. By 1950, that gap had shrunk to a factor of three. In terms of years of schooling, bet-ween 1940 and 1950 there was a 17 percent decrease in the wage pre-mium for college graduates. In less technical terms, the poor were getting relatively richer and the rich were getting relatively poorer. Goldin and Margo estimate that almost half of the compression was due to falling returns to schooling.

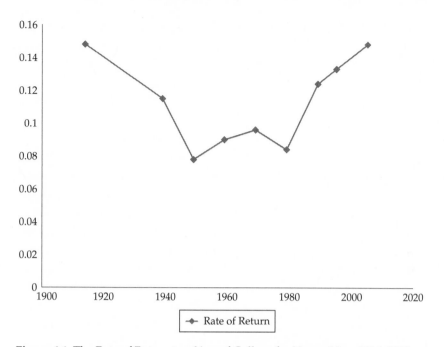

Figure 4.1 The Rate of Return to a Year of College for Young Men, 1914–2005

The Great Compression had staying power. Male wage differentials in 1975 were very similar to their 1945 levels. This led to a set of attitudes about higher education that might sound truly bizarre today. Delaying entry into the labor force in order to acquire a college degree was often considered a poor investment, even for students with the traits to succeed in college. One of us (Feldman) remembers high school guidance counselors in the early 1970s who would probe students' motivations if they expressed an interest in attending college, reminding them to think seriously about four lost years of company seniority and wages.

This extraordinary smoothing of the income distribution went into reverse starting in the late 1970s. By 1999 the gap between the 90th percentile and the 10th percentile of earnings for male workers had risen to 5.4, and as we will show in a moment the rise in the gap is accentuated for people who have even more education than a college degree (the super highly educated). Over the last thirty years the less educated have been getting relatively poorer, and the well educated have been getting relatively richer. The fact that the reversal of the Great Compression started around 1980 is a big part of our story. To attract highly educated workers, employers in higher education, medical care, and legal services have had to overcome stiffer competition after 1980 than they did prior to 1980. Since these industries have among the highest ratios of educated workers to total employment, this structural change in the whole economy plays a large role in the acceleration of costs in higher education, medical care, and legal services compared to other services such as barbershops, domestic services, and dry cleaning whose employees' educational requirements do not include a college degree.

While telling, the data in figure 4.1 actually understate the situation faced by the industries of interest. Not only do these industries employ a lot of people with a college degree, but a great number of the jobs require individuals with advanced degrees. The data showing the difference between the returns to a college degree and an advanced degree are not available for as long a time period as the data on the returns to college. Fortunately for us, the information starts in early 1973, just before the explosion in the college wage premium. Figure 4.2 presents this information.[4]

We arranged these data so that the wages of all the other categories are expressed relative to the wages of a high school graduate. This is why the wages of a high school graduate are always equal to 1.0. When we

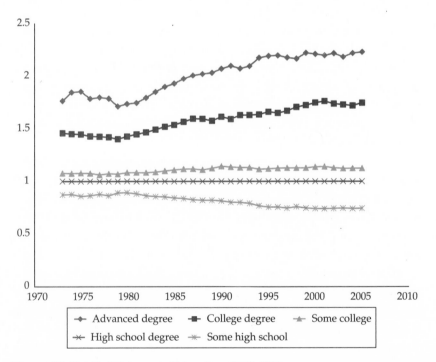

Figure 4.2 Detailed Returns to Education, 1973–2005

separate college graduates into people whose highest degree is an under-graduate diploma and those with an advanced degree, we see a similar pattern of declining relative wages of all college graduates followed by an increase starting in the very late 1970s. Splitting off the group with advanced degrees shows us that the increase in the returns to education was more pronounced for those with an advanced degree than it was for those whose education stopped with an undergraduate degree. Wages of workers with only a college degree increased from roughly 1.4 times the wage of a high school graduate in 1980 to 1.75 times in 2005. Wages of workers with an advanced degree climbed from just under 1.75 times the wages of a high school graduate in 1980 to 2.25 times by 2005.

To this point, we have made a fairly simple claim. One reason why the costs of higher education, health care, and legal services share a common time path, and one that is very different from the path followed by barbershops, domestic service, and dry cleaning, is that their labor force has a much higher percentage of highly educated workers than the other industries. The costs of employing these highly educated workers started to rise rapidly around 1980, just when the time path of costs in the two groups of industries started to diverge. This much is quite clear in the data, yet it still leaves an important question unanswered. Why did the returns to higher education, and particularly the returns to advanced degrees, begin to accelerate in the late 1970s? Understanding this process will shed additional light on why college costs so much today.

Why Did the College Wage Premium Grow?

There is an old joke about how easily one can train a parrot to be an economist. All you have to do is teach it to say "supply and demand." The joke works, of course, because there is a small shred of truth in it. A simple supply and demand framework can provide a number of important insights into why the wage premium for earning a college degree has evolved the way it has. The difficulty lies in pinning down the different forces that shift the supply and demand curves.

There is a large and fascinating literature in economics (really!) that looks at a host of different reasons why the returns to education started to soar in the late 1970s. This is not a settled area by any means, and there is ongoing controversy about the importance of some of the alleged causes. Here is a brief listing of the leading suspects:

- increases in immigration of low skilled workers,
- more outsourcing and more trade with less developed economies,
- the erosion of the real value of the minimum wage,
- declines in unionization,
- skill-biased technological change.

Of this list, the most widely accepted factor, and the one most economists would rank as easily the most important, is skill-biased technological change. Put very briefly, new technologies are skill biased if they increase the amount of training and education that people need in order to perform the tasks required of them on the job. Increases in the skill requirements of contemporary jobs have raised the demand for skilled labor, and this is a force for driving up the wages of people with more advanced schooling.

In *The Race Between Education and Technology*, Goldin and Katz (2008) fit the skill-biased technological-change argument into a broader story of supply and demand. They make a forceful case that changes in the wage distribution are best understood as the outcome of a race between technological progress and educational attainment. There is considerable evidence that technological change has been skill biased throughout the twentieth century, and that this process has steadily raised the demand for skilled workers. As long as this increase in the demand for skilled workers is met by a roughly equal increase in supply, the college wage premium and other measures of the returns to education need not grow. Goldin and Katz show that educational attainment (supply) grew very fast during the first three quarters of the twentieth century, and that this explains most of the *decrease* in the rate of return to education that we see in figure 4.1. But in the late 1970s, the upward march of educational attainment began to slow, while the demand for educated labor did not. The current burst of technological change, powered mostly by the spread of computerization throughout the economy, is just the latest manifestation of an ongoing process that has continually increased the demand for people with ever more years of schooling. This means the critical factors in explaining the mid-century fall and late-century rise in the economic return to education are on the supply side of things, namely changes in the growth of educational attainment.

Since there are two participants in this race—skill-biased technological change and educational attainment—we will divide our discussion into two parts. First, we will tackle skill-biased technological change by offering a short guide to the history of technological change since the beginning of time, or at least since the origin of the Industrial Revolution. We will follow that with a thumbnail sketch of how American educational attainment has evolved over the past century.

Changes in technology often are embedded in new kinds of capital equipment, and this new equipment can have a profound effect on both the quantity and the kind of labor that is demanded. The relationships among changes in technology, the use of new equipment, and the demand for skilled workers has an interesting history in manufacturing.

At the start of the Industrial Revolution, the relationship between new capital investment and the labor market was very different than it is today. The early period of industrialization saw the substitution of relatively *low-skilled* factory workers for highly skilled artisan labor. If you want to see examples of the pre-industrial workshops that this process supplanted, stroll through Colonial Williamsburg near the College of William and Mary where we teach. You will see highly skilled artisans with many years of on-the-job training working in small groups to produce small quantities of individually crafted handmade items. Machinery in a large factory setting operated by workers doing repetitive tasks began to displace this kind of labor. The increase in capital usage associated with building and equipping large-scale factories thus led to a reduction in the demand for skilled workers and the consequent impoverishment of artisans whose accumulated skills were no longer needed.

These changes led to considerable social unrest. The Luddites in England were the most famous of those who actively opposed "progress."[5] The Luddites took their name from Ned Ludd, who was supposed to have destroyed a machine that made stockings in Leicestershire in 1779. Starting in 1811 in Nottingham, the movement spread throughout England in the next two years. Luddites destroyed many textile mills until the movement was suppressed by the English government, which made "machine breaking" a capital crime. Facing disincentives like this, in the end the Luddites were not successful. The march of machinery could not be stopped.

In an earlier article, Goldin and Katz (1999) show how the relationship between the introduction of new machinery and the demand for skilled workers changed with the advent of continuous-process and batch-process methods in manufacturing in the late nineteenth and early twentieth centuries. Batch processing is used in processing liquids like molten metal, for example, and in things like wood pulp and chemicals. Continuous processing is used for products requiring little assembly and having no moving parts. Good examples include canned foods, flour, and matches. These types of processes require little human intervention. The machinery needs to be started, raw materials have to be fed to the machinery, and finished products come out. The continuous- and batch-process methods are the forerunners of the robot-assembly-line factories of today. These methods allowed firms to reduce cost by again substituting ever-cheaper machinery for more-expensive labor, but now the labor that was being displaced was the relatively unskilled factory worker.

Goldin and Katz explain how the shift to continuous and batch processing changed the demand for skilled workers by distinguishing between what they call the "machine installation and maintenance" phase of manufacturing and the "production or assembly" phase. Compared to a factory assembly line, continuous and batch processes use relatively more labor in machine installation and maintenance than in production and assembly. As a result, these production processes require a greater share of the firm's labor to be skilled than do the more traditional factory processes that first replaced artisans. The shift toward these continuous and batch processes switched the relationship between increases in capital and the demand for skilled labor. Changing from artisan labor in cottage industries to larger scale factory production increased the amount of capital and unskilled labor that was used and decreased the demand for skilled labor. The switch from factory labor to continuous and batch processing again increased the amount of capital used, but in this case it increased the demand for skilled labor.

When a company adopts new capital equipment that has novel technology embedded in it and this new approach requires the firm to hire skilled labor in place of less skilled labor, we call this process capital-technology complementarity. New equipment and skilled labor are complementary factors, that is, they go together. This process characterizes technological change over the last 120 years or so. The changes in technology we have seen over this long time frame are all different, of course, but they tend to be just variations on a theme. The incorporation of robots and other computer-controlled machinery on assembly lines in the last thirty-five years or so is very similar to the switch to continuous- and batch-process methods that began to spread at the turn of the twentieth century. These changes have increased the importance of the machine installation and maintenance phase of manufacturing, which raises the demand for skilled workers, while decreasing the importance of the production or assembly phase of manufacturing, which pushes down the demand for unskilled workers. Goldin and Katz argue that skill-biased technological progress has continued at a fairly steady pace over the last century and that the skills that are increasingly in demand require ever more years of formal schooling. They take a longer view of technological change, and this distinguishes their argument from many others who look more narrowly at the advent of computers as a driver of skill-biased technological progress in the last quarter of the twentieth century.

The other participant in Goldin and Katz's race is educational attainment. They present very persuasive evidence that the educational attainment of native-born Americans grew very rapidly for birth cohorts entering the labor force in the first three quarters of the century, but that educational attainment began to stagnate for birth cohorts after mid-century. Figure 4.3 presents the evidence. It shows that additional gains in schooling slowed down substantially for the mid-century birth cohorts that entered the labor force in the last quarter of the century.[6]

Part of the story this figure tells is about the impact of expanded elementary and secondary education in the early years of the twentieth century. Those born in the late nineteenth and early twentieth centuries were not likely to have entered high school let alone completed high school or attempted college. Therefore, early in the century a large part of the increase in educational attainment can be attributed to increases in primary and secondary education. The end of the long upward march of

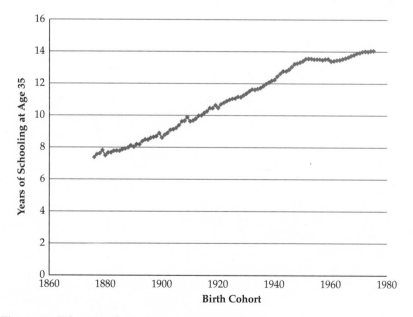

Figure 4.3 Educational Attainment by Birth Cohort

the high school graduation rate substantially explains the flattening of the line in figure 4.3 that starts with birth cohorts in the late 1940s. From a low of less than 10 percent at the turn of the twentieth century, the high school graduation rate progressed upward to over 75 percent in the mid-1960s. There it has remained.

College completion is the other part of the story behind the leveling off of educational attainment. Figure 4.4 shows the percentage of the males and females born in the United States in a particular year who graduated with a four-year degree by age thirty.[7] For example, for American males born in 1920, roughly 10 percent of them had earned a college degree by 1950. For the 1950 cohort, roughly 28 percent had earned a degree by 1980.

For the birth cohorts between 1900 and 1950, college completion rates soared among both men and women. Since the bulk of college completion occurs by age twenty-four (rather than thirty), this means that college graduates were flooding into the labor market between the mid-1920s and the mid-1970s, which is the period of the Great Compression in wages. After the 1950 cohort, male college completion went into reverse, and it has only recently clawed its way back to mid-century levels. This means that today's young men entering the labor force are no more likely to have a college degree than their fathers.

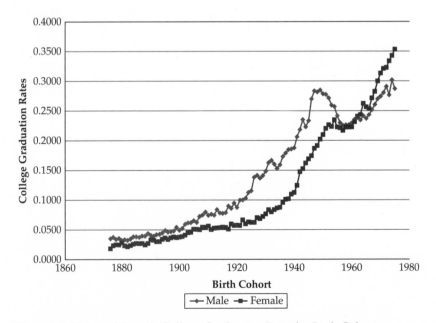

Figure 4.4 Male and Female College Graduation Rates by Birth Cohort

The overall college completion rate for native-born Americans has continued to rise, though at a more modest pace than in the past, because the female college completion rate has resumed its upward ascent. The female completion rate is now a full 7 percentage points higher than the male rate. But the recent surge in women with college degrees has not translated into an equally big increase in the supply of college degree holders in the labor market. The reason has to do with the rate at which men and women participate in the labor force. Although the gap in participation rates between men and women with college degrees has closed substantially since the mid-1960s, a sizable gap (95 percent versus 82 percent) remains. In addition, labor-force participation has begun to decline for both groups. For college-educated men, the participation rate has been inching lower since the 1970s. Since the mid-1990s, the labor-force-participation rate has begun to decline for women as well. The fall has been the greatest for young college-educated women with young children (under age three). For this group of recent graduates, labor-force participation has fallen eight full percentage points between 1994 and 2005. This decrease in labor-force participation among the increasing numbers of young women with college degrees has helped to diminish their impact on the wages of the highly educated.

Immigration is another factor that can affect the supplies of skilled and unskilled labor. The effect of immigration is quite complex. Immigrants tend to hold college degrees at higher rates than native-born workers, but the additional college-educated workers constitute a very small fraction of the national labor force. Where immigration may play a larger role is in raising the pool of extremely unskilled labor, those who lack a high school degree. Yet even here, the impact on native-born workers is disputed, and likely quite small in overall magnitude.

So, who won the race between technological change and educational attainment? To Goldin and Katz, it depends very much on when you ask the question. Looking out from the world of 1975, educational attainment clearly had won the race. The current generation was significantly more highly educated than the prior one, and this caused a general ratcheting up of living standards. In addition, surging supplies of ever more highly educated labor had contributed significantly to a narrowing of income differentials between the highly educated and the less educated. In a sense, the United States had it all: rapid economic growth that benefited everyone and which supported a burgeoning middle class that could afford to send its kids to college at rates unimaginable a generation earlier.

What has happened in the years since is that educational attainment has slipped, and skill-biased technical change has won the latest round. Skill-biased technical change clearly creates winners and losers. By pushing up the demand for highly educated labor, new technologies have changed the distribution of wages in ways that favor the well educated. The whole national income distribution gets stretched in ways that have been described as hollowing out the middle class. Today's college wage premium stands at just about the same level as in 1915.

This chapter has established that broad forces at work in the labor market have played a major role in shaping the trajectory of cost in many industries, including higher education. Compared to most other industries, higher education utilizes a very highly educated workforce. The same is true of a number of important service industries, including health care and legal services. In the first three quarters of the twentieth century, rising demand for skilled workers caused by skill-biased technological progress was more than matched by increases in the educational attainment of the workforce, so wages for highly educated workers fell compared to less skilled workers. But in the last quarter of the century the growth of educational attainment began to slow while skill-biased technological progress continued apace. The wages paid to highly educated workers began to soar relative to the wages paid to less highly educated workers. This forces up higher education costs (and the prices of health care and legal services) relative to the prices of services produced by industries that do not rely so heavily on highly educated workers.

5

Cost and Quality in Higher Education

We have just spent a chapter showing how technological change and educational attainment have rubbed together in the labor market over the past century to produce wage trends that have helped shape the trajectory of cost in higher education. Technological change also affects higher education *directly*, and this is the next part of the story we need to tell.

For much of the twentieth century, the kind of skill-biased technological change we discussed in the last chapter had little impact on higher education. Higher education remained an artisan industry. While batch- and continuous-process methods were changing manufacturing, professors and students were still assembling in classrooms, seminar rooms, and in professors' offices and laboratories for lectures, discussions, and lab exercises, much as they had done in times past. Things changed in the latter part of the twentieth century. A host of new technologies have transformed college campuses over the last fifty years. To take just one example, the computer revolution, which is an important part of the most recent surge in skill-biased technological change throughout the economy, has had a profound impact on how universities function and on how professors teach and do their research.

How Technological Change Has Transformed Higher Education

The easiest way to see that something new is going on in higher education, and in several other vital service industries, is to look at the expansion in equipment usage in these industries. Figure 5.1 gives the ratio of equipment to buildings for higher education, legal services, hospitals, nursing homes, and physicians and dentists combined (ambulatory health care).[1] Higher education, hospitals, and nursing homes consistently have lower ratios of equipment to buildings compared with legal services, physicians, and dentists because higher education, hospitals, and nursing homes have a large fraction of building space dedicated to housing, which is not as equipment intensive as treatment. The more important point is that in medical care and higher education the series start rising roughly in 1970. The upturn in the ratio of equipment to buildings is somewhat delayed in legal services, but there is an upturn nonetheless. This upturn in the real value of equipment to buildings occurs despite a fall in the

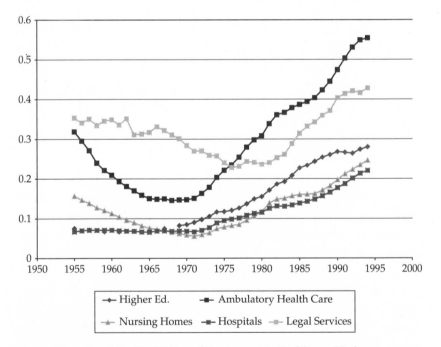

Figure 5.1 Ratio of the Real Value of Equipment to Buildings, Higher Education, Ambulatory Health Care, Nursing Homes, Hospitals, and Legal Services, 1955–94

price of equipment relative to buildings, so we are clearly seeing build-ings in these industries that are being filled with more and more capital equipment.

The way that the Bureau of Economic Analysis presents the data does not allow us to create similar series for barbershops, domestic ser-vices, and dry cleaning. This is unfortunate, because we would rather have data than rely on our observations. Still, unreliable as it may be, it is our observation that the barbershops of our youth and the barber-shops of today have much the same equipment. The same likely is true for domestic service and dry cleaning. These industries did not experi-ence the same increase in the value of equipment to buildings we see in figure 5.1.

How do these service industries compare to what was taking place in the rest of the economy? Figure 5.2 compares the time path of this equipment-to-buildings ratio for higher education with the time path for the total private economy. Both start to rise in the late 1960s and early 1970s, but the rate of increase in higher education starts to diverge from the rate of increase in the economy as a whole in the late 1970s and 1980s. The first figure shows that higher education does not behave

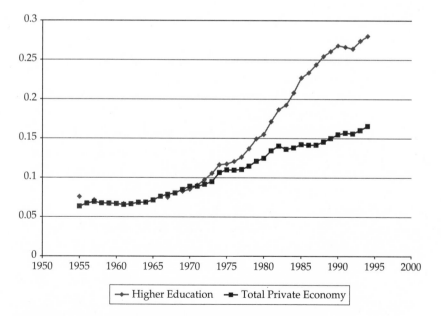

Figure 5.2 Ratio of the Real Value of Equipment to Buildings, Higher Education and the Economy as a Whole, 1955–94

very differently than medical care and legal services. The next one (5.2) offers some good evidence that what is going on in these service industries is a bit more intense than in the economy as a whole. What we are observing is an economy-wide change, but an economy-wide change that is accentuated in higher education, legal services, and health care.

A rise in the use of computers is an important part of the story in both of these figures. The Bureau of Economic Analysis only starts to include the value of the stock of computers, peripheral equipment, and software in 1962. Starting from a base of zero in 1961, by 2004 the proportion of equipment stocks composed of computers, peripherals, and software grew to 9.24 percent in the offices of physicians and dentists, 8.86 percent in hospitals, 10.79 percent in nursing homes, 41.36 percent in legal services, and 11.48 percent for the entire economy.[2] Data on computers as a percentage of equipment are not available for higher education.

Computers are not the complete story by any means. Anyone who visited a doctor or spent any time in a hospital in the 1970s would recognize a significant difference in the equipment of all kinds used in medical care today. Similarly, any 1960s graduate who goes back to his or her alma mater and visits the science laboratories or even the English department will notice a decided increase in the amount and sophistication of the equipment used. Computers have replaced typewriters on the professors' desks in the English department, while high-speed centrifuges, high-intensity lasers, and high-powered computer simulations have replaced the simpler test-tube and vacuum-tube world in science labs. Even lawyers now have to know how to present evidence using various new technologies, and a growing number of legal proceedings are done via video conferencing using high-tech equipment.

Skill-biased technological progress is responsible for an increase in demand for highly educated laborers in the economy at large. If a similar process is at work in higher education and the health care and legal services industries, we should see increases in the utilization of skilled workers in these industries as well, and we do, as figure 5.3 shows us.[3] Along with an increasingly intensive use of equipment within their buildings, these personal-service industries have changed the mix of employees they use. Compared to the mid-1970s, the percentage of highly educated workers increased in each of these sectors. The result is broadly true even for the sector "health care less hospitals," which includes nursing homes that still use a relatively large amount of unskilled labor.

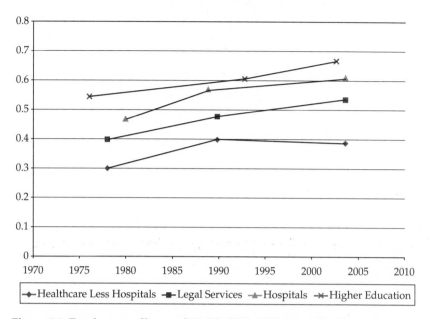

Figure 5.3 Employment Shares of Highly Skilled Workers, Healthcare less Hospitals, Legal Services, Hospitals, and Higher Education

This evidence is fairly clear. In medical care, legal services, and higher education, firms have chosen to adopt new production methods that use more equipment (figure 5.1) and this has been associated with increases in the amount of skilled labor they employ (figure 5.3). Capital-technology complementarity seems to be at work in these service industries just as in manufacturing.

Technology, Cost, and Quality

Firms usually adopt new technologies because they lower production costs. New methods allow them to produce the same output with less input. If steel producers figure out how to make a ton of hot rolled steel with 5 percent less labor time and 12 percent fewer kilowatts of power, the result is higher productivity that raises living standards. Even in artisan-like personal services, technological changes do have the potential to raise labor productivity and hold down costs. Yet we will argue that the primary impact of technological progress in higher education has been to change *what* we do and *how* we do it rather than to lower the cost of the *existing* "output" or the *current* way of doing things.

A simple example of how some technological changes can indeed reduce cost in higher education will help make this discussion less abstract. When we were graduate students, academic departments employed a rather large number of workers in a typing pool that prepared everything from professors' tests to their professional manuscripts. Typing pools have all but disappeared. Faculty members now do all of that work themselves with the assistance of personal computers and a corps of highly educated and expensive IT specialists who manage university software systems and networks. This new technology has allowed schools to substitute away from using a lot of relatively low-skilled workers (the typists) and toward using more machinery (computers, servers, and printers) and a few highly skilled workers to administer the networks and to install and fix the hardware and software needed to run the systems. More generally, IT departments did not exist in the 1960s, but by the 1990s they had become vitally important parts of many enterprises. A modern college or university would be lost without its IT services, as would a modern hospital and even a modern law office.

The disappearance of the typing pool, however, is not just a higher education phenomenon. Technology has made typists scarce in lots of organizations. In 1989, roughly one in seven employees of the federal government worked in jobs that were primarily clerical. By 2000, the fraction of employees in clerical jobs had fallen to one in thirteen. In 2000, Michael Brostek, the General Accounting Office's associate director for federal management and workforce issues, explained the reason for the change: "The advent of computers and the access of professional staff to computers is much greater than it used to be. Individuals who used to rely on secretarial and clerk staff to prepare documents now tend to do it themselves."[4]

This is yet another economy-wide change, and higher education has merely participated. According to data from the Bureau of Labor Statistics in 1972, the job category "typist" accounted for 1.38 percent of the total non-farm workforce. By 2005 that percentage had fallen to 0.22 percent.

The typing pool example tells us that there is at least some scope for technological change to hold down costs. The problem for college cost is that this sort of reaction to new technology is not broadly representative of the impact of technological change. The evidence about productivity growth in many personal services over the last thirty years is quite clear. The actual measures of productivity change are *negative* for health care and educational services since the 1980s, which means we currently use more input than in the past to achieve the same level of output. For the higher education industry as a whole, new technologies are not transforming the industry in ways that allow significant reductions in input use, especially of highly educated labor, and the shift toward an ever-more-highly-skilled workforce has not led to any measured productivity gain for the sector as a whole. Costs must go up as a consequence.

Modernization itself has played a very important role in the rapid rise in costs in higher education, medical care, and legal services. This should seem strange, since modern new techniques typically are adopted by an industry because firms are trying to cut their costs. That kind of cost cutting may increase a firm's or an industry's profit for a while, but as we noted in chapter 3 competitive forces tend over time to pass the benefit of that productivity growth on to us as higher wages and/or lower prices. This is the standard story of how rising labor productivity gradually raises the standard of living. We clearly are not observing this kind of change in higher education or in the other service industries on which we are focusing. Costs and prices are rising along with changes in the technology used by these firms and organizations. Why are these particular industries behaving in this seemingly peculiar way? To answer this we have to introduce a different aspect of technological change to the discussion.

Technological progress can have two very different effects on an industry. First, it can make goods and services of a given quality or type easier to produce. This is the steel story or the typing-pool example. Our standard measures of productivity growth can capture this effect rather easily. Second, technological change can lead the product or service itself to evolve in ways that perform old tasks better or that satisfy new wants entirely. In other words, quality may improve. These gains can be much harder to measure.

Quality is particularly difficult to quantify in many personal services, and the problem of quality evaluation is fiendishly difficult in higher education. We have no meaningful way to assess the social value or quality of additional research output coming out of universities. Even the quantity of research output is notoriously difficult to measure. The quality of teaching is no easier to evaluate. This point requires a bit of an extended argument, beginning with a brief discussion of the meaning of productivity and quality in the context of higher education.

Measuring Productivity

Productivity in service industries often is very hard to measure. As we have noted, using simple measures of labor productivity like students taught per faculty member, or students taught per labor hour worked, the productivity of higher education institutions actually has been stagnant or declining. But productivity of other kinds may have improved. Productivity growth in higher education may be the type that goes unmeasured using typical gauges of productivity growth.

What might go unmeasured? One possibility is that the quantity of knowledge acquired by the average student has increased over time. If the typical student today learns more than a typical student did in the past, and we had an easy way to measure the learning, then measured productivity in higher education would not be as stagnant as it appears. Universities are just now beginning to think about how one might measure "value added," and no such measure exists for the past. In any case, this is *not* a claim we are interested in making. We will remain steadfastly agnostic about whether or not the *quantity* of learning that goes on in a modern college is any greater than it was in the past. We have something very different in mind when we talk about *quality* change.

The critical thing is not that the quantity of knowledge has changed but rather that the knowledge itself has changed, along with the ways in which it is transmitted. A college or university today must pass on to its students a different type of knowledge and a different package of skills than in the past. Rapid changes in technology in the world around us force these changes in what colleges and universities teach and in how they teach it. The difficulty with using traditional measures of productivity in higher education is that students taught, degrees granted, or credit hours acquired may mean something quite different today than they did in the past. This newer knowledge and more current set of skills may be costlier to provide even in an efficient production setting, so higher costs per student is not an automatic sign of trouble in paradise.

Productivity growth is notoriously difficult to measure in the best of circumstances. In higher education and many other personal services the problem is compounded because there is no clear and meaningful definition of what these industries actually are producing. In higher education, we can measure things like the number of students taught, the number of degrees granted, or the number of credit hours awarded. But we do not have a readily available way to measure other important things such as the amount of knowledge transmitted, the usefulness of that knowledge, or the extent to which students' problem-solving skills and love of learning are improving and growing over time. And these teaching outputs only measure one facet of what a college or university actually does. They leave out the research and public service that are produced in conjunction with the teaching mission.

Productivity measured as students taught per labor hour is the type of productivity that has failed to rise in higher education in any sustained fashion over the last century. This stands in stark contrast to the rapid increases in labor productivity in most manufacturing industries. We could indeed increase the number of students taught per faculty member by enlarging classes or by using less expensive part-time professors whose qualifications may be substantially lower than the full-time members of the faculty. But this is not extra economic gravy generated by new ways of doing things. Unlike the steel industry example of technology-driven labor-saving productivity growth, forcing more students into each class would not be seen as unalloyed productivity growth. Most of us would recognize the potential hit to educational quality if class sizes grew, or if full-time professors were replaced by adjuncts.

This brings the word "quality" into the discussion again. Cost reduction is not the only motive for introducing new ways and new techniques. New technologies also can improve quality or change the nature of a product in desirable ways. We must at least recognize the possibility of hidden productivity growth in industries that adopt new techniques. Sometimes these quality improvements require more physical input of things like highly educated labor hours and new expensive machinery, but because productivity continues to be calculated as widgets per labor hour this quality may be missed in the data which report stagnant or even declining productivity.[5]

Yet in some instances, quality improvements actually are very easy to measure. A computer chip that executes twice as many operations per second is demonstrably better. Where quality improvements are easily measured, they are much like cost reductions. In fact, where we can, we do build these quality improvements into our price indexes. Again, computers provide a simple example. Because computing power has increased exponentially, the *real* costs of computers (adjusting for what the machines can do) has fallen substantially, even though the money cost of a computer system has not fallen nearly as much. Compare a contemporary iMac system or PC costing $1,500 with a similarly priced computer system produced in 1992. They are both computers, but there the similarity ends. The Bureau of Labor Statistics (BLS) now adjusts the consumer price index (CPI) for these quality gains. If it did not, the CPI would overstate inflation and begin to diverge substantially from the reality it is trying to capture. Likewise, the CPI also adjusts apartment rents for basic quality changes, such as the tendency for newer apartments to raise the average square footage available to people. If it did not, the cost of housing would be overstated. The BLS also adjusts the price indexes of some services for quality improvements. When cable services add channels or cell phone providers upgrade plans without increasing the price, the price indexes for these services are adjusted downward accordingly to reflect the improved quality.

Where we can easily measure the quality improvement, the gains actually will show up in our measures of labor productivity growth over time. But in many of the important services that now dominate the economic landscape, quality improvements are much harder to measure. When banks added ATMs, for instance, that change did not affect the way the BLS measured the price of banking services, even though quality of the service clearly rose. In health care, many kinds of quality change are inherently difficult to evaluate. The BLS does not factor in changes in patient outcomes, such as improved mortality or reduction in pain, so productivity growth goes unnoticed to some extent.

In higher education, we can identify many ways that technological change has raised the quality of the service. Something as simple as e-mail allows professors to provide information to students outside of class time and/or office hours and to do it efficiently without repeating the same response to each student face to face. This leaves more time for working one on one with a student doing independent research. New course-management software packages such as Blackboard® enhance student-professor and student-student interaction in ways that allow almost-round-the-clock learning. As an example, professors can pose questions for online conversation in order to make upcoming in-class discussions more effective. Advances in statistical software such as the STATA® package allow many more students to do meaningful research in a wide variety of fields than was the case a generation ago when students had to write their own FORTRAN algorithms and wait many hours for a mainframe computer to execute a set of commands, all the while hoping that every comma or semicolon in their program was perfectly in place.

Universities themselves also have begun to modify the curriculum in ways that arguably raise quality while increasing cost. Many schools have moved toward small group seminars at the first-year level and at the capstone level in order to concentrate on writing and research. And many are allocating more faculty time to one-on-one research projects with students. These are resource-intensive activities. Whenever you add to the size of the faculty in order to reduce the average class size you decrease measured labor productivity because the productivity measuring stick only captures things like total student credit hours funneled through the system.

Outside of the curriculum, schools have added significantly to support services such as student health care, counseling centers, and career services, while substantially improving facilities for people with disabilities. These extra services are quality enhancing in the eyes of the purchaser, even though they take real resources to produce. Because they don't funnel more students through the system per faculty member, these extra services are a drag on measured productivity.

Many universities often use arguments like the ones given above about quality improvements to deflect criticism over rapid and sustained tuition increases. Higher quality as hidden productivity growth offers a comforting way to rationalize higher college costs as value for money. Bobby Fong, the president of Butler University, captured one aspect of the quality-cost tradeoff this way:

> For the last three years, we have capped the freshman class at 915. While this has led to increased selectivity as the applicant pool has continued to grow, it also means that the university does not realize potential savings found in increased scale of production. Teaching institutions like Butler do not become more economical by producing more graduates every year. The very quality of the education they provide depends on limiting production.[6]

Although we think there is much merit in this "hidden productivity" argument, we caution against thinking that either technological progress or university choices about its curriculum or its size naturally pushes higher education ever closer to some abstract ideal. In fact, much of the contemporary popular writing on higher education leans decidedly in the opposite direction. Books like Alan Bloom's *The Closing of the American Mind* and Charles Sykes' *ProfScam* are representative examples of a veritable publishing industry devoted to analyzing the seeming decline in the quality of American higher education.[7] Bloom laments the collapse of disinterested rigor in the classroom, while Sykes highlights the increasing and wasteful misuse of faculty time on supposedly fraudulent research.

Despite the feeling that many of us likely share that our own college days were a halcyon epoch, there has never been a time in which higher education provided a magical optimum quality at low cost. To take but one example, the notion of what a higher education should convey to students has evolved continuously over the last two hundred years. Course content steeped in the classics was challenged in the nineteenth century by reformers who wanted to implement a more practical curriculum geared to the economic needs of the students and of the nation. This trend was furthered by the 1862 Morill Act, which established many of our prominent state universities. At the same time, undergraduate curriculums began to move away from prescribed lock-step pathways and toward student choice of what they wanted to study.

Later in the nineteenth century, with the founding of Johns Hopkins University in 1876, the modern research institution was brought to the United States from its German rootstock. Each of these changes met some perceived need. And some of them, like the development of research universities with a major commitment to educating graduate students, would have been quite costly using our standard measures of productivity such as full-time students taught per faculty member.

Former Harvard president Derek Bok (2006) concludes his look at the history of quality in undergraduate education this way:

> History, then, offers weak support at best for the reports of a decline in the quality of undergraduate education. Loose allegations to that effect have little foundation in fact but instead rest on fanciful visions of some previous golden age. Other charges alleging a growing neglect of teaching or the loss of some grand unifying purpose are likewise unsubstantiated.[8]

We agree. We have argued that many technology-induced changes of the recent past clearly are quality enhancing for higher education, and we have even called it hidden productivity growth. We also argue that university decisions to reduce class size or to offer more intensive counseling or career services offer something of value to students. Yet we are leery of any grand claims about the natural evolution of quality in higher education. The truth about quality in higher education is that it is neither on a stairway to heaven nor on a road to hell. The natural tendency of the institution is to respond to society's changing needs, often in ways that then have consequences for the economic, scientific, and social course of events.

We are left with institutions that are driven to implement new systems, new approaches, and new technologies that are often quite costly.

Sometimes the quality gains of these changes are clear, but sometimes the impulse to do these things seems "just because," and "just because" is not a persuasive argument. Why might colleges and universities feel pressed to adopt new technology rapidly, even if that technology seems tangential to the central mission of a teacher in front of a class, and that technology is extremely expensive to boot? Let us begin with a recent example.

In the 1980s and 1990s, colleges and universities began an expensive effort to wire campuses. This was followed almost immediately by an equally expensive effort to make campuses wireless. This pattern of expenditures illustrates technological change that is cost increasing. In the 1960s and 1970s, computing was done on large mainframe computers, which had few remote access points. Typically, the user had to go to the computer center with his or her stack of IBM cards to have a program run. In the second half of the 1970s and into the1980s, the ways people accessed computers changed. The first step included remote access through terminals distributed across campus coupled with minicomputers in laboratories and on the desks of selected computer users. This required a certain amount of wiring of the campus. With the advent of the personal computer and the Internet, the entire campus needed to be wired, including dormitory rooms, classrooms, and faculty and staff offices. Wiring campuses for high-speed Internet access required very large expenditures. Finally, more recently students and faculty have migrated to laptop computers and access the Internet through wireless hubs. To accommodate the evolving technology, colleges and universities have had to put resources into making fully wired campuses go wireless.

These gyrations from wired to wireless campuses were not motivated by a desire to cut costs. They were motivated by a perceived need to keep up with the changing requirements of an important new technology. The new techniques do permit universities to do more, and this clearly is a quality issue, but we will emphasize a different motive. For higher education institutions, *not* adopting these new approaches was simply unthinkable. The disappearance of the typing pool is quite different. In that case, the new technology allowed the colleges and universities, together with the government and other employers, to employ a cost-reducing strategy. The wired to wireless example of new technology creating costs for colleges and universities is just one example, but it is quite representative of the impact of new technology on the higher education industry.

Standard of Care

Why is *not* adopting new techniques often unthinkable, even if costs rise as a consequence? Let us take an example from health care. A new piece of medical equipment may allow a physician to do more accurate imaging, leading to fewer mistakes in designing the care a patient will receive. The new imaging equipment likely will be more expensive than the old. But if it produces better outcomes for patients, it improves the quality of care. Patients will want to have it, and physicians will want to use it, so it will be used. In addition, physicians have an ethical and legal requirement to meet standards of care that evolve over time. When the new imaging technology's superior proficiency is clearly demonstrated, the standard of care will require its use. At that point, physicians will have no choice but to use newer techniques, even if they are more expensive. They cannot choose to continue to do things the old way simply because the old way is cheaper. Nor can they offer budget procedures for the price conscious. They have to adopt the new and supposedly better technology, or they will face a malpractice suit. At times, there is uncertainty about whether a new technology is better than the old one. As a result, this process has its fits and starts, and the adoption of new technologies is not smooth. Yet viewed over time, there are a large number of cost-increasing medical procedures that have become commonplace.

The relationship between technological change, the quality of care, and medical care costs has long been a part of the standard explanation of rapidly increasing costs of medical care. In a 1979 report for the Department of Health Education and Welfare, Stuart Altman and Robert Blendon used the title, *Medical Technology: The Culprit Behind Health Care Costs?* The consensus answer is that technological change is at least one of the major culprits. If new technologies seem to increase the quality of care, patients and physicians alike will want to use them. As a result, the new technologies are adopted despite the fact that they increase the cost of providing care.

The evolution of the standard of care in the medical profession is quite complex and involves many aspects of how medical care is delivered and paid for, including professional societies, insurers, and the tort system. These are all industry-specific processes and institutions. Yet we think a very similar thing is taking place in higher education, though it is less well recognized.

We don't use the language "standard of care" in describing higher education, but this may be a mistake. At colleges and universities, the chalk, paper, pen, and test-tube world has been replaced by wired buildings, laptops, high-tech classrooms, and pulsed laser systems in physics labs, together with the specialists needed to make the systems work. This change has its roots in the fact that the *outputs* of higher education (both research and graduates) are the *inputs* of other industries. This forces higher education institutions to educate students to a standard influenced in part by those who will hire its students and in part by the past developments that have come out of their own research activities. The undergraduate chemistry student, for instance, has to be able to understand and operate the equipment used in a modern industrial chemistry lab. Without this knowledge, he or she would not be useful to the pharmaceutical industry or the biotechnology industry. This effect is not restricted to the natural sciences. An economics student for instance who is not well versed in how to work with data (and with the computer software packages that perform the complicated mathematical calculations) is handicapped when competing for employment at private consulting firms or government agencies that increasingly demand that new employees really understand these things. These industries and agencies have changed the way they operate by adopting a series of technological advancements, and higher education institutions must adapt or they will in effect be guilty of educational malpractice. Colleges and universities cannot ignore the technologies that are changing the world around them. Many of these technologies have roots in the laboratories, classrooms, and research centers of universities themselves.

In an important sense, higher education institutions do not have a real choice. They cannot simply provide an education like the one the professors received when they were in college. As enduring as some of the processes and concepts we teach may be, a modern university must provide students with an up-to-date education that familiarizes students with the techniques and associated machinery that are used in the workplace the students will enter. In other words, schools must meet a standard of care expected of them by the students who attend (and the families that pay), and by the private donors and state governments who support the institution.

We understand that a classical liberal education may not require access to nuclear accelerators. Nor does it require advanced computing facilities and the IT personnel required to maintain them. Some great ideas and great books are indeed timeless, and they may require nothing more than a motivated professor lecturing to a class of hard-working students. There are still schools like the two campuses of St. John's College seemingly committed to this approach.

Yet even schools that are the most committed to this approach are not stagnant technologically. Nor have they have escaped the cost-disease phenomenon so characteristic of low-productivity-growth personal-service industries in general. In fact, costs of instruction per student at St. John's have increased more rapidly than costs of instruction at many comparable institutions.[9]

Colleges and universities do more than pass on current knowledge to their students. Without wading into the thicket of criticism about whether research in different disciplines really expands the frontier of knowledge, or is of any redeeming social value, we will assert only that the attempt has some value both because of the outcomes it produces and through the skills and attitudes it passes on to the next generation. To be successful in these research efforts, an institution has to provide its faculty the appropriate tools. In many cases, these tools are on the leading edge of science and technology, and they are expensive. Much of this research is not easily duplicated in the private sector because it is basic research instead of product-specific research. Private firms have a weaker incentive to produce knowledge for free that might benefit their competitors. American universities do not have to invest so heavily in their research mission, but in the end such a choice would shortchange the nation, because the discoveries that take place in the offices and laboratories at colleges and universities have been an important reason for the technological advancement that has so dramatically improved average living standards in the country and around the world.

The synergies between the faculty research and student learning are perhaps most evident in the education of graduate students. To do a good job of creating the next generation of scientists and scholars, a college or university has to apprentice these graduate students to active and successful researchers. These successful researchers pass on their attitudes, their knowledge, and the techniques that have made them successful. This interchange is critical to create the next generation of college teachers and researchers in government and industry. More generally, this interchange is critical to insure that as a nation we keep creating the knowledge that fuels the productivity growth that yields higher living standards in the future.

Although the complementarities between research and teaching are clearest in graduate training, they are present in undergraduate education as well. A professor who stays close to the frontier of knowledge in his or her chosen discipline is more likely to be a better communicator of the insights and skills that the discipline has to offer to contemporary students. A professor who remains actively engaged in the often arduous and elaborate process of trying to push the frontier of knowledge outward likely does a better job of instilling in students the desire to gain knowledge and an appreciation of how that is done. Advanced undergraduates also benefit from getting a taste of real research so they can decide whether or not they want to pursue graduate study. All of this teaching and mentoring is facilitated if those who teach undergraduates are themselves involved in and successful at doing research of their own.

We noted earlier in this chapter that many universities recently have begun to emphasize undergraduate research, and that this new emphasis on small group interaction is costly. It is costly because it adds input (faculty labor hours) without increasing measured output (students taught per faculty member). In other words, this "innovation" reduces measured labor productivity. Nonetheless, it is an experiment in offering a changed product to the current generation of students. If it meets a new need expressed in the marketplace for graduates and becomes a part of the standard of care, then it likely will persist despite the increased cost.

Finally, the importance of meeting the expected standard of care affects more than the education and research mission of a college or university. Expectations have been raised for the quality and quantity of many administrative functions. We can provide several examples. First, colleges are expected to provide students career advice, and potential employers want access to students. Career services offices, which were often very small informal operations in the 1960s, are now sophisticated operations employing a large professional staff. Second, college admission has become a higher and higher stakes experience for students and families in the last ten or fifteen years. Bookstore shelves are well stocked with college guides, and some families hire professional admission counselors to help guide their children through the admission process. Colleges and universities have to respond by having larger and larger professional admission staffs to deal with the questions, provide interviews, run information sessions for visiting students, and to read and evaluate the mountains of applications for admission. Third, as colleges and universities have expanded their funding sources, particularly state-supported institutions whose state support represents a shrinking percentage of total funding, they have found that they have to hire larger development staffs as well as more accountants and auditors to be sure that they are raising more money and are accurately keeping track of the funds from various sources. Fourth, as societal norms concerning the opportunities it offers to students with learning disabilities have changed, colleges and universities have been required to offer services to these students. This requires professional staff able to assist the faculty to teach these students.

By their very nature, colleges and universities want to meet expectations for the standard of care. They want to provide their students with an up-to-date education. They want their faculty to be engaged in cutting-edge research. And they want to have the administrative infrastructure required to allow their institutions to run smoothly. In chapter 1, we mentioned the magnifying-glass view of higher education by way of contrast to our aerial view. The magnifying-glass or microscope view highlights many potentially unsettling things. For instance, the prestige-game explanation for increasing higher education costs suggests that colleges and universities are motivated to improve or to defend their ranking in *U.S. News and World Report*. The rankings competition is about relative position, and it is an argument that is specific to higher education. Our explanation of rising cost is very different. It is outward looking. In this third and final leg of the tripod or stool, we have argued that higher education is trying to stay current in a changing world, and the changes that colleges and universities have had to manage have increased the cost of providing an education that meets the current expectations of students and employers.

Some Concluding Thoughts

Though they do not use our precise language, higher education analysts have not completely ignored the impact of a standard of care on higher education costs. What Massy and Wilger (1992) term "the growth force" at least tangentially incorporates this notion. The growth force describes the process by which new knowledge is created. Massy and Wilger argue that this accretion of knowledge requires new faculty, new courses, and new technology. The fact that new knowledge adds to what we already know explains why they use the term "growth force." We would use the term "change force" rather than growth force. Growth in knowledge has always been a part of higher education. New knowledge has always been added, and this new knowledge demands a place in the curriculum. This has been true since Plato's Academy, and it was certainly true in the period from 1970 through 1980 when higher education costs were rising no faster than the overall inflation rate. We would also note that old knowledge often disappears from university curricula and from the university's costs over time. Semesters are not growing to account for increases in the knowledge base, and days are not getting longer to accommodate the extra knowledge. Again, there is no hard evidence that university costs are significantly affected by the need to grow larger just to pass on to the next generation the sheer bulk of human knowledge.

The important question to ask is whether or not the new knowledge is more expensive to impart to students than the old knowledge. The years since 1980 are different from earlier decades because of the type of change that has occurred. We have seen an increase in the intensity of equipment use and in the skill requirements for those who work in higher education. Because colleges and universities want to meet the highest standard of care, these changes have increased higher education costs more than the costs of most goods and services. In the end though, the idea of a change force is more optimistic than a growth force. If growth in the amount of knowledge is driving costs, then costs will always be going up. If the type of knowledge is changing, then the next set of changes might not be as expensive to implement.

To summarize, more equipment-intensive workplaces and shifts in the skill requirements of jobs impact industries differently, and it is useful to place industries on a continuum. On one end of this continuum would be industries in which the new technology has reduced costs but has had no effect on the quality of output. In the middle would be industries in which the new techniques have created both cost reductions and quality enhancements. On the other extreme would be industries in which the impact of the new technology has been to transform the product or to increase its quality without reducing costs. One of the reasons that prices in certain personal services like medical care, higher education, and legal services have increased more rapidly than other prices is that these three industries are positioned on this continuum toward the extreme in which either quality is improved or the whole enterprise is changing, but costs are not reduced.

6

The Bottom Line: Why *Does* College Cost So Much?

The food in my refrigerator spoils too rapidly. My shoes hurt my feet. American firms are not as competitive as they have been in the past. These are things we don't like. They are problems, and people naturally search for the cause of a problem by looking where the problem seems to be occurring. The food is spoiling, so the refrigerator is not working correctly. My shoes hurt my feet; they must be too tight. American firms are less competitive, so the managers of these firms must not be doing a good job.

While it is natural to diagnose problems this way, at times the proper diagnosis is quite different. Perhaps your house has faulty wiring, and the perfectly fine refrigerator only gets power intermittently. Perhaps you are developing a bunion, so the fault is with your foot not your shoes. Perhaps changes in the exchange rate have put U.S. firms, even excellently managed ones, at a competitive disadvantage in international markets.

Tuition and fees at colleges and universities consistently go up faster than the inflation rate. We don't like this, so it is a problem. The first cause one might consider is that colleges and universities are somehow doing something wrong. Colleges and universities have indeed served up some pretty fat targets in recent years, so this approach might appear to be quite fruitful. We will evaluate this approach in detail in the next chapter. The aerial view we have adopted suggests a very different approach. We have argued that broad economic forces that are buffeting every industry are the primary driver of rapidly rising higher education costs. Changes in the economic environment combined with reasonable reactions by colleges and universities result in rapidly rising costs that have to be passed on in rapidly rising tuition and fees.

Yet the upward march of college cost is neither uniform nor uninterrupted. In chapter 2, we first laid out the whole history of higher education costs and prices since the end of the Second World War. Figure 6.1 shows the time path of higher education prices to help the discussion along. The most striking feature of that long trajectory is that the two periods of sustained increases (late 1940s through late 1960s, and early 1980s onward) neatly bracket one period of flat or even slightly declining costs in the 1970s. We are now in a position to put all the pieces of this puzzle together to finish the tale of why college costs so much today and how this came to be. But first we will take you back to the three hypothetical vignettes of Ohio families embarking on the college experience at the College of William and Mary. Those three experiences nicely reveal the basic message of the national data.

Our first family arrived on campus with their son in 1960, and the middle family enrolled their daughter in the summer of 1981. Looking back from a later vantage point, college costs had indeed risen since the early 1960s, but the pace of increase was measured instead of torrid. With the full national evidence in front of you, you can see that the second

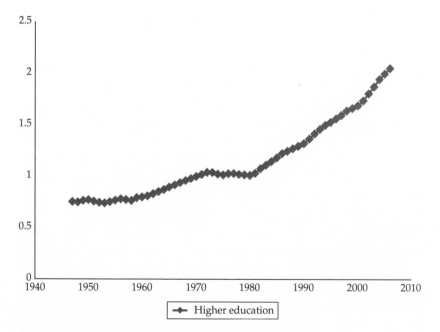

Figure 6.1 The Real Price of Higher Education, 1947–2006

family was entering the market for higher education immediately at the
end of the remarkable decade-long pause in the much longer term trend
of rising cost. Between 1970 and 1980 the real cost per student of the
educational expenses of colleges and universities actually had declined.
The last family of our trio started their college quest in 2006. This family
would view the middle family's experience as a halcyon epoch of bar-
gain-priced education. The cost of higher education began rising in a
sustained fashion in the early 1980s as the middle child was finishing her
education, and it is this more recent rise that puts the "crisis" in college
costs for many families.

Any full story of the national data has to explain both the long-term
trend and the remarkable pause during the 1970s. We will start this
chapter with a summary of our explanation of the long-term trend. In the
next section, we will explain how the flat portion in the data does not
contradict the story we have been telling.

A Summary of the Analysis

If we had to summarize four chapters of evidence and argument into a
compact claim we would say that the villain, as much as there is one, is
economic growth itself. Economic growth has a wide variety of effects on
the economy, but in the case of higher education *and a set of kindred industries* these effects all seem to conspire to make cost rise faster than the
general inflation rate. First, and perhaps foremost, higher education is a
personal-service industry. Over the broad sweep of time, productivity-
enhancing technological progress has affected primarily manufacturing
so the cost of manufactured goods has gone down compared to personal
services like higher education, health care, and legal services. Despite
recent productivity gains in some services like communications and
retailing, the more artisan-like personal services remain laggards in productivity growth. These industries must nonetheless pay for a highly
educated work force, so costs rise. This is the cost-disease process.

Second, for well over a century technological progress has tended to
displace less-educated (unskilled) labor while increasing the demand for
more-educated (skilled) labor. Alone, this is a force for rising wages of
the highly educated and for increased income inequality. Yet for much of
the twentieth century, the American labor force acquired skill and schooling at so rapid a rate that the economic return to extra schooling actually

declined. The supply of educated workers rose as fast as or faster than the demand. This process reversed in the late 1970s, and the wages of the college educated began to soar. Industries where educated labor is concentrated naturally tended to see rising cost compared to industries that use less of it or that can shed it easily as wages for highly educated labor rise. The higher education industry uses an awful lot of highly educated labor, and the industry cannot easily economize on its use of that skilled labor because the primary service deliverer in this modern artisan industry is one of the most highly educated workers in the economy. The computing revolution of the last thirty years has only served to increase the industry's dependence on skilled labor.

Finally, technological progress affects industries very differently. Some industries produce a rather homogeneous and unchanging product. Cement or basic chemicals like sulfuric acid come to mind. A technological improvement that allows you to make one of these products with less labor or with fewer megawatts of power will allow you to produce it more cheaply. On the opposite end of the spectrum, technical progress sometimes does NOT lead you to produce something with less labor or electric power. Instead, it pushes you to make a higher quality product or simply a different product for different needs. We have argued that higher education and the other personal services it resembles are at this "opposite" end of the spectrum. At this end, technological progress does not translate into lower cost.

All of these claims about higher education flow mostly from our chosen aerial perspective. We have situated higher education within the broader economy, and we have sought out the large forces that have shaped the trajectory of higher education costs together with costs in other related industries. We have indeed sometimes dipped into the micro- or street-level data to illustrate our arguments, but the street-level view is not the starting point for how we think about the historical evolution of cost in this vital service industry.

The Decade of the 1970s

We have argued that cost disease is the best way to think about the long upward march of college cost when compared to the average of all prices over the whole time period we are examining. Stable costs for an extended period like a decade should indeed make one sit up and take notice. Yet forces that reverberated though the entire global economy in that decade easily explain the pause of the 1970s. These big forces did not turn off the cost-disease engine for all time or reduce its explanatory power over long sweeps of history. Cost disease is driven by productivity growth that is more rapid in some sectors (like manufacturing) than in others (like personal services). College cost temporarily peaked in roughly 1973, which is the year the great slowdown of global productivity began. Output per labor hour in manufacturing grew at an annual rate of roughly 3.0 percent between 1960 and 1972. That rate slowed to 1.85 from 1973 to 1981 before rising again to 3.2 percent between 1982 and 1995.[1] If productivity growth recedes elsewhere in the economy, the major driving force of cost disease is muted.

In an important sense, the great pause of the 1970s actually reinforces our main contention that economic growth itself is the driving engine of cost in the still artisan-like higher education industry. When growth at the national level slows down significantly, as it did during the turbulent decade of the 1970s, we should expect a moderation in cost pressure in any industry that is prone to the cost-disease phenomenon.

In addition, the decade of the 1970s also saw a significant decline in the wage premium earned by college graduates. We have talked about the "Great Compression" in wages that characterized the middle of the twentieth century. That compression was particularly severe in the 1970s. Between 1970 and the early 1980s, the average earnings of male workers with five or more years of college education fell nearly 20 percent in real terms. Faculty salaries moved downward with them. Between 1970 and 1982, faculty salaries at public universities had fallen 25 percent in real terms. Private university salaries had taken a slightly greater 30 percent hit.[2] Taken together, slowing manufacturing-sector productivity growth and declining wages for the well educated would naturally put the brakes on growth in the real cost and price of a college education. Yet like manufacturing-sector productivity, the returns to higher education rebounded in the 1980s, so the cost of higher education began to surge upward in response.

Imagine cost disease as the basic flow rate of a river. A tidal surge or even a strong wind can reduce that flow for a while. But in the end, as long as the rains are regular, that long-run flow exerts a powerful force. Interruptions to productivity growth or strong headwinds in the labor market that temporarily depress wages of the highly educated can create the impression that cost disease is a spent force. But unless and until productivity growth comes to the remaining artisan-like personal services, the basic impetus behind cost disease is always there.

A Statistical Summary

To this point, we have summarized how economy-wide factors have influenced the time path of costs in higher education. The question remains whether these factors are more important or less important than higher education–specific factors that other analysts emphasize. This is not an easy issue to resolve, but we can provide some data that suggests the answer.

We create diagrams like figure 6.1, which we presented at the beginning of the chapter, by taking the price index for higher education and dividing it by the price index for personal-consumption expenditures in a base year (1970). The upward slope of the line tells us that prices in higher education have consistently gone up more than the prices of all of the goods and services included in the price index for personal-consumption expenditures. The argument in the last three chapters suggests that this is exactly what one should expect to see. Because of cost disease in services and the rapid increase in the earnings of highly educated workers starting in 1980, we should expect to see higher education prices rise more rapidly than a broad price index.

Although the upward slope of figure 6.1 is consistent with our claims, it could be consistent with many other claims as well. To see how much of the observed upward slope is explained by cost disease in services and the rapid increase in the earnings of highly educated workers, we constructed a price index just for industries that should have been affected by these same two factors.[3] These industries are all service industries. They don't necessarily use the same amount of or the same mix of highly educated labor as higher education, yet prices in these industries are likely to be dominated by the same economy-wide factors we are claiming are very important in higher education. We constructed a second "real price of higher education" by dividing higher education prices by the price index of presumably similar industries.

If the factors we emphasize are the most important factors driving prices in these industries and in higher education, and the structures of the industries were identical, we would expect the real price of higher education calculated this way to roughly be equal to 1.00 every year. Figure 6.2 compares the real price of higher education computed this way with the real price of higher education computed as it is in figure 6.1 using the broadest measure of economy-wide prices.

The results in figure 6.2 suggest that the economy-wide factors we have emphasized are indeed a very important part of the explanation of

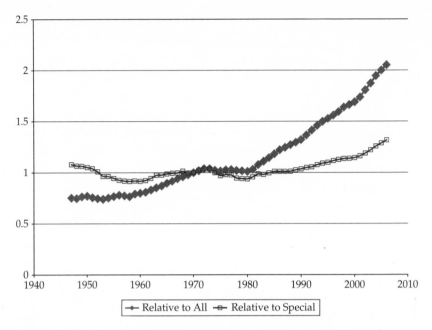

Figure 6.2 The Real Price of Higher Education Relative to All Prices and Relative to Special Price Indexes of Service Industries that Rely on Highly Educated Labor

the time path of higher education prices. Using the set of industries similar to higher education as the comparison group, the new real price of higher education is very close to 1.00 for much of the sixty-year time span of our analysis. This tells us that whatever factors are driving the price index created from this group of similar industries are the factors driving higher education prices as well. Higher education–specific factors surely exist, and there are undoubtedly industry-specific factors in the other industries as well, but over this span of history the things higher education shares with other industries dominate any specific factors.

There are wiggles in the index to be sure, but the overall picture is of a constant real price of higher education until very close to the end of the data. This rise tells us that higher education prices have indeed gone up slightly over the past fifteen years when compared to the prices of other similar personal services. But even here we should be very cautious about interpreting this. The small increase in the last few years might or might not herald a late-blooming higher education–specific cost factor.

We can suggest three possible explanations for the slight rise in the price of higher education compared to other personal services. First, the rise could also be caused by industry-specific factors in the *other* industries. In figure 2.4 we saw that the price of physicians' services stopped climbing in the mid-1990s. This tail-off in physicians' fees would cause the real price of higher education as we have calculated it to rise by comparison. Second, decreases in subsidies as a percentage of cost provided by state governments to their state-supported colleges and universities starting in the 1990s are playing a role. As we will explain in detail in the next part of the book, decreases in these subsidies can be a cause of prices rising more rapidly than costs. This is a higher education–specific factor to be sure, but it has nothing to do with costs.

Third, as we showed back in chapter 4 (table 4.2), highly educated workers represent a higher percentage of the workforce in higher education than they do in the offices of dentists, physicians, or lawyers, which are three of the important industries in the comparison group. This means that increases in the wages of these workers relative to the wages of less highly educated workers will have a larger impact on costs in higher education than in the comparison industries. This too would cause the higher education price series that we constructed to begin rising. But this increase is not because of anything that is happening inside higher education. Instead it is caused by an outside factor that happens to have a larger impact on higher education than on the other industries.

The primary message to take away from figure 6.2 is that over the long span of years higher education behaves very much like a set of similar industries, and the slight increase in the series at the end of the data does not mean there has been any real change in the behavior of higher education industry itself. The weight of the evidence suggests to us that very specific changes or processes taking place solely within higher education do *not* explain much if any of the tendency for higher education prices to rise more rapidly than prices in general. The critical factors are that higher education is a personal service, that it has not experienced much labor-saving productivity growth, and that the wages of the highly educated workers so important at colleges and universities have soared. These are economy-wide factors. They have little to do with any pathology in higher education.

A Look at Policy

Our explanation for rapidly rising college costs seems to have one big disadvantage compared to higher education–specific explanations.

Higher education–specific explanations place the blame for rising costs on identifiable agents who are making a certain set of decisions. According to these "inside the industry" accounts, the problem lies with college administrators, members of boards, legislators, and governors. These are the people who have been at the controls as inefficiencies in higher education supposedly have multiplied, and their decisions have abetted, and sometimes enabled, the spread of wasteful practices. College presidents with an outsized appetite for prestige make inviting targets.

Our account does not emphasize the role of individual agents. Costs are going up because of impersonal factors, such as patterns of productivity growth that favor manufacturing, or changes in the economic benefits of education, not because anyone is doing anything in particular (nefarious or otherwise). We don't deny that there are people in charge. College administrators, members of boards, legislators, and governors are certainly responsible for decisions that affect costs in higher education. Rather than denying these agents their role, our analysis highlights a set of constraints these agents face when they make the decisions that result in higher costs.

Our analysis suggests that higher education decision makers are faced with choices that result in either rising costs or declining quality. If the decision makers do not offer competitive salaries, they will not be able to attract the best workforce. If the decision makers try to increase output per worker, they may well decrease the quality of the education they provide. And if they do not provide the best equipment for their workers, they will not offer an up-to-date education or produce leading-edge research. The fact that ever-increasing costs have resulted from the collective decisions of these agents suggests to us that the majority of these choices have come out on the side of trying to preserve or increase quality as opposed to the side of decreasing costs.

What does this mean for policy? Explanations of increasing costs based on stories of waste, fraud, and abuse suggest a set of policies. If there are incentives for waste, find them and change those particular incentives. If universities are inefficient, give them less to force them to become leaner. If certain schools increase tuition "too fast," then punish them with a cutoff of federal support or put them on "shame lists." The latter suggests that there are also bad actors, and policies should be designed to punish the bad actors.

If the cost problem is not ultimately driven by failures peculiar to the higher education market, then these sorts of remedies can bring down a host of unintended and unwanted consequences. Remedies designed to force efficiency, for instance, are hard to distinguish from decreases in quality. Colleges and universities respond to budget cuts by lowering the number of courses offered, increasing average class sizes, using more graduate assistants in the classroom, and reducing support for libraries, laboratories, information technology, and other support services. In the longer run, if schools cannot compete in the market for talented faculty, this could compromise the fundamental purposes of higher education and destroy American leadership in basic research.

Our approach to the college-cost problem suggests a different set of policies. These policies have to recognize the basic tradeoffs faced by higher education. Policy makers would like to control the three basic features of the American higher education system—price, the size of the public subsidy, and the quality of the programming. Unfortunately, this is an unholy trinity of higher education. Policy makers can at most control two of them. If you force universities to hold the line on price (while underlying costs are rising), then you cannot maintain quality unless the subsidy rises. If you cut the subsidy, you cannot hold the line on price unless you are willing to see quality fall. Realistic policy proposals will have to be aware of these basic tradeoffs. The only way to avoid these difficult choices is to find a way to increase productivity in higher education without decreasing quality. We may ultimately succeed in doing to the artisan industry of higher education what the Internet did for brokerage services. The Internet itself may offer a number of ways to begin enhancing labor productivity in this business. But to this point no technological magic bullet has appeared that will rescue the personal-service industries.

7

Is Higher Education Increasingly Dysfunctional?

Summarizing the complex public discourse about higher education in a few short pages is an undertaking fraught with risk. Many scholars and policy-makers have written and spoken on the ills supposedly infecting higher education. While there are many shades of difference in the arguments, we think most of the analysts and much of the public would agree to a shared narrative. The simple four-sentence summary would run something like this. Our traditional public and private four-year colleges and universities are increasingly dysfunctional institutions that have drifted away from their true social mission. As a result, their costs have spiraled out of control. Even as they plead for more financial support from private donors and from state and federal governments, tuition increases push the college degree, which has become an essential entry ticket to the modern economy, increasingly out of reach for families with middle-class incomes. Government policy must steer institutions into controlling runaway tuition increases.

Our equally brief response is that there is no compelling evidence that higher education as a whole is a dysfunctional system or that the sustained cost increases we see over long stretches of time are driven by increasing dysfunctionality or by any newly emerging pathologies and inefficiencies in the provision of higher education. There are some incentive problems in higher education that could be improved by appropriate public policy remedies, and in later chapters we will suggest what those remedies might look like. But public policy approaches driven by the dysfunctionality story often focus on simple price controls and other command mechanisms that address symptoms and not causes. Policies focused on controlling price are likely to damage the quality of our colleges and universities. They are also full of possibilities for surprising, and surprisingly harmful, "unintended consequences."

At the very beginning of this book, we laid out our case for taking an aerial view of higher education. The view from above led us to emphasize broad economic forces as the primary determinants of college costs over time. While our approach is not entirely new, it is not the standard story of rising college cost. The close-up or magnifying-glass view expressed in the dysfunctionality narrative has been repeated so many times by so many commentators that it has become almost a new orthodoxy for why college costs have risen, and risen needlessly. Because this narrative is now the conventional wisdom, we need to give the orthodox story its due and explain why we think our aerial approach provides a better explanation of the time path of college costs.

Our first task then is to present the major arguments underlying the dysfunctionality narrative. A reasonable person right now would probably be on the alert for simple straw man versions of the orthodox narrative constructed so that that we could easily brush them aside. On the contrary, we think we have written a fair account of the inefficiency stories. They are not unreasonable positions riddled with internal inconsistencies. Quite to the contrary, most of the hypothesized inefficiencies in our higher education institutions or failings in the higher education market are well grounded in theory. Our contention is that the orthodox narrative is not a good explanation of the evidence, not that the stories that make up the narrative make no sense.

A Dysfunctional System—Prestige Games and Gold Plating

The current view of higher education as a dysfunctional system starts with stories of wasteful competition among colleges and universities. The schools assert that their attention really is focused on providing high-quality programs. The orthodox critique of this is that they are focused instead on a prestige game. Prestige games are about positions in a pecking order, and no matter how good a school may be by some absolute measure of quality, there are still only ten slots in the top ten. The prestige-game arguments take many forms, but the common theme among them is that positional competition within the higher education industry does not produce much of value for society and serves instead primarily to raise costs that must be paid by taxpayers and students.

There is a sound basis in theory for the idea that some competitions are socially wasteful. Arms races are a prime example. Gordon Winston (2000) uses the wonderful analogy of Alice and the Red Queen, "who had to run very fast, indeed, just to stay in one place."[1] In an ongoing arms race, everyone is working furiously to ensure that they don't fall behind, and nothing much actually happens. The key to an arms-race competition is the importance of position, or rank. In many circumstances how well you do something actually is less important than whether you do it slightly better than the next guy. On the other hand, any advantage may be temporary. To avoid losing their current position in the pecking order, whatever that might be, all parties continually invest resources to ensure that no one catches them from behind. Since arms races have no clear end, the process can continue ad infinitum, soaking up inordinate quantities of money along the way.

Everybody would be better off if no one tried to acquire any advantage, yet who would disarm first? The unilateral disarmer would be punished immediately. Their rung on the rankings ladder would be in peril. For universities, that is a big deterrent indeed. What keeps a destructive arms race alive is coordination failure. People make worse decisions if they cannot make credible commitments to each other either to take a certain action, or alternatively *not* to act. This arms race notion now pervades public discourse on how both public and private universities behave. For all universities, positional competition supposedly siphons resources away from more productive uses. For the nation's elite schools, and especially for the ones flush with resources, there is supposedly precious little incentive unilaterally to move away from this seemingly costly game.

Universities do compete with each other in many ways, some of which can be fashioned into competitive-arms-race stories. First, for a school to succeed in the prestige game it must possess a top-notch faculty. In the orthodox story of our dysfunctional university system, this competition has many destructive aspects. First, if Princeton acquires a world-class professor then somebody else, like Duke, must lose one. Competition in zero-sum games may indeed be socially destructive if resources that could be used to better purpose are instead used up in a battle that does nothing more than rearrange the "chairs." The fight for the services of these top-gun professors also may create a superstar market for this fixed pool of top talent. This superstar market supposedly sends salaries for a group of select faculty members soaring. There are plenty of anecdotes one can find of universities paying "obscene" sums to snag a hotshot physicist, or even a hot literary theorist. Stanley Fish, for instance, earned a six-figure income in the Duke English department in the 1980s at a time when average professor salaries were less than half that. These added salary costs are borne by everyone else in the form of reduced resources for other purposes, higher prices passed on to students and their families, or both. If the resources are sucked out of existing programs, the quality of the university's offerings decline, which hurts all students. If tuition rises, access to higher education is restricted and young people—often from an underprivileged back-ground—do not get the chance to participate fully in the twenty-first-century economy.

Like faculty members, talented students are another important "input" into the production of higher education. Students learn from their peers as well as from their professors, so having an increasingly talented student body improves the quality of education offered within a university. Because the quality or prestige of a university is determined in part by the quality of its students, competition for talented students is intense. Here too the orthodox narrative focuses on ways that colleges and universities may be engaging in a socially destructive process. Robert Zemsky, Gregory Wegner, and William Massy (2005) actually use the term "mutually assured destruction" in describing the admissions process as an arms race.[2]

Even the seemingly innocuous application process can embody wasteful spending. The logic is disarmingly simple. The proportion of applicants who actually enroll at the nation's most selective colleges and universities is a surprisingly small 10 to 15 percent, yet their selectivity does not inoculate these top schools from the virus of destructive competition. Quite to the contrary, passivity is a recipe for losing top prospects to institutions that aggressively recruit. The costs of recruiting take many forms. As Ronald Ehrenberg (2000) notes, Cornell University receives over 20,000 applications, but sends application packets and glossy descriptive brochures to over 110,000 high school seniors every year. Then there are the labor costs associated with sending recruiting specialists to college fairs throughout the nation, doing interviews, and staffing campus tours and other promotional events. To give a sense of the magnitude of these costs, Ehrenberg says that information provided to him from a confidential study of a set of selective private institutions produces numbers per entering student for 1996 in the $1,700 (universities) to $2,500 (colleges) range. If accurate, this amounted to between 5 and 10 percent of the gross tuition revenue (before subtracting financial aid costs) from first-year students. This type of competition is not, of course, limited to the most-selective institutions. It can ripple downward through the tiers of schools, all of which want to attract some students who might otherwise attend "better" places or avoid losing good students to peer institutions.

An amenity competition is yet another process supposedly at work busily adding fat to the costs of college attendance. This is sometimes termed the gold plating of the college degree. Amenity competitions often are presented as though they are arms races. Even basic infrastructure investment by schools can be fashioned into an arms-race story as schools supposedly competed vigorously to be among *PC Magazine*'s most "wired" campuses. This seems especially ironic as universities then worked assiduously to become wireless a few years later.

In the orthodox narrative, palatial dormitories, well-appointed student athletic facilities, and high-quality dining options are other forms of gilding that needlessly push up the cost of a traditional residential college experience. If these fees are not fully discounted to reflect family means, access to higher education may be restricted. To the extent that the gold plating reflects a competitive arms race, the social benefit of the last dollar spent on dormitory improvements may be low compared to the value of redirecting that same dollar toward an instructional use, to increasing financial aid, or simply to lowering the price. As easy as it is to see in these processes nothing more than waste or a meaningless chasing of the whims of technology, the alternative explanation for this behavior is that schools were responding to the real demands of their clientele. We will show that there is much less gilding here than may meet the eye, and that the upscaling of amenities at colleges and universities does not even fit the arms race logic.

Dysfunctional Institutions—The Lattice and the Ratchet

The first part of this dysfunctionality narrative was about how the larger market for higher education misfires in ways that push up the cost of attendance. The next part of the orthodox story is about how the universities themselves operate in dysfunctional and inefficient ways. Here the story focuses on the behavior within universities of groups operating in their own self-interest, and how university governance structures permit these groups to reshape what universities do and how they function. Zemsky, Wegner, and Massy (2005) have coined the wonderfully descriptive terms "faculty ratchet" and "administrative lattice" to label these phenomena, which they then use to describe an often-destructive competition for resources between administration and faculty on university campuses.

The faculty ratchet refers to the process by which full-time faculty have seemingly redefined their role in the institution over time to suit their own desires. The ratchet argument encompasses a number of processes, but two stand out as potentially expensive. The first of these is the gradual reduction in teaching loads over the past half century as university faculties have come to see themselves increasingly as producers of new knowledge (research) instead of mere disseminators of existing knowledge (teachers). The second is the tendency of university faculties to shift tasks formerly performed by professors onto professional administrators. Both of these processes are expensive, and the expense is magnified because the modern faculty is not simply a group of passive employees. The faculty helps govern the institution, and for the most part the faculty members have strong egalitarian impulses. Teaching loads don't go down just for the best scholars or for the newest hires, even though it may start that way. They tend to go down for all faculty members. And like a ratchet the process moves in one direction only, toward lower teaching and mentoring responsibilities for full-time faculty. To Zemsky, Wegner, and Massy, with each turn the ratchet progressively detaches faculty members from the collective goals of the home institution, pulling them instead toward the individual goals of research, publication, and professional pursuits.

The administrative lattice refers to the growth over time in administrative support for all kinds of new or expanded activities at colleges and universities. These activities, which range from academic advising and career services—much of which originally was a faculty responsibility—to expanded regulatory compliance, new auxiliary services, and ever-expanding information technology services. In part, this is related to the supposed amenity competitions we discussed earlier. Universities now have extensive counseling centers, writing centers, career-planning centers, and high-tech dormitories (with the on-call IT servicing to match). Zemsky, Wegner, and Massy claim that colleges now offer a list of services "to rival those of a first-class resort."[3] The professionalization of these activities also leads to a bureaucratic entrepreneurialism on the part of the staff and administration that further enlarges the role and size of the professional staff over time. Once a core of trained professionals exists at IT, for instance, or in counseling, they will naturally find cogent arguments for how they can expand what they do in useful ways, but only if they had one or two more well-trained professionals to staff the new initiatives. Why should a university resist, if it can pass the cost along to students or to state legislatures?

Both of these processes are indeed taking place. Between 1973 and 2003, the percent of university employment classified as executive/ administrative/managerial did rise from 6.4 percent to 7.3 percent, and faculty teaching loads do seem to have declined, though actual statistical evidence for this is hard to find.[4] In fact, survey data suggest that full-time faculty now spend a *greater* percentage of their time on teaching than they did in the early 1990s (D. Leslie 2006). On the other hand, it is a speculative leap to posit that these changes are an important factor in driving college cost increases.

The lattice and the ratchet also provide scaffolding on which to hang many of the destructive arms-race stories that are used to explain rapidly rising costs. If, for instance, faculty members increasingly see themselves as individual entrepreneurs instead of team players for their schools, then what is important to them is their individual research and the professional networks they create for themselves in their own disciplines. They will see themselves less and less invested in the collective teaching and mentoring mission of their university. If professors have redefined their own mission away from teaching and toward research, that could feed the competitive arms race for superstar professors. To those who buy into the orthodox story, this also reduces labor productivity at universities. Although it is overly simplistic, one way to describe what a professor does is to count up the number of students taught per full-time faculty member. This places no value on all the other things a faculty member does—everything from research and public service to mentoring and course development. But if you take a narrow view of a professor's labor productivity, then as university faculties elevate the importance of research this would depress the productivity of what may be the key input in delivering higher education—the professor in front of a class.

The lattice and ratchet also provide the orthodox narrative with a mechanism for explaining how institutions seemingly have moved farther and farther from their "true" social mission. Defining that mission is not easy, and identifying a time period in which that mission once was fully realized is akin to finding Eden. Nonetheless, at some risk of over-simplification one can sketch the outlines of a traditional view of the university's social mission and then show how the pathologies in the market and the dysfunction in our higher education institutions could have caused us to drift away from that mission.

The social mission of higher education has two components, one based in efficiency and the other in notions of equity. The efficiency argument for a social role in promoting higher education stems in part from potential positive spillovers to society that higher education creates. Earning a college degree clearly yields a big private benefit to the graduate since there is a large gap in earnings between someone with a college degree and someone whose education stops with high school. This wage gap has widened substantially over the past quarter century, which is one of the factors fueling an increased demand for places in four-year schools. So going to college clearly is an investment decision for each individual. But if a person's education makes others around them more productive, that is a spillover benefit that goes to other people. Since this external benefit does not accrue to the person producing it, people may not have the right incentives to acquire higher education and the number of people earning degrees may be too small. This is a standard case for some form of public subsidization of postsecondary education. But this is not the social mission that motivates the current view that higher education is in a crisis of its own making. It is the equity side of the social mission that gets the political pot bubbling.

This equity argument is rooted in the idea that education produces social mobility, and open access to higher education is a force for equality of opportunity. Both of these arguably are very desirable policy goals, especially in an age of increased income inequality. This equity case for the social mission of universities also has an efficiency component. Capital markets don't do a very good job of allowing young people to borrow for investments in their education, especially at the undergraduate level. This is because the return on investment is highly variable and subject to the choices a student might make (like their academic major) that lending institutions cannot control. These efficiency and equity arguments form a substantial part of the case for why states subsidize their public institutions and why we have federal programs such as the Pell Grants and Stafford Loans that are designed to increase access for qualified students who would otherwise not be able to try for a college degree.

The Revenue Theory

The final piece of the orthodox narrative is an overarching view of what drives cost. That driver is the rising revenue stream made available to colleges and universities by states, the federal government, and private donors. This "revenue theory of cost" is sometimes half-jokingly called cost *maximization*. In one sense, the argument is just a tautology. As non-profit institutions, cost equals revenue by definition. This is not very illuminating, and the revenue theory actually is a bit more sophisticated. Advocates of the revenue theory argue that revenue essentially is in control of the process. Higher education institutions spend everything they can raise, so revenue is the only constraint on cost. Expand revenues and universities will add buildings, programs, and personnel into the vacuum created by extra money, whether or not the programs create any real value or fill any genuine need. Waste is inherent in their design because, as the author of the revenue theory Howard Bowen (1980) argues in his first "law," "The dominant goal of institutions is educational excellence, prestige, and influence."[5] Since universities spend all they are given, the gain in quality from the last dollar of spending may be quite low in comparison to the social value of the same public dollar spent somewhere else, like health care or K–12 education. In the orthodox narrative, public restraint is the only real guarantor that keeps universities from wasteful overspending.

The revenue-theory argument is slightly different for private universities than for public ones, in part because of the role of state governments. In brief, for private universities the demand for places at prestigious universities supposedly is not responsive to price, so universities can essentially charge what they want without fear of having empty desks each fall. Thus the processes of the ratchet and the lattice, as they change the nature of higher education institutions in expensive ways, are not constrained by the market. Cost pressures just drive up tuition, and tuition drives up cost, in a vicious spiral. For public universities, the orthodox narrative adds the formidable lobbying process that allows state university systems to pass on the costs of their increasingly dysfunctional institutions to the taxpayers. The revenue theory is the indispensable macro partner to all the micro stories of dysfunctionality. If college cost is driven by a college's appetite for resources, then cutting costs requires interrupting the flow of resources in ways that force universities to get by with less.

Evaluating the New Orthodoxy

At this point, we have presented two very different explanations for rapidly rising higher education costs. In chapters 3–6, we deliberately took an aerial view of higher education that situated the industry within the broader economy and explained rising costs largely in terms of technology-driven economic forces that have worked on the U.S. economy over the past century. As we have just described, other analysts narrow the focus and look deeply within colleges and universities and in the markets in which they operate. Their arguments are higher education–specific, and based mostly on seemingly perverse incentives that increase waste and inefficiency. Now we need to make the case that the aerial view does a better job of explaining what has happened to higher education costs than does the orthodox view through the magnifying glass.

Before we delve into the details, we need to clarify what we are *not* saying. The argument we will advance is not about whether colleges and universities are efficient. We are rather agnostic about the question of efficiency in higher education. To take but one example, the institution of tenure often is derided as a counterproductive inducement to sloth among the professoriate. Lifetime tenure can indeed be a perverse incentive to work effort. Yet there is another side to the story. Most academic scholars are forged in a crucible of intense effort. The normal workday clock does not hone the skills developed in graduate school, and the work effort needed to achieve tenure is not insubstantial. People who come through this lengthy process are not a random draw from the population. They are group that has been whittled down based on a set of attitudes that tend not to get turned off once tenure is achieved. And continued productivity is rewarded in higher education precisely because faculty salaries at most institutions are not driven largely by seniority. Faculty members also can be lured away if their productivity goes unrewarded at their home institution. Tenure even serves a productive purpose within the modern university by allowing faculty members, one of whose jobs is to select their peers, to choose young colleagues who are superlative without fear of jeopardizing their own position.

On balance, many of the practices that have evolved in colleges and universities may not be completely optimal, and we do not necessarily believe that colleges and universities are run as efficiently as they could be. By the same token, we don't think that colleges and universities were run as efficiently as they could have been ten, twenty, thirty, or forty years ago either. To be convincing, the higher education–specific arguments have to do more than show that colleges and universities are inefficient. They also have to demonstrate that they have become increasingly inefficient and that this growing inefficiency can explain a large portion of the cost pressure in higher education. We are willing to grant the first point, but we do not think the notion of increasing inefficiency does a very good job of explaining the evidence. To return to the example of academic tenure, even if we suppose that that institution is inefficient, its influence on higher education is not growing. The percentage of the faculty that is tenure track has declined over time, and many universities have begun to institute post-tenure reviews with teeth.

Higher Education Is a Service

Now that we have clarified what we are *not* arguing, we can turn to a comparison of the aerial view and the magnifying glass. In chapter 2, we established four facts about higher education costs and prices. In the ensuing chapters, we presented our explanation of these facts. Fact one is very important. "The price behavior of higher education is more similar to the price behavior of services than it is to the price behavior of goods." A story about rising college costs based on increasing dysfunctionality in higher education cannot easily explain this fact.

We addressed this issue in a study published in the *Journal of Higher Education* in 2008. If higher education–specific factors such as the revenue theory were the driving engine of college costs, then the set of industries whose costs behaved similarly to higher education would be random. If all of the sources of cost increase come from within, there is no reason to believe that costs in any other industry would behave in a similar fashion. Using the same data source we used chapter 2, we developed a measure of how similarly prices in sixty-nine different industries mirrored cost changes in higher education. We then ranked these measures of similarity to see which industries were closest to higher education. The twenty industries ranked most similar to higher education included eighteen services and two goods. If similarity with cost movements in higher education were randomly distributed across industries, the likelihood of drawing eighteen services and two goods from sixty-nine industries, thirty of which were goods and thirty-nine of which were services, is .0003.[6] Based on this, we concluded that the similarity between higher education and other services is not likely a coincidence. In technical language, we can reject the hypothesis that any similarity between higher education costs and other goods and services is purely random.

To put this discussion on a more concrete footing, consider the time path of higher education prices and the prices of the services provided by dentists. Figure 7.1 displays the time path of the real price of higher education and the real price of the services of dentists from 1947 to 2006. This figure is a less cluttered version of a diagram like the diagrams in chapter 2. The picture is quite clear. The prices of the two services have both gone up, and they have followed an almost identical time path. How is one to explain this striking similarity?

Maybe dentists and the dental-care industry are increasingly dysfunctional as is higher education. They are involved in prestige games, or suffer from ratchets and/or lattices, or have costs that jump up to match revenues. Conversely, perhaps through some mysterious mechanism the spread of fluoride treatments, the advent of high-speed drills, and changes in the prevalence of dental insurance somehow also affect prices in higher education. If neither of these explanations is appealing, perhaps the striking similarity of their price increases over time is one great big coincidence.

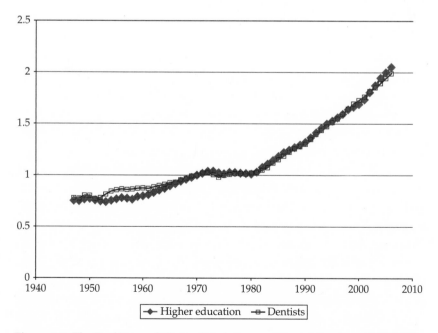

Figure 7.1 The Real Price of Higher Education and Dental Services, 1947–2006

An explanation of rapidly rising higher education costs that relies on higher education–specific factors as the fundamental drivers would have to put its money on coincidence. Yet our larger statistical test suggests that we are not observing a coincidence. There are just too many such coincidences to make this a tenable position. There is something systematic going on instead. The similarity of behavior is solid evidence that higher education and dentists (and many other service industries) share a common economic environment and a common response pattern to changes in that environment. In summary, one should be very wary of stories that ignore these similarities or that suggest that they are accidental.

Our evidence linking higher education to other service industries does not rule out the prospect that higher education–specific factors could be important as well. But it is enough to suggest that our story based on broader economy-wide factors cannot be ignored and perhaps enough to suggest that it should be given the greatest weight in an overall explanation of rising college cost. In fairness to those who emphasize higher education–specific factors, in many cases they do not completely ignore cost disease. Often it is included as one small factor among many other higher education–specific arguments in lists of the contributors to cost pressure. Still, there are whole books on college costs that do not even mention cost disease. Our test tells us that cost disease is much too important to leave out of the discussion.

Explaining the Entire Time Path of Higher Education Costs

A good story that explains the evolution of higher education costs over the last sixty years should be able to encompass all of the data without any ad hoc hand waving to deal with difficult decades that don't cooperate. Recall the final fact from chapter 2. "From 1947 to 2006 the real price of higher education experienced two periods of growth separated by roughly a decade of almost no growth." One of the most striking features of figure 7.1 is that the prices of dentist services experienced this same dramatic slowdown. In the last chapter, we explained how we account for the decade of no cost growth. Rapid technological progress outside of the personal services like higher education drives higher education costs upward, and the slowdown of national productivity growth coincides with the slowdown in the growth in the real price of higher education. How would an account of rapidly rising higher education costs based on increasingly dysfunctional behavior deal with the decade-long period of no growth of the real price of higher education?

If increasingly inefficient higher education institutions inside an increasingly dysfunctional market are a crucial part of rising college costs, then there must have been a burst of functionality or at least a major slow down in the growth of dysfunctionality in the 1970s. Faculty members must have stopped ratcheting up the time they spent on research, administrations must have stopped growing, and temporary truces must have been called to halt arms races. A narrative based on rising dysfunctionality relies on a set of unidirectional processes. Perhaps there are cogent arguments that explain why the virulence of higher education dysfunction is so variable, but if so we have not encountered them. Any convincing account of higher education cost has to deal with the flat period of the 1970s as well as the two periods of increasing costs that bracket that decade. This is not easy for accounts based on increasing dysfunctionality.

At this point, we have made two claims about the orthodox narrative. First, there is a striking regularity in the data that this narrative cannot explain. The behavior of higher education costs is very similar to the cost behavior of a specific set of other industries, and the dysfunction stories provide no suggestion that these regularities in behavior should occur. Second, these explanations only fit part of the entire time path of higher education costs. They cannot account for the slowdown of real higher education costs in the 1970s. We think these facts are very telling, but they are not the only ammunition we can fire at the higher education–specific view.

Not-for-Profit and For-Profit Private Universities

Consider the different predictions the two explanations would make about costs at not-for-profit and for-profit institutions. The argument of the revenue theory that increases in revenue drive costs upward in the traditional public and private nonprofit four-year universities does not seem to fit for-profit private universities whose bottom line is real and whose advertising would suggest that they are a no-frills alternative to traditional colleges and universities. One might suppose that Harvard and Yale can pass along the costs of their unrelenting appetite for prestige and "quality" onto eager students who value the ivy badge. One might also suppose that flagship public universities might have some clout with compliant state legislatures to keep the spigot of public money flowing (though this is a much more questionable assertion). But we are hard-pressed to imagine a similar story forcing private for-profit schools' costs ever upward based on any plausible arms-race stories or through sustained political activity to force public subsidies available to them ever upward. In addition, not-for-profit institutions typically are focused only on teaching, so none of the stories built around expenses associated with research should have any traction.

An explanation of cost pressure based on broad economic forces does not lose its power when focused on for-profit institutions. The same economic forces faced by not-for-profit colleges and universities will buffet these institutions. They have to hire in the same markets, and they also have to have staffs of highly educated people. While they will not deal with cost pressures in exactly the same way as not-for-profit institutions, they should face similar cost pressures.

Table 7.1 gives the cumulative five-year percent increase in tuition and fees at private four-year nonprofit universities and then at a sample of four private for-profit institutions.[7] For this comparison, we selected the longest lived campuses of four of the major for-profit universities: DeVry Institute–Arizona, University of Phoenix–Phoenix Hohokam Campus, Strayer University, and ITT Technical Institute–Indianapolis.

All things considered, the rates of tuition increase at the two types of institutions are very similar. This would seem to be more in line with a story that emphasizes economy-wide factors than one that is more narrowly focused on higher education–specific factors. Although these data are interesting, the test is hardly definitive. The data are for tuition instead of costs, and the similarity in rates of increase may be explained by lower cost increases at for-profit institutions combined with increasing profit margins. Still, while clearly imperfect, it is a piece of evidence that seems more in line with our explanation than with ones based on increasingly dysfunctional colleges and universities.

Table 7.1 Comparisons of Tuition Increases at Not-For-Profit and For-Profit Private Universities

5 Year % Change in Tuition and Fees, Year Ending In:	Private 4-Year, Not-For-Profit	Private, For-Profit
2007	31%	32%
2002	31%	27%
1997	32%	49%

Two-Year and Four-Year Schools

The behavior of costs at two-year and at four-year institutions provides an additional opportunity to sort out the two explanations. The increasing dysfunctionality narrative highlights things that should be much more important at four-year institutions. The pathologies of prestige games and faculty polishing their own research at the expense of their teaching mission might well be a significant driver of cost per student at four-year schools. But two-year community colleges would not seem to be infected by these same ills. They tend to be open-enrollment institutions focused on teaching. Their faculty members do little if any research.

Not all four-year institutions are selective or have a heavy research emphasis, but institutions that are likely to be engaged in a positional prestige game or big research efforts are all clustered into the category of four-year colleges and universities. Four-year institutions care deeply about how they are viewed in the pecking order. In our own state of Virginia, the arrival of the annual "America's Best Colleges" edition of *U.S. News and World Report* is cause for much anxiety and occasional indigestion in the administrations of the University of Virginia, Virginia Tech, and the College of William and Mary. In addition, four-year institutions often have a strong emphasis on research, and many of the larger four-year institutions fund a large portion of their operations with monies from research grants.

Two-year community colleges emphasize teaching. Unlike four-year institutions, expenditures on research account for a very small fraction of the spending. And there are no *U.S. News* rankings of community colleges. If positional arms races and excessive emphasis on research were powerful causes of college cost increases in excess of the inflation rate, one would expect to see costs in public four-year institutions rising at a much faster clip than costs at public two-year institutions.

What does the economy-wide explanation of cost increase predict? Cost disease, changes in wage rates for skilled workers driven by technological change, and the need to keep higher education current in a changing world all are forces that affect both two-year and four-year schools. Our forecast would be that cost should rise at roughly the same rate at the two types of schools. The same broad economic forces buffet them both, so cost behavior should be similar.

The *Digest of Educational Statistics* (Department of Education) reports information on current fund expenditures for two-year and four-year public institutions.[8] The data series begins in the 1971–72 academic year and goes through 2001–2. Current fund expenditures include basically everything that schools spend that is not part of the capital budget. Figure 7.2 shows the current fund expenditure per student in each year for two-year and four-year public institutions, compared to what it was in the 1980–81 academic year. The time paths of cost increase are strikingly similar, and over the full thirty-year span the cumulative percentage cost increase is roughly the same. Between 1971–72 and 2001–2, spending per student tripled at two-year schools and rose only slightly more than that at four-year schools.

This doesn't leave much of a wedge for increasingly virulent pathologies to be the dominant force driving up college costs. The evidence seems to provide more support to our economy-wide explanation than to any of the higher education–specific ones. Still, this evidence alone is not quite enough to slay the higher education–specific narratives. For such a test to be completely compelling, one explanation would have to say "up," and the other explanation would have to say "down," and the data would have to be unambiguously up or down. In our case one theory says "different," the other theory says "the same," and the data show "quite close." We think the evidence leans our way. Costs at two-year and

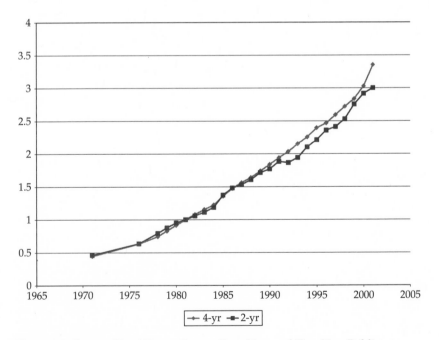

Figure 7.2 Current Fund Expenditures, Four-Year and Two-Year Public Institutions, 1971–2001

four-year public schools grew substantially faster than the inflation rate despite the lack of any clear arms races distorting what community colleges spend. And the remaining small gap likely reflects the different missions of four-year and two-year schools. Scientific research for instance, which has always been concentrated at four-year universities, is done with increasingly expensive laboratories and equipment.

Charges for Room and Board

The increasing dysfunctionality narrative includes several strands of argumentation. Some of the arguments concern features of higher education costs that are not particularly important. A prime example of this is the notion that schools are becoming resorts with luxurious housing and gourmet meals. There is no doubt that college dormitories are better appointed than the dorms we lived in when we were students in the 1960s and 1970s. Also, college dining is a much more enjoyable experience than it used to be. Still, the supposed gold plating of amenities has little to do with the rise in college costs.

Consider the three students attending William and Mary from Ohio we discussed in chapter 1. The student attending in 1960 paid tuition and fees of $722 and room and board of $782. Room and board charges were higher than tuition and fees. The student attending in 1981 paid $3,368 in tuition and fees and $2,384 for room and board. In 1981, tuition and fees cost quite a bit more than room and board. The final student entered college in 2006. Tuition and fees were $25,048 and room and board was $7,385. In 2006, tuition and fees dwarfed room and board charges.

The experience of our three William and Mary students mirrors what is going on in higher education in general. Figure 7.3 shows indexes of tuition and fees and room and board for both public and private universities from 1965 to 2007.[9] The figure clearly shows that for both public and private universities, room and board charges have grown much less rapidly than tuition and fees. If one is looking for an explanation of rapidly rising cost in higher education, one has to look at the costs of providing an education. The costs of providing an education have grown much more rapidly than the cost of providing room and board. Gold plating of room and board is not a big part of the story.

In addition, room and board expenses don't fully fit the logic of an arms race. One reason is that in most cases there is a private market for room and board and many students can access that market. That private market acts as a discipline on how universities price their nonacademic

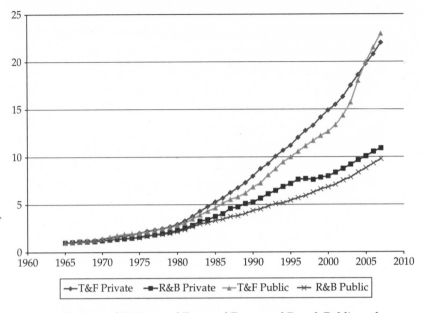

Figure 7.3 Indexes of Tuition and Fees and Room and Board, Public and Private Universities (1965=1), 1965–2007

services. And lastly, increases in the quality of room and board tend to mirror rising living standards in the United States as a whole.

Advertising Expenses

We presented some evidence earlier that selective private institutions spend between 5 and 10 percent of their gross tuition revenue from first-year students on recruiting the incoming students. Suppose this number is accurate. For many people, a number of that magnitude may sound very alarming. Yet this seemingly high cost of recruiting a class at a selective institution is another instance in which the effects of any excesses are likely to be very small. Students in their second, third, and fourth years also pay tuition, so these figures imply an advertising-to-sales ratio of 2.5 to 3 percent.[10] Ratios much higher that 2.5 to 3 percent are quite common in other industries. Here are some examples. The ratio in soaps and detergent is 11.5, in amusement parks 9.7, in aircraft 6.2, in furniture stores 5.8, in drugs 4.3, and in cigarettes 4.0.[11] The advertising-to-sales ratio for selective private institutions is not at all out of line with those in other industries.

In addition, highly selective private institutions are the schools that we would expect to have the highest expenses on advertising. Public institutions, and particularly ones that are not very selective, will not spend nearly as much as these selective private institutions. So for higher education as a whole, the amounts spent by the most-selective schools are unrepresentative. As a result, the impact of any changes in advertising practices is not likely to have much effect on the pace of cost increases in the larger world of higher education as a whole.

Lastly, even at selective private institutions, there is no reason to expect that this advertising expense is a pure waste. A college education is a big-ticket item that is usually purchased once. Buyers have a strong incentive to accumulate a lot of information about the product or service before pulling the trigger. Some of that information can come from unbiased written sources, but those sources do not fully displace the information-rich campus visit, the illustrated brochure, and the virtual tour on the college website. All of these methods of communicating information to potential "buyers" soak up resources that could be used for something else, but the information that is provided has real value. In addition, and unlike other products, college advertising is about *matching* as well as recruiting. All selective universities can fill their programs quite easily, but they want the best—and best-suited—students to matriculate. Some of the information passed both ways serves to winnow as much as to attract.

In summary, we do not think that much if any of the increase in college cost can be pinned to wasteful and unnecessary positional spending on advertising and promotion. Lots of industries that are not under the microscope spend a great deal more on advertising than do colleges and universities. In addition, seemingly large expenditures of this type are concentrated in a small group of our more selective institutions. And finally, this spending is not necessarily wasteful. At least some of it provides real benefits to the institutions and students involved in college searches.

Dollar Bills on the Floor

There is a story that economists sometimes tell to poke fun at our own profession. An economist once was walking in a park with a friend, and as they were crossing a path the friend noticed a $100 bill lying on the ground. The economist admonishes his friend that he shouldn't bother to bend over to collect it since if it were real it would have been picked up already. This apocryphal tale reflects the usual stereotype of the economist who blithely presumes that markets always work and that the world is always efficient. This is the attitude that helped make the Great Depression great! In any case, the truth about us is far darker. With apologies to George Lucas, much of the interesting stuff written in economics explores the dark side of the force—all the situations in which markets fail to work well and lead instead to inefficient outcomes. All of the arms-race stories fit nicely into that niche. If the nation's public and private schools—and especially the selective private institutions and selective public flagship universities—are quite inefficient, then there are potentially lots of $100 bills on the ground just waiting to be picked up. Those bills could go toward many useful things, including lower tuition and fees. They would represent opportunities waiting to be exploited.

We are not naïve optimists about the market. But we are skeptical that the occasional $100 bill on the floor of the college administration building has much to do with the long-term trend of college cost rising more rapidly than general inflation. One small reason for our skepticism is that $100 bills on the floor *do* tend to get picked up after a while. If there are growing inefficiencies, then there are also growing opportunities. Where are the barriers that keep no-frills universities from arising and displacing the supposedly inefficient university system, especially the private universities that do not get large state subsidies? Surely there is a market for the price conscious. Alternatively, if Bill Gates could bankroll a new private university that spent the same amount per student as Yale, but which allocated that spending more productively than existing universities, then he could offer a higher quality education for the same cost. Reputation may be worth something, but endowment can overcome the advantages of handed-down aura relatively quickly. The current Yales and Harvards of the nation know this as well.

Private for-profit universities are indeed growing, but they are not yet serving the typical young undergraduate. They also don't support research or produce the next generation of faculty scholars. Their comparative advantage at present seems to be in providing specific skills, often to older students seeking credentials within their firms. Also, in many cases they are particularly generous in accepting transfer courses, even giving credit for "life experience." They do not offer the complete educational package. And as we noted earlier, they don't seem to be immune to the process that is pushing up higher education costs in their not-for-profit brethren.

Conclusions—Occam's Razor

In this chapter, we have introduced the rich and interesting literature that holds a magnifying glass up to the higher education industry. This up-close view sees increasingly dysfunctional economic behavior at colleges and universities as the driving engine of higher education cost increases. We acknowledge the intuitive power of this narrative, but we think that these higher education–specific arguments do not do as good a job of explaining the facts as our aerial view. While readers may not find every example we have offered equally or completely compelling, we think the weight of the evidence points strongly in one direction. The similarity between the behavior of higher education costs and costs in other industries that we first outlined in chapter 2 is strong evidence that important economy-wide processes are at work in higher education and in other kindred industries. Likewise, the similarity of the trajectory of prices at for-profit and not-for-profit institutions and the similarity of the time path of costs at two-year and four-year institutions poses a problem for higher education–specific stories of dysfunction since the dysfunction should be much less virulent at for-profit institutions and at two-year schools. By contrast, our economy-wide explanation applies to all types of institutions.

In addition to fitting the data much better, we think our aerial view is superior as a theory. Our approach is right in line with the scientific wisdom of the fourteenth-century Franciscan friar William of Occam. Occam's famous "razor" states that the best explanation of any phenomenon is the one that makes as few assumptions as possible, eliminating the assumptions that make no real difference to the observable and measurable predictions of the theory. The striking similarity of the time path of costs in dental care and other service industries and the time path of costs in higher education provides a good example. One *can* construct separate explanations of rising costs in the higher education industry, and in the dental care industry as well, based on a set of distinct industry-specific factors. But a more parsimonious explanation based on a simple set of broader economic features that have rippled across the entire economic landscape of the past century strikes us as a better explanation.

8

Productivity Growth in Higher Education

Costs in higher education must rise faster than the general inflation rate as long as productivity growth at colleges and universities lags behind productivity growth in the rest of the economy. To slow the growth of inflation-adjusted higher education costs, this productivity growth differential between higher education and the rest of the economy has to decrease. As the decade of the 1970s amply demonstrates, a falloff in productivity growth in manufacturing can put the brakes on cost growth in higher education. But this surely is a cure for rising college cost that is worse than the disease. Higher productivity, no matter where it occurs in the economy, is the engine of rising average living standards.

The real hope of reform is to increase the pace of productivity growth in higher education in order to bring it closer to the rate of productivity growth in the rest of the economy. This would slow down the rise in college costs while adding another force for higher overall living standards. In chapters 2 and 3, we pointed to cases of service industries whose price behavior was quite different from higher education. Perhaps the most intriguing example was brokerage charges. Technological change through online trading of securities explains the fact that since the mid-1980s, the inflation-adjusted charges of stockbrokers have decreased. This tells us that technological fixes to slow productivity growth are quite possible, even in service industries. Our task in this chapter is to explore and to evaluate whether or not new technology that augments productivity can be used to slow the rate of growth of higher education cost without sacrificing the quality of the instruction offered.

Yet before we proceed to identify the possible ways that new innovation can boost productivity, we need to recognize that there are other ways to control costs. Universities can decrease the costs of the inputs they use by substituting lower cost inputs for higher cost inputs. This may have an adverse impact on quality, but that may be an acceptable consequence given the alternatives. Next, schools could attempt to wring more output from the existing inputs by making the labor and physical plant of the college or university work harder. This is the heart of many reform proposals that emerge from the dysfunctional-university narratives. In this view, there are significant cost savings currently lying unutilized because of the increasingly inefficient culture of higher education. We will take each of these in turn.

Colleges and universities can control the cost of their inputs by substituting less expensive teaching assistants and adjunct faculty for full-time professors. Full-time professors are much more expensive than teaching assistants and adjunct faculty, so shifting teaching responsibilities to assistants and adjuncts should allow the same number of students to be taught at less expense. This is indeed a strategy that many schools have chosen to follow. Data from the U.S. Department of Education indicate that the percentage of instructional faculty classified as full time declined from 77.9 percent in 1970 to 52.4 percent in 2005.[1] Doing this is a decision of necessity, not desire. Schools facing budget stringency may opt for changing the mix of professors in preference to other, even worse, choices such as cutting the number of class offerings or significantly increasing class sizes. Even so, a rising reliance on part-time professors is deeply problematic to most schools.

Teaching assistants and adjunct faculty are unlikely to do the same job as full-time faculty. As one example, temporary and part-time faculty usually are not available to do academic advising and counseling for students. In a 2005 study, Ronald Ehrenberg and Liang Zhang found that institutions that used a large percentage of adjunct professors have lower freshman retention rates. In addition, the research and public-service contributions of a college or university suffer if it saves money in this fashion. Financial exigency may from time to time force institutions to decrease their reliance on full-time faculty, but this is a response that clearly compromises quality or that reduces some other output the university provides. The choice to replace full-time faculty with cheaper alternatives is not a productivity increase in any meaningful sense of the term. This is why we will focus this chapter on the other alternative, innovation that has the potential to raise productivity without compromising quality.

The dysfunctional-university narratives we outlined in chapter 7 also suggest an array of cost-cutting approaches, many of which involve changing the culture of higher education institutions to make them leaner and meaner. These arguments range from eliminating the faculty role in university governance to abolishing tenure. Faculty governance, for instance, is supposedly a drag on productivity because it pulls expensive labor away from more productive classroom and research uses, and because it allows university faculties to set the rules by which they work. Tenure is supposedly a problem because it frees the faculty from effective job-performance reviews.

There is a veritable cottage industry of books and articles that assign a large portion of the blame for higher education's stagnant productivity to workplace-culture issues. In *Going Broke by Degree* (2004), Richard Vedder stakes out this ground very forcefully.

> Why is productivity falling? The basic problem is that universities are mostly nonprofit organizations, subject to only muted competitive forces, and lacking market-imposed discipline to economize and innovate. University presidents, deans, maintenance supervisors, department chairs, and other administrators do not benefit from reducing costs. Major policy issues are typically decided in committees, where advocates of the status quo (often faculty with tenure) usually have the upper hand.[2]

The problem is that there is very little evidence about workplace culture other than juicy anecdote and cherry-picked comparisons. If our reading of the evidence in chapters 2 through 7 is near the mark, these workplace-culture issues are at best a secondary driver of college costs, yet they garner a substantial portion of the public discussion. Institutions like faculty tenure, for instance, often are rebuked for encouraging laziness and for having outlasted their historical moment in securing academic freedom. Yet most of the supposed workplace-culture issues in higher education have been with us for the better part of a century, and in many cases they have evolved over time in pro-productivity ways. Tenure, for instance, is increasingly supplemented with post-tenure reviews that have teeth, and at many schools the faculty has shed some responsibilities on governance, career advising, and remediation to professionals with specific skills for those tasks.

We are not interested in diving into the workplace-culture debate in this book. It suffices to say, that debate often is very polemical and politicized. And if we are right about the primary sources of rising college costs, the debate is off target if we want a meaningful long-term solution to the college-cost problem. As long as colleges and universities retain their basic nature as artisan-type institutions in which large numbers of highly trained professionals engage in deep personal interaction with small numbers of students in a face-to-face setting, then the pressures of cost disease will remain.

Distance Education

In teaching, getting more output for the same set of inputs means either larger classes or more classes per professor. Traditionally, faculty and students alike have resisted the first option. Both sides of the education equation believe that larger face-to-face classes lead to an inferior learning environment. More classes per professor reduce the time available for individual mentoring, advising, research, and public service, all of which are other outputs of a university. There is a growing body of research challenging the claim about class size. A number of studies have shown that learning outcomes from distance education delivered over the Internet can be quite similar to learning outcomes from face-to-face instruction in a traditional setting. Also, there are studies showing that combining the intelligent use of new instructional technology and traditional classroom activities, what is called "blending" technology with a traditional course, improve learning outcomes in very large classes. These studies claim that the new techniques can provide higher quality instruction with lower costs. Quality-preserving productivity growth may indeed be possible in higher education.

The notion that an education can be obtained without face-to-face interaction between students and faculty members is by no means new. Well before computers became ubiquitous, many students received college credits through correspondence courses. Also, considerable hype accompanied the advent of courses delivered by educational television in the 1960s. In this case, the results did not live up to the promises. Computers and the Internet have expanded the potential of distance education. Again there is considerable hype. In this case, the early results appear to be better.

At present, there are institutions at which all of the instruction is done via distance education. These programs are easy to find. A simple search came up with listings such as distance-learning-college-guide.com, elearners. com, and guidetoonlineschools.com.[3] Also, many colleges and universities offer a portion of their curriculum as distance-education courses. An annual survey of colleges and universities supported by the Alfred P. Sloan Foundation found that 21.9 percent of all students enrolled in the fall of 2007 were taking at least one online course. Just five years earlier, the same percentage was 9.6 percent.[4] The survey also shows that over one-half of these enrollments are at institutions offering associate's degrees, so two-year institutions were overrepresented. Nonetheless, there are significant numbers of distance-education enrollments at four-year institutions.

The dichotomy between distance education and traditional classrooms is not the same as the split between for-profit schools like the University of Phoenix and traditional not-for-profit higher education institutions. As the Sloan Foundation survey indicates, distance education has a major foothold in public and private not-for-profit institutions as well as in the for-profit sector. The rest of this chapter explores the potential of distance education to restructure the whole higher education enterprise. The distinction that is important for us is between distance education and face-to-face education, not between nonprofit institutions and schools motivated by profit.

Distance education has several advantages over face-to-face classroom instruction. First, it can be asynchronous. Students do not have to be at a certain place at a certain time. As any instructor who has had students fall asleep in his or her early morning or late afternoon classes will attest, there can be advantages to letting students decide when and where they do their work. The asynchronous nature of many distance-education courses is one of the reasons these courses are so popular for older students who are combining college courses with a career and family. The students can do their coursework after they have completed their workday and after the kids are asleep. Not only can the instruction be asynchronous during the day, but also it can be asynchronous during the year. There is no reason to be bound by semesters or quarters. With a completely distance-education curriculum, a student could start at any time during the year.

Second, students can easily repeat presentations. With face-to-face instruction, the student can review his or her notes, visit the instructor during office hours to go over parts of the class presentation that were unclear, and ask questions during review sessions, so there are opportunities for repeats. But with material available on the Internet, the entire presentation can be repeated as many times as the student wants, whenever and wherever the student wants to see it. The student is not constrained by faculty office hours or scheduled review sessions, so the potential for repetition is much greater.

Third, with distance education there is less need to build and maintain classrooms, libraries, gymnasiums, and other campus building. A distance-education institution does have to have offices for the faculty "teaching" the courses, though instructors can do much of their work at home or in the park if they want. Space is also needed for the computer system required to store information and to allow interaction with students at a distance, but the space needs are dramatically reduced. Costs to build, heat, cool, and clean campus buildings and to maintain campus grounds are major expenditures. Eliminating or significantly reducing them relieves budgets in a big way.

Distance education has its disadvantages too. First, some topics require synchronous learning. Some aspects of class discussion can be stimulated using chat rooms and e-mail, but face-to-face communication cannot quite be replicated. Differences in gestures, tone of voice, and facial expressions that are all part of normal communication do not show up in a chat room or over e-mail. Video conferencing cures some problems, but it requires people to commit to a time schedule that undermines the asynchronous nature of distance education. Second, many courses require class participation in ways that are difficult to simulate, at least with existing technology. Student presentations are not useful experiences without an audience, and gathering an audience requires doing things in a particular space or at least at a particular time. Laboratory experiences are also very difficult to replicate over the Internet. The typical student is unlikely to have the equipment and materials necessary to do anything beyond the simplest laboratory work. Finally, many educational experiences require teamwork. This can be simulated or approximated over the Internet, but as with class discussions and class participation, there are times when face-to-face meetings will enhance teamwork.

A second difficulty with distance education is that it requires students to have considerable discipline. Any college teacher will tell you of the powerful effect of deadlines. Assignments have to be turned in on time. Exams are scheduled in the syllabus, and the students have to be ready. Many people have enough self-discipline to thrive in an environment in which they set their own deadlines and proceed at their own pace. For others, performance is improved by deadlines imposed from the outside. In many ways, this difference is related to maturity, so not surprisingly distance education has had its biggest successes with older and more mature students.

A third difficulty with distance education is that it takes a lot of effort to create a satisfactory distance-education course. Effective interactive course materials require lots of programmer and content-expert time. As any teacher who has made the simple transition from lectures that rely on the use of a chalkboard to lectures using Power Point® or other presentation software can attest, the transition takes time and the results often are not seamless, at least at first. An effective distance-education course requires a course's worth of presentations, a series of exercises and problems, and other interactive learning aids to deal with questions and other issues that arise. The computer programs that link students to the courseware have to be thoroughly tested to find programming bugs, and this is often an arduous task that requires a lot of skilled labor. Also, the distance-education provider has to have the computing power to handle large files and multiple simultaneous users. This requires considerable bandwidth.

Distance education clearly is not free. There are considerable fixed costs involved in getting a distance-education course up and running. But once the course is completed, the extra cost of adding another student is quite low. This is what distance education accomplishes. More students can be added to the course at potentially very low cost without diminishing the quality of the learning experience. Traditional face-to-face instruction is also a high-fixed-cost enterprise, since professors spend a considerable amount of time developing courses. But as more and more students are added, quality deterioration is likely to set in much faster than it will in a distance-education setting.

There is an additional difficulty caused by the high cost of creating a distance course. Given the work involved in altering an interactive course, the creators may be quite reluctant to change it in any significant way except at specified intervals. If the course is continually changing and evolving, the cost advantage of distance education wanes. In the traditional setting in which we teach, current events often alter what we do in our economics classes. New research in our discipline also changes what we teach, and sometimes how we teach it. The same can be said for what goes on in many classes in other disciplines. If new data or new research alters our view of what is going on in the economy, all we have to do is change the lecture we are presenting or lead the class to a different discussion topic that applies the course concepts in a different way. This can be done by a professor on the fly with little, if any, preparation time. Once we have built the structure of a course, we can move within that structure fairly nimbly. This kind of flexibility is much more difficult in a distance-education framework. Given the time and skilled labor involved in creating the course materials and the programming required to put the new material on the Internet in a seamless interactive format, distance classes are likely to be much more difficult to keep up to date.

In our view, these considerations limit the situations in which distance education has a clear advantage. Distance education has an edge where the primary feedback from the students is fairly straightforward written work and when the course content is not likely to be altered by current events or by an evolving professional literature that is rewriting the boundaries of knowledge. Despite these limitations, there are quite a few courses that may fit. Courses in basic statistics, computer programming, accounting, algebra, or calculus could work well in a distance format, though all would lose the benefit of group work and group study. A basic writing course and introductory courses in many of the social sciences might also fit the distance format well. Some introductory science courses are also possible candidates, but the laboratory portion of the courses likely would not work well. Generally, the courses best fitted for the distance-education model would be at the introductory level. These are courses in which the basic material to be covered changes very slowly. Distance education does not fit upper-division courses as well. In these courses, laboratory experiences, class discussion, class presentations, the cutting edge of the professional literature, and current events play a larger role. A distance-education provider *can* construct a course for any topic at any level. Our contention is that in these more advanced courses, distance education would have a very difficult time replicating the quality found in a face-to-face learning experience. For this reason, we are very skeptical of the quality of many distance-education courses, and we are particularly skeptical of the quality of many purely distance-education degrees. Too much of what goes on at a good college or university involves face-to-face interactions, requires the high personal touch of laboratories or field trips, or reflects the flexibility of teachers adjusting what they do in response to the class's needs or to changes in the world the class is supposed to explain.

The respondents to a large survey done by the Sloan Foundation agree with our general assessment of the learning outcomes of distance-education courses. For the entire sample of over 10,000 college faculty members, only 7.0 percent of the respondents rated online courses somewhat superior to or superior to face-to-face courses.[5] A full 70.0 percent of the respondents rated online courses somewhat inferior to or inferior to face-to-face courses. The numbers were not as skewed for the faculty members who have had experience teaching an online course. For these faculty members, 16.8 percent rated online courses somewhat superior to or superior to face-to-face courses, but still 48.0 percent rated online courses somewhat inferior to or inferior to face-to-face courses. This is, of course, a biased sample. It is composed of faculty who as a group are likely to be less favorably disposed toward distance methods that might replace them. Yet we can draw two ideas from the evidence. First, familiarity bred more respect. Faculty members who actually had some experience with components of distance learning were less hostile to the idea. But even the group that was more familiar with the tools ultimately had an unfavorable view.

We want to make one final point about distance-education environments. Perhaps we are biased, but we think that the job of the distance-education instructor would be quite unappealing. Making up new test questions or designing new course materials can be creative and stimulating. But once the course is developed, the job boils down to answering e-mail all day or perhaps moderating a chat room. If the courses are changed too frequently, distance education loses its cost advantage, so course development should not be a continuous thing. As face-to-face instructors who occasionally teach small-group seminars, we are energized by our interactions with students. We do a fair amount of answering of student e-mail, but we have many more in-depth interactions with students in class and in our offices. Face-to-face interactions with students are part of what makes our jobs worth doing. The distance-education instructor does not have any of these interactions. We wonder just how easy it will be to keep high-quality instructors interested in being at the other end of a stream of student e-mails. And if distance-education institutions really pursue their cost advantage, the job will involve a constant stream of student e-mails.

Despite our personal views, many distance-education courses and quite a number of distance-education degrees are out there, and as the data from the Sloan Foundation study show, they attract a significant number of students. Distance courses have a clear cost advantage over the traditional approach, which creates much of their appeal. What is much less clear is that they offer an education of comparable quality. Some distance courses may offer comparable quality or even perhaps superior quality, but distance-education institutions may have great difficulty in constructing high-quality versions of all the courses required for a well-rounded college education. Because of this, distance-education institutions usually do not offer the full range of degrees.

Combining Online and Traditional Instruction

A 2009 report released by the U.S. Department of Education (DOE) gives the results of a meta-analysis of online-learning studies.[6] A meta-analysis essentially is a study of all the available studies. The DOE evaluation restricted the sample of studies used in the analysis to ones that directly compared online learning with face-to-face classroom learning of the same material. The results of the study show that online courses or course modules had statistically significantly better learning outcomes than did the face-to-face courses or course modules with which they were paired. In addition, it showed that what the study calls blended learning environments, those combining online and face-to-face learning, had an even greater advantage over face-to-face-only environments. At first glance, this study seems inconsistent with our claim that distance-education courses and degrees are inferior. But we need to dig deeper before coming to a firm conclusion.

First, the courses in each of the studies in the meta-analysis were by no means a random sample of all possible courses taught in a university environment. Researchers picked courses for which they thought online learning would be appropriate. The courses studied did not include laboratory sciences, seminars, or classes in which oral presentations would be important. Also, the experiments often were done on course modules instead of entire courses. These modules are the particular parts of a course that best fit the online-education paradigm. Pointing to the fact that online education outperformed face-to-face education in this large study only shows that there are particular circumstances in which online instruction may be better. The DOE study cannot be used to endorse a purely online approach. For us, the most important part of the DOE study is the result that the blended courses and course modules outperformed all the alternatives. This suggests to us that the productive new tools the Internet has made available can improve measured educational outcomes within the traditional classroom setting. This sort of quality improvement might not show up as a productivity gain (students taught per faculty member), and it need not overturn the artisan-style method of delivery in higher education.

The National Center for Academic Transformation (NCAT) at Rensselaer Polytechnic Institute has been actively pursuing a strategy of promoting blended courses.[7] A grant from the Pew Charitable Trusts allowed the Center to fund pilot projects at thirty colleges representing a broad spectrum of the higher education community. The pilot projects focused on the large-enrollment introductory courses that make up a substantial share of all undergraduate enrollments.[8] The pilot projects were very successful. Twenty-five of the thirty projects showed increases in student learning, and the other five showed no change in student learning. All of the pilot projects were able to decrease cost per student. Reductions in cost per student ranged from 20 percent to 77 percent.

Again the courses involved were not a random sample, so there is no claim that the techniques employed would work across the curriculum. As opposed to random selection, there was a clear design. For one, the courses were selected to maximize the impact on college budgets. Introductory courses are critical to the education provided at all colleges and universities. The NCAT data show that 42.5 percent of college enrollments are in the top twenty-five most heavily enrolled courses. Since the pilot projects demonstrated cost savings in many of these courses, there is the potential for substantial cost savings at many universities from adopting the techniques used in these pilot projects. The crucial question to tackle is *how* these pilot projects generated cost savings.

In general, cost per student can come down in two ways. The course size could remain the same, and the cost of delivering the course could decline. Alternatively, the costs of the course could remain the same, and the number of students enrolled could increase. Some of the strategies used in the NCAT pilot projects reduced costs the first way, and others reduced costs the second way.

There were six different cost-reduction strategies reported by the participants in the thirty pilot projects. First, costs were reduced by the use of online course management systems such as WebCT® and Blackboard®. These systems automate the mechanics of recording grades, posting assignments, and communicating with students. This was more of an innovation in 1999 when these pilot projects were completed than it is today, so most of the cost advantage from the use of course-management systems probably has been realized already since these tools are now widely used. Second, costs were reduced with the use of automated grading of exercises, quizzes, and tests. This offloads rote activities from faculty, freeing up time. There are limits to the kinds of questions that can be graded this way, but for certain classes this may save a considerable amount of time. Also, because the grading is less painful, instructors will assign more quizzes and exercises. This may well be behind some of the documented improvement in learning outcomes. Third, the use of tutorials presented online or on CD-ROMs can reduce the need for students to meet in practice sessions moderated by professors or graduate teaching assistants. Fourth, there were considerable gains from sharing resources. At a great number of institutions, there are many sections of the same course. As a result, things like making up tests, exercises, and quizzes are repeated many times by different teachers. In several of the pilot projects, sharing resources reduced faculty time. Fifth, costs were reduced through staff substitutions. In some cases, the time of graduate teaching assistants was substituted for faculty time. And perhaps surprisingly, in many cases those involved in the pilot projects found undergraduate course assistants could be used instead of graduate teaching assistants. Sixth, the pilot projects were able to cut costs by reducing space requirements. Since students were doing more of the course activities online, there was less need for classroom space. If a college or university used the Internet more intensively in a large number of courses, the physical footprint of the academic program could shrink.

These results are very encouraging, but one has to be wary of extrapolating from pilot projects of this type. Those who got the funds to do one of the pilot projects were clearly the professors who were more enthusiastic about the potential for the use of instructional technology, and their motivation may be behind some of the measured success of the pilot projects. This is a common problem in all forecasting based on pilot programs. The mass of people who must implement the new techniques may not be as interested in the approach or as adept at implementing it as the group that pioneered the pilot projects. Part of this problem may be generational, and the march of time should cure this. There are few professors in their fifties and sixties who are as adept with technology as are their colleagues in their thirties and forties. The younger professors have grown up with computers, so they are less likely to resist the kinds of changes that made the pilot projects a success.

We must stress that these apparently successful changes in course delivery were all made in the context of a traditional class. The pilot projects did not adopt online teaching and learning wholesale. They are examples of the blended approach. The basic idea is to have the computer do the things for which it is best suited and have people do the things they do well. The development of artificial intelligence may well change this boundary as time passes, but at the moment, the computer is better at rote tasks and humans are better at tasks requiring judgment. This means that computers can grade multiple-choice tests, or tests in which the correct response is numerical, but humans are better at evaluating essays and parsing errors in logic that are shades of grey instead of black and white. Computers also are more patient than human beings, so exercises that need to be repeated many times before a student masters a skill will work better if they can be automated. Unlike those who have gone all the way with distance education, the projects funded by the NCAT understand the advantages of the blended approach. As the results of these projects demonstrate, this approach can save money without sacrificing quality.

Open Educational Resources

The research that demonstrates the effectiveness of blended instruction has increased interest in these new methods. Several major universities have chosen to make their courses available on the Internet, and this gives a considerable boost to the adoption of blended approaches by making information and learning modules freely available. For example, in 2000 the Massachusetts Institute of Technology (MIT) decided to make all MIT courses available on the web.[9] The Open Course Ware information includes syllabi, reading lists, lecture notes, assignments, and video lectures. After a few years, almost all MIT courses have been made available, and millions of students and teachers had accessed the MIT site. Carnegie Mellon University's Open Learning Initiative provides another example.[10] The Open Learning Initiative provides twelve complete courses that are available for free. A randomized trial comparing the online statistics course from the Open Learning Initiative with the same Carnegie Mellon course taught in the traditional fashion showed that the online students did better on a standardized test of knowledge of statistics.

The significance of these open-courseware initiatives is that major universities such as MIT and Carnegie Mellon have done a large amount of the heavy lifting for institutions interested in shifting portions of some courses online, and they are offering the courses for free. In a 2009 article in *Science*, Marshall S. Smith argues that these efforts and others like it might well form the backbone of a revolution in the delivery of higher education. The open educational resources are particularly important for potential students from less developed countries where higher education is reserved for the privileged few who can travel to another country. They can also be used to expand the offerings of U.S. colleges. In August of 2009, an article in the *Chronicle of Higher Education* suggests that the Obama administration might well provide significant assistance to those who are developing open educational resources.[11]

The economic advantages of online and blended learning are considerable, and they are enhanced if major institutions are willing to do some of the course development for free. Particularly if the government provides money and encouragement, it is easy to forecast that the use of online and blended learning environments will continue to expand. As is currently the case, completely online institutions will appeal most strongly to what are called nontraditional students who are not willing and able to spend four years dedicated to obtaining an education. These are the students targeted so effectively by for-profit institutions. There are several reasons to believe that the traditional college-aged students will still exhibit a desire to go to traditional colleges and universities, and particularly those with a strong residential flavor. The campus activities and the chance to live in a community of people of one's own age make the college experience very appealing. Still, as the quantity and quality of freely available online courses grows, the demand for online degrees will follow, particularly from overseas and from nontraditional students. Also, successful online techniques will be integrated into traditional classrooms. As the pilot projects have demonstrated, courses that blend online learning with traditional face-to-face instruction can reduce costs.

Imagining a Distance-Education Future

We have expressed some skepticism about large claims for the revolutionary nature of distance education. We do not think that distance training is a perfect substitute for face-to-face instruction in a large number of very important cases. Yet others do not share our skepticism about the quality of distance-education degrees. And we admit that the technology could well improve to the point that distance-education classes of superb quality would become available for the entire curriculum. This is unlikely in the near term, but people often underestimate the ability of technological innovations to change the way we do things. In 1915, for example, the cost of a three-minute long-distance telephone call was the equivalent of the wages from ninety hours of work for the average worker, and the call had to be made at home or in a phone booth. Today, this phone call costs less than two minutes of work, and the call can be made from almost anywhere. Few people in 1915 could have envisioned a world with small easy-to-use handheld devices that allow people to pay bills, send text, and take and transmit pictures from almost anywhere in the nation at minimal cost.

We don't want to be accused of a similar lack of foresight, so in this section we will consider what the higher education world might look like if all instruction moved online. The undeniable cost advantages of distance education combined with a reduced quality advantage for face-to-face experiences could make enough people unwilling to pay the price of an on-campus education that the residential four-year college experience largely vanishes. What would the world look like without traditional colleges and universities?

Before we proceed, there are a couple of things we should get straight. First, we are not forecasting the future. We are actually quite suspicious of the claims of futurists who speculate about brave new worlds. Complex systems like the American higher education industry are almost organic in nature. A system like this that has persisted and evolved for a century or more actually may meet a set of related social needs, that is, the system may exist for a reason. Imagining a new system allows us to see what advocates of simple piecemeal changes actually ignore as they pull down the existing structure. Second, we are leaving out a lot of the story. There would be a long and complicated transition to the world we want to explore. The higher education system is a complex organism that cannot be changed with a snap of one's fingers.

Higher education as it is currently structured provides benefits above and beyond the instruction it provides. If instruction were only delivered online, something would have to be done to replace the other outputs of colleges and universities. For one, without traditional colleges and universities, there will have to be a very thoroughgoing restructuring of the way basic research and some applied research is conducted in the United States. Currently, the scholars who teach the courses are ultimately the ones responsible for creating the course material by pushing the boundaries of what we know. Shifting all instruction online changes the job of professors to being the mentors of students who are interacting with course materials on the Internet. As we said before, the teachers' job would essentially be to answer a stream of e-mail or some other form of online communication from students. Would creative people, the kinds of people who would be likely to push the frontiers in their discipline, be attracted to this kind of a job? Would the institutions offering the online degrees be willing to pony up the time and money required to support vigorous research efforts? The answers may well be no.

In an important sense, shifting to an online educational industry would be like the shift from artisan production of goods to factory production of goods in the early nineteenth century, with one big difference.

The workers who produce college education also produce knowledge gains to society that corporations and entrepreneurs can use for free, and it is this research that has been an engine of economic growth.

All is not lost if someone other than college teachers are the ones responsible for creating new knowledge. The federal government, state governments, or perhaps consortia of online institutions could create research institutes to push academic frontiers. As it is, a great deal of very important science research is done at national laboratories. Also, many private companies support large research efforts, though the fruits of this research are usually proprietary information and therefore not widely shared with the intellectual community. This is the difference between product-specific research, which companies have plenty of incentives to do, and basic research that augments everyone's productivity but which cannot be patented. Government and private research centers would have to be expanded to cover the fields of research currently found at universities. This would be a big task. Still, we can contemplate a world in which research is conducted in research centers not associated with colleges and universities.

The difficulty with the non-college research centers scenario is that it does not account for the education of each new generation of research scholars. Perhaps this education could be done as an apprenticeship at the research centers. Something like this occurs now as government science research centers offer many newly minted PhDs their first jobs in the sciences. These people are called "post-docs" or more formally postdoctoral fellows. They have already done all of their graduate course work and conducted at least one major research project at the university granting their doctoral degree. As post-docs they continue their training by working on research teams at the national laboratories. Post-docs are so common in most sciences that many college science departments will not hire newly minted PhDs. They only hire scientists who have completed one or more post-doctoral fellowships. Perhaps the research centers could take on the task of mentoring graduate students much the way they currently mentor post-docs. The post-doc model would have to be expanded to cover many more fields, but this would be a natural result of expanding the number of research centers to cover all fields.

If graduate students would have to be mentored by researchers at the research centers, we may have just recreated graduate institutions out of the research centers. The current post-doc already has done his or her initial graduate work at a traditional university. For the online-only model to work, the initial graduate training, which involves a lot of traditional course work, would have to be done online. Because the online institutions would be unlikely to have research faculty, the research centers would have to take on the job of mentoring graduate students at least in the dissertation phase of their graduate work. This would be the last possible time that graduate students could be transferred to the scholars at the research centers. The research centers would house the experimental apparatus needed by some dissertation students. Doctoral courses could still be primarily the responsibility of the online institutions, but there would have to be cooperation between the research centers and the teaching institutions as students prepared to do the research phase of their studies.

Sharing responsibilities for graduate training this way could work, though the number of institutions with doctoral programs would probably shrink considerably. This would happen naturally. In many fields, colleges and universities provide a large percentage of the jobs for people with a PhD. Despite the considerable joys involved in the completion of a PhD, without college employment as an option, fewer students would undertake graduate training of this type.

In the traditional model of undergraduate education, our students often get a taste of what academic graduate education would be like. A major senior honors project involving independent research is the capstone experience of many undergraduate programs, and many institutions push undergraduate research throughout the curriculum. Completing research projects gives the undergraduate a sense of the life of independent thinking and research that graduate training can launch. Sometimes this experience helps a student decide that graduate work is not his or her cup of tea. In other cases, students discover that they actually like the research process, and the most talented among them go on to do graduate work. This is easy to do with a current faculty of teacher/scholars. It might be difficult or impossible with teachers who were not expected to be scholars and whose major job was to mentor students in an all-online environment.

The last paragraph highlights a difference between online education conducted by course facilitators and face-to-face education conducted by teacher/scholars. Online courses are suited to situations in which information is imparted and students are coached to acquire information. A large number of face-to-face courses aim to do this as well, but many undergraduate courses are not simply vehicles to communicate received information. They teach processes, such as how to frame a question as much as pass along currently known answers. This also describes undergraduate research experiences. The aim of research training is to impart a love of learning and discovery. The objective is to ask questions and imagine new insights, to invent new knowledge, not simply to understand and communicate existing knowledge. The student has to define an acceptable research topic, find out the current state of professional understanding, and try to discover something new. Good undergraduate and graduate research projects often lead the students in directions that could not be anticipated before the research is begun. These efforts require considerable agility on the part of the student and the instructor. This experience may not be easy to replicate in an online-only environment, and undergraduate education would be impoverished as a result.

On the plus side, if all instruction were delivered online, many of the nonacademic services provided by colleges and universities today could wither away, because they are associated with the residential nature of traditional colleges and universities. In a completely online environment, students do not have to go to a particular place, so they do not need to be housed or have dining options provided by the institution. A large amount of the administrative apparatus of a typical college or university involves student life and is the result of the residential nature of the campus. Online colleges would not have to hire people to sort out problems with roommates, violations of dormitory rules, violations of rules regarding alcohol, and violations involving the unauthorized use of automobiles. Online institutions would focus exclusively on the academic progress of students. They would need academic counselors of various types, but a student's nonacademic life would be the responsibility of the student and the student's parents. As parents we are not sure this is such a plus! Developing independence inside the somewhat protected confines of a traditional residential college may have some social value. This is another one of those organic elements of the college experience as it has evolved over the centuries.

This section has *not* been an exercise in futurism. One should always be very wary of futurist speculation. The record of forecasters who spin out the future evolution of complex systems is littered with failure. We do not think that face-to-face instruction will disappear anytime soon. Instead, this section is intended to be a cautionary tale for anyone who thinks that constructing a world without face-to-face instruction will be natural, easy, or self-evidently desirable. The current system is an accretion over time of responses to perceived needs. At present, online provision has a significant cost advantage over face-to-face instruction for some courses, and it may achieve that cost advantage without a decrease in educational quality. This is a prospect worth exploring.

If improvements in technology expand the number of courses for which this is true, calls for replacing face-to-face instruction with online instruction may grow. But the current artisan model of providing higher education is not a self-evident relic waiting for an enlightened leadership to initiate its wholesale transformation. Colleges do much more than pump received knowledge into undergraduates.

Technical change is a process that is not well understood. Yet innovation is the key to sustained growth and rising living standards. Many of the key insights that have shaped modern society were not driven by the profit motive, though they generate significant profits once the business community acquires the insights for free. This innovation is positively correlated with the development of the modern university over the past century and a half. There is no guarantee that a world of online education coupled with a centralized and shrunken research establishment could ever produce the steady stream of insights provided by our decentralized, messy, prestige-driven university system.

Finally, the online institutions that are currently thriving do so in part because they can hitch a free ride on the efforts of the traditional institutions that still dominate the education landscape. These traditional institutions provide the training for the online faculty and provide the research that leads to new insights the online institutions can incorporate into their courses. In an entirely online environment, no one may be there to provide the free ride. Replacing the research and graduate training that keeps our higher education system vibrant would require a major effort, and without significant public support it might not happen. Without a system that gives highly trained people an incentive to do basic research and to train young graduate students, higher education may stagnate and ultimately wither.

Back to the Near-Term Future

Speculating about the prospect of an online-only higher education system may be interesting, but the more immediate question we face concerns whether or not we will be able to incorporate technological innovations that improve labor productivity at colleges and universities. This is a difficult question because competing forces are at work. Colleges do care about educational outcomes, so they will continue to integrate new technological innovations, as they prove effective. Many professors already teach blended courses, and most schools actively support the trend. This will only grow as more demonstration projects, including those that involve open-access software, show the efficacy of these methods. There are good incentives for schools to adopt less expensive and more effective methods. Many institutions do not relish relying on adjunct teachers as much as they currently do. As younger and more tech-savvy faculty replace older faculty, that too will encourage the move toward the new online and blended techniques. And lastly, price sensitivity among "consumers" is a factor as schools compete in an ever-more-national market for students.

Unfortunately, there are incentives that push in the opposite direction. New blended and online opportunities may allow a given-sized faculty to teach a larger number of students or fewer faculty members to teach the same number of students. This is real productivity growth. But productivity is measured in terms of students taught per faculty member, so productivity improvements will show up as larger student-faculty ratios. Unfortunately, the idea that larger student-faculty ratios are associated with a poorer education is enshrined in many important places. When students and their parents look at colleges, often one of the first questions they ask is about average class size and student-faculty ratios. The answer they are looking for is that class sizes are small and student-faculty ratios are low. Second, the *U.S. News and World Report* rankings reflect this same sentiment. The rankings include the student-faculty ratio (less is better), the percentage of classes with over fifty students (less is better), the percentage of classes with fewer than twenty students (more is better), and expenditures per student (more is better). To please prospective students and to move up these rankings, an institution has to become less productive! Even if it is not the main driver of college cost, this perverse incentive is indeed fueled by a positional arms race. While we can lament the unfortunate power of rankings, any college president will tell you that his or her life is easier when the school is climbing the *U.S. News* ranking than when the school's ranking is falling.

Overcoming this barrier to generating sustained productivity growth may be difficult. The notion that there is an inverse relationship between class size and quality is deeply ingrained. And it is not just a bias. Some classes require the artisan touch, and even in classes that can be expanded in size the experience is changed. The fact that the rankings reflect the idea that small is beautiful just makes the problem more difficult. And the rankings are unlikely to go away. Rankings sell lots of issues and books for the various magazines (which include *Forbes* and *Money Magazine* as well as *U.S. News and World Report*) and college guides that attempt to compare schools in any systematic way. Some of these publications reward efficiency, but typically they reward smaller classes and low student-faculty ratios. In the end, lower class sizes are preferred for bad reasons as well as good ones.

To end this review of technology's capacity to forge meaningful productivity growth in higher education, we do not see online coursework as a magic bullet that will cause a sudden change in the trajectory of higher education costs as it did for the cost of brokerage services. For that to happen, the entire structure of higher education would have to mutate into a post-artisan method of teaching. Instead, we think productivity improvements will happen slowly. Evolution is more likely than revolution. Some institutions will lead the way and others will lag. Cost increases in higher education will moderate, but only slightly. The idea that smaller classes and lower student-faculty ratios are associated with higher quality education has real power and would still have that power even if it weren't enshrined in the *U.S. News* rankings.

As long as higher education grants a leading role to the teacher/scholar, the basic cost-disease process will play an important role in determining higher education costs. As the all-online institutions have demonstrated, one can eliminate or substantially reduce the role of teacher/scholars. Cost disease should play a somewhat smaller role in the cost structure of these institutions. Yet as we showed in one of our examples in chapter 7, the prices of for-profit universities seem to be rising about as fast as prices in the nonprofit sector where the traditional residential environment still prevails. Nevertheless, we think it unlikely that a sizeable fraction of traditional four-year schools will imitate the online institutions, and we have outlined the potential social costs and consequences of imagining a shift in that direction. If we move away from the teacher/scholar model, higher education will be impoverished. There is room for significant improvement, but the basic model has real advantages that should not be sacrificed.

PART III

Tuition and Fees

9

Subsidies and Tuition Setting

Up to now, our aerial view of higher education has focused on the things that determine the costs of providing an education. We have talked about the sums that schools actually spend to produce the experience they offer to their students. Yet the average college student only pays a fraction of the total cost of his or her education. This means that changes in cost alone don't fully determine how much more money students and families must pay to get a year closer to earning that prized college degree.

Now we switch our attention to how colleges and universities collect the revenues needed to cover those costs. This leads us into interesting economic and political waters. If a college's costs exceed what it charges, then clearly someone is providing a subsidy, and the first thing to realize about higher education is that it is one of the most heavily subsidized economic activities in the nation. The vast majority of students pay much less than one-half of the cost of the education they receive.

This leads to the three big questions that will occupy us in this part of the book. First, what makes it possible for a school to charge the customer so much less than its full costs? The subsidy that schools pass on to their students comes from many sources, each of which has a story to tell. Next, given that colleges do not have to charge a price that fully covers all costs, how do they go about setting their tuition and fees? And lastly, we need to take a rational look at the emotional issue of college affordability. Have rising college costs driven a stake through the heart of the American educational dream, and will this curtail U.S. economic progress and social opportunity in the upcoming decades? In plain language, has a college degree become less affordable over time?

This chapter starts the discussion by outlining the factors that determine the two prices that dominate public discussion and the policy process in state capitals and in Washington. The first is the list-price tuition that schools publish in their catalogues. We will sometimes call this the sticker price. The other price is the net tuition (after all grants and discounts) that must be financed by students and their families. The list-price tuition is important because of its visibility and its political impact. A headline that screams "Tuition and Fees at the University of X Reached $60,000" will be one that will arouse public anxieties and affect public-policy choices. Despite the fact that most students don't actually pay this sticker price, the 2008 renewal of the Higher Education Act imposes burdens on colleges and universities if their published list-price tuition rises too fast. Basing a policy on a price faced by only the wealthiest families seems odd indeed. For students and their families, the net tuition a student pays after all grants and scholarships are deducted is the critical tuition concept. Increases in net tuition are behind the increase in the average amount of student indebtedness, so this number also can move public opinion and public policy.

Tuition and Fees

We have to clarify several pieces of terminology before we can begin to look at tuition setting in any detail. First, colleges and universities use the combined term *tuition and fees* for the price they charge. Unfortunately, the distinction between tuition and fees is not based on any bright line. Some institutions call all of their charges fees. A good example is the University of California system. Other institutions call all of their charges tuition. And still others have some charges they designate as tuition and other charges they designate as fees. Many public universities charge "tuition" for the educational side of the budget and "fees" for everything else, such as health care or recreational facilities. To those who have to pay the bill, this is a distinction without a difference. Both are charges they have to pay to attend the school for a year. We will therefore focus on the total tuition and fee charges of colleges and universities, and we will be silent about the distribution between the two categories of charges. To save space in the remainder of this chapter we will frequently use the word tuition to stand for tuition and fees.

There is an important distinction between mandatory fees and elective fees. When we speak of "tuition and fees," this includes only the mandatory fees that must be paid by every student who enrolls. This is the standard usage. Other fees are elective because not all students have to pay them. For example, a fee to park on campus only needs to be paid by students who own automobiles and who desire to park in campus parking lots, so it is an elective fee and would not be included in tuition and fees.

Second, institutions often charge a large variety of different tuitions. For example, at state-supported institutions, typically in-state students are charged less than out-of-state students. Also, tuition charged graduate students often is different from tuition charged undergraduate students. And, at some institutions, different undergraduate or graduate programs have different tuitions. At this point, we are not interested in the determinants of all these different tuitions. Right now we focus on the average tuition charged by the institution. This simplifies the story considerably and keeps us focused on the bigger picture.

Third, at this point we will talk about how list-price tuition is set as if the decision is made entirely by the institution. This is, of course, not strictly true, especially for public universities. In some states, the list-price tuition at state-supported schools is set by a state board or directly by the legislature. In other states, the tuition decisions made by an institution can be overturned by the legislature. Also, we will not discuss the effects of guidance about tuition that is occasionally given to state-supported institutions by state boards or state legislatures. In essence, we are going to remove the political influences and focus instead on the mechanics of tuition setting. This is because whoever is making the tuition decision faces the same basic constraints on their choices. We will bring these other important issues back into the discussion when we consider higher education policy in the final part of the book.

The Mechanics of Tuition Setting

The list-price tuition set by a school and the average tuition that must be financed by students are determined by the interaction of four factors: (1) the cost per student of the education and the cost per student of the other college functions covered by mandatory fees; (2) the per student subsidies the institution receives from government or private sources; (3) the average institutionally funded student grant; and (4) the average student grant funded by a sources outside the institution. In this chapter, we explain how these various factors interact.

Tuition setting is only slightly different from normal price setting. In the normal business model, the price charged to the consumer has to be sufficient to cover the cost of producing the product or service and provide just enough profit to the business to keep it doing what it is doing. Barring some kind of subsidy, the owners of a business cannot sustain losses for long, and businesses cannot avoid losses unless they can generate revenues that match costs. Colleges and universities are different. The vast majority of institutions of higher education are not profit making in the usual business sense. These colleges and universities either are entities of a state government or are private nonprofit corporations. There is a small and growing for-profit sector in higher education, but there is no need to single them out at this point. They follow the normal business model without extensive subsidization. In almost all cases, the not-for-profit institutions are highly subsidized, which allows them to charge a price (tuition) that does not cover full costs. Understanding the role of subsidies is crucial for understanding higher education pricing.

The major difference between state-supported schools and private ones is the source of subsidies. State-supported institutions receive direct subsidies in the form of state appropriations. There are two types of state appropriations: those covering operating expenses and those covering capital expenses. The typical state institution receives state appropriations sufficient to cover a portion of its operating expenses and state appropriations that cover the vast majority of capital expenses. In contrast, the subsidies for private institutions primarily come from current gifts and from the earnings on endowments. For private schools, often it is difficult to distinguish operating subsidies from capital subsidies. State-supported institutions also receive gifts and have endowments, but in almost all cases, state appropriations are the much more important subsidy. Also, some private institutions receive state appropriations, but gifts and endowment earnings are much more important for these institutions. Both public and private institutions receive funds from research grants, and a portion of these funds can be used to cover the expenses of the institutions. Finally, some institutions are able to generate revenue from the sale of educational activities beyond their tuition-paying student base, but these revenues are usually much less important than state subsidies, endowment income, gifts, and research grants.

The prevalence of subsidies in higher education has some obvious consequences for how tuition is set and how it evolves over time. As we mentioned in chapter 1, changes in costs and changes in subsidies both can be part of the underlying reason for changes in tuition. On the subsidy side, state appropriations and private endowment earnings can be quite volatile. Changes in the overall economic climate affect state revenues, and this often shows up as substantial changes in the amount a state appropriates to its institutions of higher education. The condition of the national economy also affects returns in stock and bond markets, which in turn changes the earnings on endowments and the likelihood that donors will be generous. Institutions often react to changes in subsidies by adjusting tuition.

The kind of subsidy we have been discussing is the general subsidy from all sources that is available to the institution. This is passed on to the "average" student as a tuition that falls short of the average cost (cost per student) at that institution. Most students, even the ones who pay the full list price, receive some of this subsidy. Student-specific subsidies are also important. Student-specific subsidies are the moneys offered to individual students in the form of a grant or a scholarship. These grants and scholarships allow students to pay less than the full list-price tuition. Some student-specific subsidies are financed by the institution the student attends, and other student-specific subsidies are financed by outside entities such as the federal government, state governments, and private charities.

Figure 9.1 provides a simple way to explain tuition setting. All of the cost and tuition concepts referred to in the figure are measured on a per student basis. To give a sense of the magnitudes involved we have included estimates for the averages at private four-year institutions for academic year 2003–4. To understand the figure, start at the box labeled

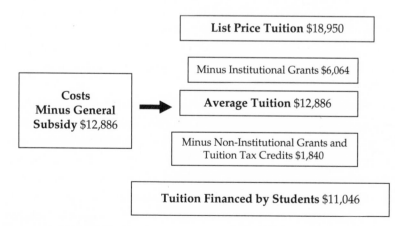

Figure 9.1 Tuition Setting

"Cost Minus General Subsidy." This is the amount the institution has to receive on average from its students. This explains the arrow to the box labeled "Average Tuition." To break even, a nonprofit entity such as a college or university has to have revenue equal to its cost. This is the channel through which costs and general subsidies drive prices in higher education. If cost per student rises, holding everything else the same, then average tuition must rise as well. If subsidies fall, also holding everything else the same, tuition again must rise. Of course, everything else does not have to remain the same. If the subsidy falls, schools could cut costs in order to maintain the same average tuition. As we argued before, without large amounts of waste and fat to trim, cutting cost is cutting quality. This is part of the unholy trinity of higher education. If you set the subsidy and you set average price, you cannot also set quality (cost). That is determined by your first two choices.

The right-hand side of the figure explains the relationships among the various tuition concepts. It is the part of the figure in which student-specific subsidies are inserted. List-price tuition is at the top. It is the tuition and fees number listed in the college catalogue. For 2003–4, this averaged $18,950 at private four-year institutions. Institutions do not collect the full list price from every student. For a variety of reasons, they give tuition discounts to particular students. These tuition discounts are often called scholarships. They may be need-based, in which case they are simply additional grants in a student's financial aid package, or they may be merit-based. They can also take the form of tuition waivers that institutions sometimes give to certain identifiable groups. Tuition waivers that some schools offer to the children of faculty and staff are one example. We simply refer to all these tuition discounts as institutional grants. To find the revenue the institution actually receives from its students, we must subtract the average institutional grant from list-price tuition. This yields what we have called average tuition. Private four-year institutions provided on average $6,064 in institutional grants to their students in 2003–4.

We have just made a point about college sticker prices that bears repeating. If a school chooses to offer tuition discounts to selected individuals or groups, then its published list-price tuition must be higher than the average tuition. For some people to pay less than the average means others must pay more if the school is to cover its costs. In terms of figure 9.1, if the average private four-year school charged everyone the same price, the list price could be almost 50 percent lower. Of course, if they did that the group of students that attended the school would look quite a bit different. Schools use merit aid and need-based aid to try to broaden and diversify the pool of students from which they draw talent.

Lastly, to calculate the tuition the average student must finance, we have to subtract from the average tuition all grants that are funded by entities other than the school itself and also subtract the value of any tuition tax credits. These outside grants may come from the federal government, from state governments, or from private sources. Also, many families are eligible for tuition tax credits, so some of the tuition and fee expenses are financed by reductions in tax liability. On average in 2003–4, students attending private four-year institutions received $1,840 in outside grants and tuition tax credits.

General Subsidies

Now we need to take a closer look at the leftmost box in figure 9.1, the one labeled "Cost Minus General Subsidy." This is the crucial number, since it tells us the average level of tuition universities must collect to make ends meet. We have already spoken at length about the broad technological and economic processes that drive higher education costs upward over time. The economic and political forces that act on subsidies are quite different. We can learn a lot about college tuition by seeing how the general subsidy has evolved over time and by breaking up the general subsidy into its component parts.

For public universities, state politics is the great driver of subsidy levels over time. By many measures, state governments have retreated substantially from their earlier commitment to low-priced public university education. The long retreat has been punctuated by big swings in state revenues associated with the national business cycle. The pattern of subsidy at our own university makes an excellent visual case in point. Figure 9.2 shows the state appropriation the College of William and Mary receives as a fraction of what we spend on educating our students (which does not include room and board).[1] Two features immediately jump out. First and foremost, the state share has declined substantially over the last thirty years. In the face of rising cost pressure on colleges and universities over the same span of years, this has had clear ramifications for the tuition we charge.

Yet the decline in the state share is not continual and incremental. It's more like a roller coaster. When the economy tanks, the state share plunges as budgets are slashed, and schools use tuition increases to

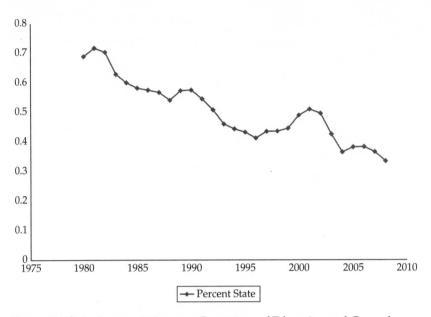

Figure 9.2 State Appropriations as a Percentage of Education and General
Expenses, College of William and Mary, 1980–2008

recoup some of the lost revenues. When the economy is doing well, the
state share creeps upward and tuition increases tend to be much more
moderate. But the state share never seems to reach previous highs before
the next financial retrenchment ensues. We will have much more to say
about the state funding roller coaster in chapter 15 when we tackle the
interesting and potentially very fruitful issue of reforming and restructuring the way states finance their public colleges and universities.

The long-term downward trend in the share of the cost covered by
state appropriations reflects shifting budget priorities at the state level,
and this is clearly reflected in national data. Figure 9.3 uses national data
to show how many dollars are appropriated by the states to support
higher education per $1,000 of personal income between 1960 and 2008.[2]
This is a measure of what is called "state effort," and it is perhaps the
most commonly used measure of how important higher education is to
the states.

State effort expanded dramatically in the 1960s and peaked in the
middle 1970s. Despite substantial increases in the proportion of young
people who go to college and the resulting increased pressure on
enrollment at state universities, the level of state effort has declined by
almost 40 percent from its 1970s peak. What figure 9.3 shows for the

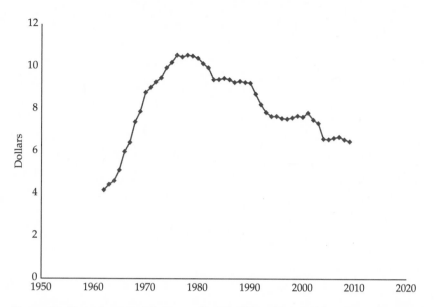

Figure 9.3 State Appropriations per $1,000 of State Personal Income, 1962–2009

states taken together is also true for each state alone. This hump shape characterizes every state's pattern.

The decline in state effort has received a fair bit of attention from people who study higher education. Three factors stand out that help explain what is going on. The first is the rise of other needs that have slowly pushed higher education spending down the list of state priorities. These other spending needs include a laundry list of items; including K–12 programs, corrections (prisons), and unfunded federal mandates. The most important of these other spending priorities seems to be health care mandates, and the Medicaid program in particular. Secondly, higher education is distinctive among most state programs in having a potential source of handy revenue of its own, namely tuition. Despite complaints from families that have periodically brought pressure on state legislatures to hold the line on tuition, this revenue potential seems to have shifted the state budget over time toward those activities that cannot help fund themselves.

The last factor that helps explain the decline in effort is the "Tax Revolt" that has influenced state spending and revenue collection.[3] Starting in 1976, twenty-three states adopted some form of tax or expenditure limitation. Some of the tax-revolt provisions have been added to state constitutions using the initiative process, and others have resulted from acts of the legislature itself. There are a variety of different types of tax-revolt provisions. Some provisions require taxes, or spending, to increase no more rapidly than state personal income, and some states place limits based on population growth and/or inflation. Other provisions require a super-majority vote in the legislature for increases in tax rates. These tax and spending limitations vary in other dimensions. For example, the definition of state revenue subject to the limitation varies. In some states, all state revenues including tuition and fees charged by state-supported institutions are limited. In other states, tuition and fees are exempted from the limitations.

Although the hump-shape pattern in figure 9.3 is evident in all the states, the timing of the peak and rate of decrease during the decline does differ substantially across the states. In earlier work of our own, we showed that a state's effort in support of its colleges and universities declined much more precipitously in the presence of tax-revolt provisions. Tax-revolt institutions such as tax and expenditures limitations and super-majority requirements are good predictors of when state effort peaked, and of the severity of the decline in effort afterward.

The other way in which politics is important is through research grants funded by agencies of the federal government. Much of the research budget of the National Science Foundation, NASA, the Department of Energy, the Department of Defense, and the National Endowment for the Humanities funds research conducted by faculty members at colleges and universities. Political support for science in particular is very important to keep these funds flowing.

The final source of subsidies is private support either in the form of gifts for current operations or the earnings on prior gifts that are accumulated in endowments. The growth of these kinds of subsidies depends on the generosity of donors and the return on the funds invested in the endowment. The ups and downs of the aggregate economy can have significant effects on both of these sources of private subsidies.

We can learn a lot by breaking down the general subsidy into its component parts and by looking at how this subsidy differs between public and private schools. Table 9.1 gives revenue per student by source for four-year institutions in 2006 dollars for 1987 and 2006.[4] These years are the two end years of the data compiled by the Delta Cost Project, which is the best source of data for the revenues of colleges and universities. We have divided revenue into average tuition, federal subsidy (federal appropriations, grants, and contracts), state subsidy (state and

Table 9.1   Revenue per Student at Year Institutions by Source in 2006 Dollars, 1987 and 2006

	Private		Public	
	1987	2006	1987	2006
Research Universities				
Average Tuition	12,857	18,490	3,277	6,801
Federal Subsidy	14,958	17,802	3,707	7,323
State Subsidy	1,422	1,376	11,410	12,091
Gifts	7,563	16,649	1,241	1,444
Endowment	2,695	28,085	130	1,406
General Subsidy	26,638	63,912	16,488	22,264
Total Revenue	39,495	82,402	19,765	29,065
Masters Universities				
Average Tuition	8,468	13,459	2,409	4,988
Federal	1,388	1,108	1,298	1,884
State	659	480	7,683	7,057
Gifts	1,996	2,512	209	226
Endowment	567	2,263	28	250
General Subsidy	4,610	6,363	9,218	9,417
Total Revenue	13,078	19,822	11,627	14,405
Liberal Arts Colleges				
Average Tuition	8,524	12,263	2,045	4,621
Federal	1,655	1,091	1,510	2,268
State	1,194	604	6,807	7,170
Gifts	3,081	5,545	198	485
Endowment	1,758	7,495	57	259
General Subsidy	7,688	14,735	8,572	10,182
Total Revenue	16,212	26,998	10,617	14,803

local appropriations, grants, and contracts), gifts (private gifts, grants and contracts), and endowment. The federal subsidy, state subsidy, gifts, and endowment are added to give the general subsidy, and the sum of average tuition and the general subsidy is the total revenue of the institution.

The first thing to notice in this table is that subsidies are very important for all types of institutions. Looking at the 2006 numbers, the total subsidy accounts for 77.56 percent of total revenue for private research universities and 76.6 percent of total revenue for public research universities. The percentages are lower at masters-degree-granting universities (masters universities), 32.1 percent for private and 65.4 percent for public, and they are slightly higher for liberal arts colleges, 54.5 percent for private and 68.7 percent for public. Subsidy percentages above 50 percent mean that students are paying less than half of the revenue collected by the colleges and university.

The second thing to see is that the source of the subsidies varies dramatically between private and public institutions. State support dominates the public subsidy. Using the 2006 data, state support represents 54.3 percent, 74.9 percent, and 70.4 percent of the total subsidy at public research universities, masters universities, and liberal arts colleges respectively. In contrast, the subsidies at private institutions are predominantly from private sources, namely gifts and endowment. In 2006, gifts and endowment represent 69.9 percent, 75.0 percent, and 88.5 percent of the total subsidy at private research universities, masters universities, and liberal arts colleges respectively.

Now compare the 1987 and 2006 data. Public colleges and universities of all types have become more dependent on tuition. At research universities, tuition accounted for 16.6 percent of total revenue in 1987, and this rises to 23.4 percent in 2006. The same comparison yielded 20.7 percent in 1987 and 34.6 percent in 2006 at masters universities, and 19.3 percent in 1987 and 31.2 percent in 2006 at liberal arts colleges. The reason why these institutions have had to increasingly rely on tuition is quite clear. The extra tuition dollars are making up for the fact that state support has not kept up with costs. The state subsidy to research universities accounted for 57.7 percent of revenues in 1987 but only 41.5 percent of revenues in 2006. The comparable numbers are 66.1 percent in 1987 and 48.9 percent in 2006 for masters universities and 64.1 percent in 1987 and 48.4 percent in 2006 for liberal arts colleges.

In contrast, dependence on tuition has not grown at all types of private colleges. At research universities, tuition accounted for 32.6 percent of total revenue in 1987 and 22.4 percent in 2006. The same comparison yields 65.7 percent in 1987 and 67.9 percent in 2006 at masters universities, and 52.6 percent in 1987 and 45.4 percent in 2006 at liberal arts colleges. Only at private masters universities are institutions becoming more reliant on tuition. The extraordinary growth in gifts and endowment at many private institutions allowed them to reduce their reliance on tuition.

Later data may show changes in these trends. The dramatic fall in the stock market in 2008 was very hard on the endowments of many private universities, and this has diminished their ability to subsidize their activities. The resulting cutbacks at the hardest hit private institutions have been very similar to the kinds of retrenchments experienced by public institutions following a reduction in state appropriations. For many of these private institutions, the fall in endowment earnings has made them much more dependent on tuition income.

In an article published in 1999, economist Gordon C. Winston of Williams College made very careful calculations of the costs, prices, and subsidies in higher education that are similar to the results we have just presented. His more comprehensive look at a single year illustrates that the averages are only part of the story. Institutions are very diverse, and there is a large variance around this average. In Winston's data, the percentage of cost covered by tuition ranges from a low of 20.1 percent at institutions in the top 10 percent of the subsidy distribution to a high of 77.4 percent at institutions in the bottom 10 percent of the subsidy distribution.[5] The variances around the average data we presented in the table are likely to be quite similar.

Conclusion

In our discussion of the factors that drive college costs, we did not distinguish between the experience of public and private institutions. Both types of institutions experienced cost disease, faced higher prices for their highly educated workers after 1980, and added to their equipment as they adapted to the computing revolution. Our discussion of pricing has to be different. The data we have just reviewed make it clear that at least between 1987 and 2006, the subsidies available to state-supported institutions have not kept up with the subsidies available to private institutions. The relative reduction in subsidies at state-supported institutions has made them become much more reliant on tuition as a revenue source than they have been in the past. This shift toward a larger reliance on tuition has been a very contentious issue in many states.

10

List-Price Tuition and Institutional Grants

Setting list-price tuition at a college is much like the price-setting process in many businesses that sell big-ticket items. When you walk into an auto dealership or a piano store, you will see a price tag on each item. Most savvy customers know that the printed number is only the starting point of the discussion. And people are aware that the price they pay may not be the same as what the next customer has to pay. The business has its costs to cover, and it would like to turn a profit. In addition, it knows that customers will respond favorably to the idea that they are receiving a discount. The business then sets a list price sufficiently high that it can sell a large number of its products at less than the full list price and still have sufficient revenue to cover its overhead and make a profit. While colleges and universities are not profit-making entities and never use this language, the process is strikingly similar in many ways. Schools charge a list price that often only a minority of students pay, and as laughable as this may seem, there are even institutions that offer 100 percent of the freshman class a "discount."[1]

There are some big differences, of course, between a college and an auto dealership. Auto dealerships are selling replaceable inventory, so volume is the goal. Colleges limit what they sell (enrollment) to maintain quality. The differences extend to how they set price as well. Although the bargaining approach is gaining ground as schools compete to draw talented students their way, the bulk of tuition discounting remains formula driven and need based. These are the institutional grants that schools offer, and they are sometimes given fancy scholarship names.

Schools value the composition of their student body, and they are willing to pay a price in lost revenue potential by offering discounts to some students who otherwise would not be able or willing to attend. This is not how most auto dealerships behave. Yet the fundamental similarity remains. The list price and the selling price are two separate things. Because colleges and universities need a certain amount of revenue to cover the unsubsidized portion of their costs, the practice of giving tuition discounts to specific students has a big impact on the list price the school sets.

The first part of this chapter explores the ways that institutional grants affect list-price tuition. We will use a very simple example of a one-hundred-student college to show how tuition discounts offered to a fraction of the student body raises list-price tuition as a by-product. This is the college and university analogue to a business raising the list price so it can offer its goods on sale for some consumers. Later in the chapter, we review the evidence on tuition discounting. We will show that the use of institutional grants has grown significantly over time. The final portion of the chapter looks at why this has happened.

Simple Tuition-Setting Examples

We can use a hypothetical small college to explore how list-price tuition, institutional grants, and average tuition are related. Suppose our hypothetical college has one hundred students. The college wants to spend $2,000,000 per year educating these students, and it has general subsidies available from various sources to cover one-half of its costs ($1,000,000). Given these numbers, the college must raise another $1,000,000 in net-tuition payments in order to cover its costs. This college is under no obligation to give any institutional grants. It can raise the $1,000,000 it needs in tuition revenue by charging each of the hundred students the full list-price tuition of $10,000 per academic year. In this case, the list-price tuition and the average tuition level are the same. Together with the $1,000,000 general subsidy the school receives, the tuition revenue is just sufficient to cover all the college's costs of providing the education.

In this very simple baseline scenario, what happens if the general subsidy falls? Perhaps the school is a state university whose appropriation is cut. Alternatively, it could be a private college whose endowment takes a tumble. To keep the discussion concrete, suppose the general subsidy falls to $800,000. If the school wishes to keep spending $2,000,000 on educating its hundred students, then it has to raise an additional $200,000 in tuition revenue. With no institutional grants, the college must raise its list price from $10,000 per year to $12,000 in order to generate the extra revenue.

The key thing to see is that you would get the exact same tuition increase if there had been no fall in the general subsidy, but the college had decided instead to spend $200,000 more per year on its students. This illustrates a very simple principle. List-price tuition can be pushed up by a change in the general subsidy or by a change in costs. If the only thing you know is that list-price tuition is rising, there is no way to distinguish between a change caused by a cost increase and a change caused by a decrease in the general subsidy the school receives. This point is often lost on those who blame runaway costs for all increases in list-price tuition.

With the base case in mind, we can now see what happens when we add institutional grants. Suppose our small college offers institutional scholarships worth $1,000 to fifty of its students. The school still wants to spend $2,000,000 on its programming, and it still receives a general subsidy of $1,000,000. This means the school still has to collect $1,000,000 in tuition from its total student population of one hundred. To do this, it must set the list-price tuition at $10,500. Fifty students pay that list price and the other fifty pay $9,500. The school gets $525,000 in revenue from the fifty students who pay the list price and $475,000 in revenue from the fifty who receive the scholarship. The take-home message of this example is that if a school wants to decrease the price for some students, and it also wants to continue spending the same amount to educate each student, then it will have to increase the list-price tuition it publishes in its catalogue. Lastly, the existence of these institutional grants does not change the *average* level of tuition. That is still $10,000 per student. Some pay more than this, and others pay less.

What happens if this school wants to make its institutional grants more generous? Suppose the school wants to double the scholarship to $2,000 for the fifty scholarship students. In this case it must raise the list price to $11,000 for the fifty non-scholarship students so that it can decrease the net price to $9,000 for the fifty scholarship students. The students who pay full price now pay a total of $550,000 of the total tuition bill and the other half whose tuition is discounted pay $450,000.

In essence, our simple college decided to put its education on sale for half of its students. The only way it could do this and still cover its costs was to raise its list-price tuition before it offered the sale price to some of its students. If the school raises its list-price tuition in order to offer more generous institutional grants, this does not raise the *average* tuition as long as the school's total spending remains the same. Average tuition is $10,000 in each case. It has to be $10,000 in order for the institution to meet its budget. Institutional grants only change the distribution of tuition among students.

These examples illustrate three fairly simple but important points about institutional grants and list-price tuition. For any given level of total college spending on its students,

1. Offering institutional grants raises list-price tuition,
2. Sweetening those grants pushes up list-price tuition even more, and
3. The average tuition level is the same regardless of how much tuition is discounted for some students.

Who Funds Institutional Grants?

Schools often claim that their institutional grants do not raise tuition because the grants are "funded" out of private resources and not from other students' tuition. This argument does not stand up to close scrutiny. It ignores the simple fact that money is fungible. We can use our workhorse hypothetical college again to show why the distinction between institutional grants that come from private funds and those funded by tuition generally is meaningless.

As usual, our hypothetical college has $2,000,000 in costs to cover, and it covers them with general subsidies and from tuition collected from its fifty scholarship and fifty full-paying students. Now we change the subsidy a bit. Suppose that the school only has a general subsidy of $900,000, but it also has a separate annual $100,000 private fund that is designated only for scholarships. Since the institution only has $900,000 in general subsidy, the school seemingly needs to collect an additional $1,100,000 in tuition.

Although things *look* different, nothing has really changed. To raise $1,100,000 in tuition, the list price is again $11,000. The fifty full-paying students generate $550,000 in tuition. The fifty scholarship students pay $9,000, which gives the school $450,000. Together the students pay $1,000,000 in tuition. The scholarship fund "pays" the remaining $2,000 of the tuition bill for the fifty scholarship students, yielding the required $1,100,000. This is just a bit of financial sleight of hand. The school has $2,000,000 in revenue to pay $2,000,000 in costs, and this is true whether or not $100,000 of the total subsidy is walled off into a separate "private scholarship fund." The actual tuition paid by students is the same here as it was in the case in which there were no funds designated for scholarships.

In the language of financial aid, the last two examples have compared "unfunded" and "funded" institutional grants. In the first situation, the school had no private funds specifically designated for scholarships. It simply lowered the tuition for a selected group of students. In the second example, the scholarships were fully funded from private sources and the money could not be used for anything else. At first glance the "funded" scholarship seemingly presents a problem since it leaves the school $100,000 short when paying the $2,000,000 it costs to run the college for the year. The problem, however, is more apparent than real. The $100,000 in scholarship money is handed to the fifty scholarship students who then hand it right back to the school by paying $11,000 in tuition. The school is actually collecting $1,100,000 in tuition. One million dollars comes from the students and their families and $100,000 comes from the designated fund. The school can then spend this scholarship money on academic programming, just as if the money was part of its unrestricted $900,000 subsidy. This shows that designating dollars within the total subsidy has no meaningful effect as long as the total subsidy available to the school remains the same.

There is one situation where rigidly designating the use of funds can have an impact, and the impact actually is negative from the school's perspective. Money is not fully fungible if the restrictions placed on how the school uses part of its subsidy force the school to do something it otherwise would not have chosen to do. This would happen if the funds designated for scholarships exceeded the amount the institution thought was prudent to spend on scholarships.

As a general rule, privately endowed scholarship funds are unlikely to exceed the level of scholarships that most schools would like to offer, so the constraints imposed by donor restrictions are not likely to trouble scholarship decision making very often. Each institution faces a critical decision about how generous it wants to make its institutional grants, and the source of funding used for these grants generally is irrelevant. For any given level of spending on programming and for any given total subsidy that is available, the more the institution wants to "spend" on institutional grants, no matter what type of funds are used, the higher will be that school's list-price tuition.

This result does not mean that colleges and universities should shy away from soliciting endowment donations or annual fund giving designated for student scholarships. In general, a school that wants to increase its resource base should offer potential donors a wide array of opportunities to give. Endowing a scholarship can be very appealing to many donors. Since these endowments increase the school's total subsidy, the institution and its students clearly will benefit.

Here is a specific example of a request for contributions that one of us received in the mail as this chapter was being written.

Gifts to the Trinity College Annual Fund support core priorities that help define Duke. This year, the dean of Trinity College, George McLendon, invites you to specify which of these core needs you would like your Annual Fund contribution to support:

- Need-based financial aid, which helps Duke enroll the best and the brightest;
- A world-class faculty committed to teaching, student-mentoring, and ground-breaking research;
- Programs that enable students to apply knowledge in service of society.

The problem for givers is that there is no way that a school can credibly commit to them that donations they mark for the aid category actually increase aid spending by the school compared to what would have been spent if the money had been given to any of the other categories. They are all part of the general budget, and the money generally is fungible. Fortunately for the schools, most people aren't fully aware of this!

A larger resource base relaxes constraints that bind the school's choices, and this can benefit students in a number of ways. Our workhorse example can show how. Return to the case where the school offers a $2,000 break to its fifty scholarship students and its list-price tuition is $11,000. This school nets $1,000,000 in tuition revenue and it has another $1,000,000 in general subsidy to spend. The students get whatever $2,000,000 in programming can buy. Now suppose that its alumni or some other set of donors creates an endowment that generates another $100,000 in subsidy for this school. This institution would have many options, all of which are very attractive. We will look at four examples.

First, it could use the $100,000 to double its scholarships from $2,000 to $4,000 for the chosen fifty students who receive tuition assistance. In this case, list-price tuition would still be $11,000, but scholarship students would pay $7,000 instead of $9,000. The extra $100,000 is fully spent on these selective tuition reductions. Alternatively, the institution could use the $100,000 to give $2,000 scholarships to all of its students. In this case list-price tuition would still be $11,000 and every student would be a scholarship student paying $9,000. The extra $100,000 would be spent on tuition reductions of $2,000 for the fifty students who did *not* previously receive scholarships. Giving everyone a scholarship is not as silly as it sounds, even though it is the same as reducing the list price to $9,000. There is good evidence that the cachet of getting a "scholarship" is worth more to students and families than a simple price reduction, and getting a "named scholarship" is worth even more.

Third, the institution could use the $100,000 to reduce list-price tuition to $10,000 and keep the $2,000 scholarships for the fifty scholarship students (here the $100,000 would be spent on tuition reductions of $1,000 to all 100 students). The first option gives all the benefits to the initial scholarship students, the second option gives all the benefits to the students who originally had no scholarship, and the third option spreads the benefits evenly among all the students.

Lastly, the school could use the entire new revenue stream to increase what it spends on programming. Total spending could rise from $2,000,000 per year to $2,100,000 per year. If spending more means higher quality, then the benefit of the extra endowment income is spread to students through higher quality offerings instead of through lower prices. Thus far we have talked only about private fund-raising, but additional money from any source, public or private, has the same effect. The important point is that if the institution has command over more resources, its options improve. As is often the case in life, more is better than less.

How Much Tuition Discounting Goes On?

Tuition discounting using institutional grants is not a small matter, particularly at private four-year institutions. In the 2007–8 academic year, over half the students at private four-year colleges and universities received some level of institutional grant, and this is on top of any direct state or federal financial aid they received. At public four-year institutions, the figures were somewhat lower. At doctorate-granting public universities, 26 percent of the undergraduates received some form of tuition discount, while at non-doctorate-granting schools the proportion was 15.4 percent. But these proportions don't tell us how *deeply* the tuition is discounted at various institutions.

To do that, we need a measure that quantifies the size of the discounts. One measure that is used is the tuition discounting rate. This number is calculated in two steps. First, we take the total dollar amount of institutional aid and divide it by the total number of students at the school. This gives institutional aid per student. The next step is to express this institutional aid per student as a fraction of the total price, which is list-price tuition plus fees.

$$\text{Tuition Discounting Rate} = \frac{\text{(Institutional Aid Per Student)}}{\text{(List-Price Tuition and Fees)}}$$

A tuition discounting rate of 10 percent, for instance, tells us that for every $1,000 of list-price tuition, the college has cut $100 off of this number on average across the student body. The number does *not* tell us anything about how big the grants are to any particular student.

We can easily go back and calculate the discount rate for the hypothetical college we have been using. In the example where the college gave a $1,000 break to fifty students and charged a $10,500 list price, the amount of institutional aid per student is $500 ($50,000/100). Expressed as a fraction of the list-price tuition, the discount rate is 4.76 percent ($500/$10,500). When the average grant was $1,000 (fifty students received $2,000 grants, and fifty students received no grant) and list-price tuition was $11,000, the discount rate is 9.09 percent. How do these compare to real discount rates?

In a study for the College Board in 2006, Sandy Baum and Lucie Lapovsky calculated tuition discount rates from the College Board's *Annual Survey of Colleges*.[2] Their data show that the discount rates in our examples are in the ballpark for public two-year institutions (community colleges) and quite a bit low for four-year institutions. Table 10.1 gives their results.

These discount numbers make two things very plain. Tuition discounting is a significant factor, particularly at four-year institutions, and

Table 10.1 Tuition Discount Rates by Sector, 1994–95 and 2003–04

Year	Public 2-year	Public 4-year	Private 4-year
1994–95	4.6%	13.1%	25.3%
2003–04	7.4%	15.4%	32.0%

Table 10.2   Calculation of Average Grant and Cost Minus General Subsidies, 4-Year Institutions

Year	Tuition Discount Rate	List-Price Tuition	Average Grant	Cost Minus General Subsidy
Public				
1994–95	13.1%	$2,705	$354.36	$2,350.64
2003–04	15.4%	$4,645	$715.33	$3,929.67
Percent Change		71.7%	101.8%	67.2%
Private				
1994–95	25.3%	$11,719	$2,964.91	$8,754.09
2003–04	32.0%	$18,950	$6,064.00	$12,886.00
Percent Change		61.7%	104.5%	47.2%

it is growing over time. The tuition discounting numbers also help us resolve two interesting questions. First, how much of the observed increase in list-price tuition between 1994–95 and 2003–4 is caused by increases in tuition discounting? Second, how much could institutions reduce their list-price tuition if they eliminated tuition discounting? You can come up with answers that are at least good ballpark estimates if you know the actual list prices charged by these broad categories of schools. This is what we do in table 10.2 for public and private four-year institutions.

To understand this table, look first at the 1994–95 academic year for public four-year institutions. The tuition discount rate (13.1%) times the list-price tuition ($2,705) yields the average institutional grant ($354.36). The column labeled "Cost Minus General Subsidy" is the difference between the list-price tuition and the average grant. This is the amount per student that schools must cover with tuition revenue to make ends meet. It is what we have called average tuition in our examples, and it is what schools could charge as a single undiscounted price. If you go to the row labeled "Percentage Change," you will see the percentage change in the dollar figures between 1994–95 and 2003–4. Public four-year colleges and universities, for instance, have more than doubled the size of their average grant.

The entries in the table also tell us that the increase in tuition discounting only accounts for a small part of the rise in list-price tuition at public four-year schools. Between 1994 and 2005, "Cost Minus General Subsidy" rose by 67.2 percent. This is the percentage increase in list-price tuition that would have been needed if the level of tuition discounting had remained 13.1 percent. The rise in tuition discounting (to 15.4 percent) thus pushed up tuition and fees by an extra 4.5 percent, from 67.2 percent to 71.7 percent. Another way to put it is that the extra tuition discounting amounted to 6.7 percent (or 4.5/67.2) of the rise in list-price tuition.

The story for private four-year institutions is rather different. Again the average grant more than doubled. But in this instance, the contribution of increased tuition discounting to the increase in list-price tuition is considerable. If private four-year institutions had kept their tuition discount rate at 25.3 percent, their list-price tuition would have grown by 47.2 percent, which is the growth rate of "Cost Minus General Subsidy." Instead, the greater use of tuition discounting at private universities pushed up list-price tuition by an extra 14.5 percent, from 47.2 percent to 61.7 percent. All schools are using more tuition discounting, but private schools are pushing the envelope harder. Explaining this is our next task.

But before we turn to this task, we want to review a major point about college cost and pricing. A reasonable observer cannot infer what is happening to college costs by looking just at what has happened to list-price tuition. We have just shown that list-price tuition will grow more rapidly than what the average student must pay—which is cost minus the general subsidy—if the tuition discounting rate increases. And we also know that changes in general subsidies will affect the required average tuition, so any fall in public subsidy or in private endowment return will affect list-price tuition, no matter what has happened to the school's actual costs. Cost is only one of the factors driving list-price tuition.

Why Has Tuition Discounting Increased?

To answer this question, we have to understand why colleges and universities choose to use institutional grants in the first place, and we need to see if the higher education marketplace has changed in ways that explain why colleges are relying on them more. Put simply, schools use institutional grants to improve the quality of their entering classes. "Quality" is a loaded word. Here we intend to give it the broadest possible interpretation. To schools that have to craft an incoming class, the quality of that class depends on many things. One goal is demographic diversity, and this includes among others the economic, racial, gender, and geographical diversity of the students. Quality also will depend on the academic abilities of the students as well as a host of other attributes, like athletic prowess, musical talent, and leadership skills.

Their concern about student quality makes colleges and universities relatively unusual businesses. Aside from their credit worthiness, a business is not typically concerned about the quality of its customers. They may want to project an image to potential customers about the sort of person who uses the product, or what you will become if you do, but the actual buyers are not selected for their attributes. What makes customers attractive to most businesses is simply their ability to pay for the products or services.

Colleges and universities are different. Students play a critical role in the educational process. They are not just passive receivers of knowledge. To learn, they have to put forth some effort studying, being involved in discussions, writing, and working on team projects. Much of the learning that goes on at a college or university involves interactions between students, and this learning occurs both within the classroom and outside of it. To use a little bit of easy-to-understand jargon, if knowledge, wisdom, and skill acquisition represent the output produced by a university, the inputs schools use to generate that output go beyond the faculty, staff, machinery, and buildings paid for by the school. The students themselves also are inputs, and the better the input the better the output. Put simply, if your classmates are good students it will help you to be a good student, and if your classmates offer challenging and diverse perspectives, that will help you to learn better and to discern better. As a result, the thought process involved in assembling a student body is much more like the way a coach tries to assemble a winning team than it is like a business trying to attract customers.

A school's admission process is designed to put together a group of students that will yield the best possible student body. This is complicated by many factors. Since prospective students cannot be sure of getting in everywhere they apply, most apply to multiple institutions. Schools recognize that some or even most students may view them as a second or third choice. Many students, particularly the most desirable ones, will receive multiple offers of admission. As a result, even highly selective schools have to admit more students than the number of slots they have in their incoming class. This is the well-known "yield" problem. Schools would like N students in the freshman class and they must admit more than N, knowing that only a certain percentage will matriculate. The trick is getting the right mix of students among the N who enroll. That mix determines the overall quality of the class.

Therefore there are two steps in the student recruitment process. The first is to convince a broad set of students to apply to your institution. After you have evaluated the applicants and have admitted a group of them, the second step begins. Now the challenge is to convince the students who you have admitted to accept your offer of admission. Institutional grants come into play in the second step. They are designed to increase the probability that the most-desirable students will accept the offer of admission.

The question an institution faces in the second step of the admission process is how to allocate the funds it has set aside for financial aid. There are two types of very appealing students worth considering. First, there is the student who would very much like to attend your institution, but who cannot afford to attend even after receiving grants from federal financial aid sources. This sort of student may have signaled his or her strong interest in the school in a number of ways, including early-decision applications, campus visits, and other more direct statements. The process of applying for financial assistance makes schools aware of each student's demonstrated financial need and of how much of that need remains unmet after all other public and private grants are counted. Armed with this information about unmet financial need, this sort of student offers a very appealing use of some of a school's financial aid budget, since meeting that need may significantly raise the likelihood that he or she will accept an admission offer.

Second, there are the admitted students ranked in the highest quality category. These students will be appealing to many institutions, so they are very likely to have multiple admission offers. These students may or may not have unmet financial need. When they receive all the fat envelopes telling them of their admission, these students likely have some preferences over the group of schools that has accepted them, but they may also be persuadable. These students will be making college-choice decisions based on the price/quality combinations offered by the institutions in play. In the short run, there is little an institution can do about the quality of its programming or of its faculty, but with an institutional grant it can affect the price the student must pay. The role of the institutional grant is to increase the probability that these highly desirable students will accept offers of admission by making this institution's price/quality combination better than the alternatives.

Grants to students typically are classified based on why they are offered. The two basic categories are need based or merit based. The first of our two examples would be a need-based grant, and our second would be a merit-based grant. The motivations were clearly different in our two examples. Yet this classification scheme is not really so crystal clear and clean. Suppose that an institution only used "merit" to make its institutional-grant offers. If one of the students receiving a grant had demonstrated financial need, would that grant be need-based or merit-based? The school's motivation may not involve need, but the outcome is identical to a need-based grant.

The motivation for the federal government in offering aid is quite different than the incentives that govern institutional grants given by colleges and universities. Federal financial aid is all need based. The aim is twofold: first to help create access to higher education for students who can succeed in college, but who would otherwise not attend because of objective financial constraints, and also to assist students in matching with the most appropriate programs for their abilities. Society has an interest in getting the best possible match between students and colleges. Extra schooling benefits the students themselves (and the tax base), but without government aid, credit markets do not do a good job of allowing students with poor collateral to borrow against potential future earnings. We will have more to say about this in later chapters. For now, we will just note two public incentives to create access for students whose constraints are financial, not intellectual. The higher productivity of college-educated workers can raise the productivity (and wages) of others around them. This potential spillover benefit of education is a motive for governmental need-based aid, but it is *not* a motive for institutional grants. And lastly, most governments also value the social mobility that equalizing educational opportunity tends to bring.

But after compensating for these access problems, society has no particular interest in affecting the decision a student makes between two institutions to which he or she has been admitted. The student can make the college choice on his or her own. On the other hand, the schools themselves have a strong interest in attracting a certain set of students. As we have already seen, building the college's entering class "team" is a challenge. Students are both an input and an output, and financial need and student characteristics interact in complicated ways.

Given this complex motivation, what might explain the increasing size and importance of institutional grants? The first big reason is rooted in financial need. Desirable students who have limited means now have more need for financial help than they did thirty to forty years ago. Three forces drive the increased need.

- College costs have increased very rapidly.
- Starting in the late 1970s and early 1980s, the income distribution in the United States widened considerably.
- Federal financial aid has declined as a percentage of the cost of attendance.

The first two forces clearly are intertwined, and we spent a rather long time talking about them in part two of the book. Cost disease pushes up college costs faster than general inflation. In chapter 12 (on affordability), we will delve into the data on how these forces have created winners and losers in the U.S. economy. To foreshadow a bit, we will show how these forces have increased the burden on poorer families and on middle-income people whose incomes have stagnated or fallen due to technological changes that have favored the well educated. Repeating some data we used earlier, in 1950 an American working male at the 90th percentile of the income distribution made three times as much as the working male at the 10th percentile of the income distribution. In 1999 the 90–10 gap for male workers had risen to 5.4. In effect the rich got richer and the poor got poorer. Given increasing college costs and declining relative income, needy students are needier and more numerous.

Federal grant aid is the third factor. As we have seen, student need has been driven up by the rise in college costs and by stagnant income of families at the bottom of the income distribution. If federal grant aid had kept pace with rising student need, then colleges and universities would not have had to use their own institutional grants to offset increased need among their applicants. In fact, federal financial aid has not kept pace. Figure 10.1 gives the inflation-corrected value of the average Pell Grant. It shows that for most of its history, the average Pell Grant has fluctuated between $2,000 and $3,000, measured in 2007 dollars. Since the cost of attendance has increased substantially more rapidly than the inflation rate, the average Pell Grant covers a smaller and smaller percentage of the cost of attendance.

The combination of these three factors has led colleges and universities, both public and private, to use institutional grants (tuition discounting) more intensely as a way to help desirable students with financial need attend their institutions. As we have shown, for any given level of spending per student, this increasingly intense tuition discounting must raise list-price tuition. Alternatively, the tuition discounting must be paid for by siphoning off resources that could otherwise have

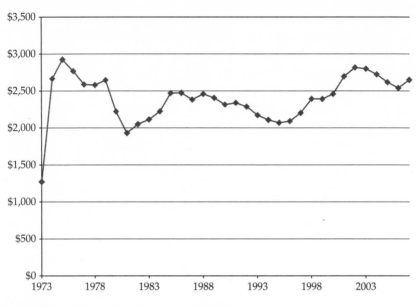

Figure 10.1 Average Pell Grant in 2007 Dollars

been used to maintain or increase the quality of the programming available to all students.

Increased financial need on the part of college applicants is not the only reason why schools may be spending more on institutional grants. The second reason for the shift toward larger grants has more to do with competition among schools for desirable students. Caroline Hoxby suggests that changes in the size of the market that colleges and universities face is a critically important piece of information in understanding their expenditures on institutional grants designed to attract desirable students. In the 1950s and 1960s, most colleges and universities operated in largely local markets for student talent. Students ventured out of state relatively infrequently, so each college and university faced limited competition in its market niche. As family incomes grew and as transportation and communications cost diminished, students began to consider a much wider geographical spread of colleges and universities. In 1949, 93.2 percent of all students attended an in-state college.[3] This percentage had decreased to 74.5 percent by 1994. The change was even bigger for private colleges, from 80 percent in 1949 to 54.6 percent in 1994. As a result, there are now a large number of colleges and universities with truly national student bodies, and there are fewer and fewer institutions with only regional or local student bodies.

As students consider colleges and universities from a larger geographical area, the market niche occupied by any one college becomes more crowded. As a consequence of this crowding, other things being equal, institutions will find that a dollar of grant money leads to a smaller and smaller increase in the probability that a desirable student will accept an offer of admission. Given this change in the effectiveness of an aid dollar, the only way institutions can preserve the quality of their student bodies is by increasing their institutional grant offers. This process has been gradual, and it is ongoing. The result is that institutional grant offers have increased at all institutions, and aggregate institutional aid spending has increased as a result.

In the foregoing discussion, we assumed that the institution was only motivated by a desire to obtain the best student body. It engaged in tuition discounting based on merit broadly conceived. Based on this assumption, we found that grants classified as need based and grants classified as merit based would both increase over time. Thus institutional grants would increase at institutions committed to awarding only need-based grants *and* at institutions that place little weight on economic diversity. No matter what the underlying motivation, to meet their goals institutions have to increase institutional grants.

Is There a Financial Aid Arms Race?

The increasing use of institutional grants often is characterized as an arms race. We have encountered arms-race stories already. Although we find that arms races, like the prestige competition among highly selective schools, are not the primary cause of rising college cost, the arms-race model does help explain what has happened with financial aid. The arms-race analogy typically is used to describe the increased use of merit aid. In an arms-race story, the only reason that College A has increased its offers is that it has to match College B, or it will lose the particularly talented students it wants. Some spark is needed to set off the race, but once the spark has ignited it, the race will be self-perpetuating. Does this idea square with our story about why institutional grants have grown in importance over time?

Part of our explanation is based on the geographic expansion of the market. The number of institutions that are direct competitors for particular students has risen over time. As this competition expands, some institution has to find itself on the bottom of the ranking of institutional grants, and it will have to respond. As it responds it will put some other institution at the bottom, and this institution will have to respond. This sounds a lot like a positional arms race, and once it starts the momentum may be difficult to overcome.

To stop an arms race, the participants have to find a way to band together that allows them jointly to pull back from the race. They must be able to develop a mechanism to verify compliance with the agreement, because no school will want to join an agreement if others may cheat it. Many college leaders think colleges and universities should sign an agreement to limit financial aid to the cases of demonstrated need. For example, writing in the *Chronicle of Higher Education* in 1999, Michael McPherson and Morton Owen Schapiro said, "Specifically, we should urge Congress to pass a law affirming that colleges can enter into agreements to apply common standards in assessing need and awarding aid without running afoul of the antitrust laws."[4]

Yet the geographical extension of the market for higher education also pressures schools to upgrade quality over time, and it allows schools and students alike to do a better job of matching. The enlargement of the area from which schools draw their students also reduces the market power that schools might have had in their protected local areas. This is the upside of competition, and it is what the antitrust laws are designed to protect. Using targeted aid grants is part of this competition among schools for talent within a larger market. A fair evaluation of the consequences of market enlargement must weigh these positives along with the less desirable arms-race aspect.

The idea that institutions should band together to control financial aid practices has an interesting history. Starting in 1958, a group of institutions formed what became known as the Overlap Group. The institutions in the Group were all committed to offering financial aid that covered all demonstrated need of their students and to limiting their aid budgets to this objective. These institutions offered no merit-based aid. At their meetings, they agreed on what constituted "need" for the students who were admitted to more than one of the participating institutions. These students had an admission "overlap." The group's rules placed a limit on the financial aid offers any institution could extend. No school was allowed to offer more than what the commonly-agreed-to formula defining the student's financial need. The mix of grants and loans contained in the financial aid offer could vary, but the total aid offered could not. This effectively limited bidding wars that turned need-based aid into merit-based competition.

In July of 1989, the U.S. Department of Justice's Antitrust Division started an investigation of the Overlap Group. They were looking for evidence that the Group's activities amounted to illegal price fixing. In May of 1991, the Justice Department formally charged one of the Overlap Group's members, the Massachusetts Institute of Technology (MIT), with a violation of the antitrust laws. In September of 1992, the judge ruled against MIT. This ruling was altered on appeal, but importantly, the judges on the appeal rejected MIT's claim that the tuition setting and financial aid policies should be exempt from the antitrust laws. The case was finally settled with an agreement that allowed institutions to communicate with one another about financial aid policy but explicitly prohibited discussions about individual students.

This ruling effectively thwarts efforts to stop a financial aid arms race by coming to a verifiable agreement and it explains why McPherson and Schapiro called for congressional action. Absent explicit legislation exempting higher education from the antitrust laws, the arms race cannot be stopped in the normal fashion. If anything, despite the protests of those who do not like where the arms race is headed, it appears to be heating up rather than stopping. The recent changes in the way the most highly rated institutions are treating need-based aid is clear evidence of this. Now Stanford, Princeton, and Harvard among others offer aid packages to students with demonstrated financial need that do not include any loan component. In addition, they are offering tuition-free education to students from families with incomes well above levels typically associated with needy students. For example, in 2008 Stanford University's webpage includes the following information.

Tuition Charges Covered for Parents with Income Below $100,000

For parents with total annual income below $100,000 and typical assets for this income range, Stanford will ensure that all tuition charges are covered with need-based scholarship, federal and state grants, and/or outside scholarship funds. In most cases, the parent contribution will be no higher than the standard cost of room and board (around $11,000). Many parents in this group will see contribution amounts far lower than $11,000.

Similar offers can be found on the websites of other major universities. Essentially, these institutions are throwing out the typical financial aid formulas and are making their financial aid much more attractive. This gives these very wealthy institutions, many of whom are former members of the Overlap Group, a big leg up in the financial aid arms race.

Some Final Thoughts on Institutional Grants

Institutional grants are designed to improve the quality of the student body, either by meeting the demonstrated need of a qualified student with limited financial resources or by enticing a student with particular skills or talents to come to the institution. Because the quality of the educational experience at a college or university is determined by the quality of the students as well as the quality of the staff and facilities, colleges clearly have an incentive to use institutional grants. The students who have to pay the higher tuition also may benefit if they can work with the students enticed by institutional grants.

Yet there are some downsides to using merit-based institutional grants, especially if merit aid displaces need-based financial aid. This description would fit any school that gives an increasing volume of merit-based grants, but which does not meet demonstrated financial need for all accepted students. An institution might do this if the admission staff thinks that the marginal student the school can attract with merit-based aid is more valuable to the institution than the marginal student it can attract with need-based aid. Shifting the aid budget away from need and toward merit will have no effect on tuition, but it will have a detrimental effect on the options of students who are less well-to-do. If enough schools do this, two socially undesirable things may occur. Access to higher education will be reduced for the slice of the population that could succeed in college but whose financial situation makes college attendance difficult. And perhaps more insidiously, less-well-off students will find themselves trading down to schools for which they are not as well matched. The result may be lower wages for themselves, fewer spillover benefits for their coworkers and communities, and less social mobility.

On the other side of the ledger, merit aid may provide some incentives that yield a positive payoff. Students may work harder in high school if that work will increase their chances of qualifying for a scholarship. Even without merit-based aid, the college admission process provides a considerable incentive to work hard in high school. Getting in to favored schools with highly selective admissions processes is not easy for high school slackers. Yet merit-based aid may add to this incentive to work hard. We know of no research that measures the contribution of institutional merit-based aid to increases in high school work incentives. But there is some evidence of an effect for a state-wide program. In 1999, Daniel T Bulger, Gary T. Henry, and Ross Rubenstein demonstrated that the initiation of the Georgia HOPE scholarship, a state merit-based aid program, has been associated with an increase in high school grades and SAT scores in Georgia. The effects are not large, but they are consistent with the notion that a broad-based merit aid program can improve effort in high school.

We have talked about the pros and the cons of tuition discounting without firmly concluding that one dominates the other. There is so little real evidence about this that prudent caution is in order. Yet whatever the current balance, this benefit-cost calculation may change as the arms race in institutional aid matures. As institutional grants become more and more common, the benefits for the students who do *not* receive one, such as rubbing shoulders (and minds) with desirable scholarship students, may dissipate. Institutional grants are beneficial to an institution when they allow the school to attract students who would otherwise attend other institutions. If yours is the only institution offering these grants, you will be very successful in attracting the type of students you want. Once everyone is in the game, an institution can only succeed in changing the odds if its institutional grants are more attractive than its competitors.

There are two ways an institution can make a grant more attractive. It can increase the amount of the grant or increase the privileges associated with it. Both of these strategies are likely to be harmful to the position of the typical student not receiving an institutional grant. First, as grant amounts get larger, the tuition and fees paid by the non-scholarship student will increase. Second, as the privileges associated with a grant grow—for example, scholarship students get special housing, are allowed to take special courses, get to be first in line at registration, or are segregated in an Honors College—the chances that non-scholarship students will benefit by associating with the scholarship students diminishes. Essentially, the costs to non-scholarship students grow, and the benefits they receive decline.

In the extreme, if every institution were engaged in aggressive tuition discounting, the tuition discounts wouldn't actually affect the composition of the student body at any institution. All that will happen is that each institution will give sufficiently attractive tuition discounts to maintain its student body, and the students who do attend are exactly the same ones who would have attended prior to the scholarship race. The only effects would be that the privileges on campus that accrue to talent, or to whatever characteristics the institution prizes, would tend to grow, and the students who are not aggressively sought would pay higher tuition. In this case, the non-scholarship students are unambiguously losers. They share the campus with the scholarship students, who would have been there in any event, but they do not bump into them very often, and they have to pay more for the privilege.

This is the description of a mature arms race. Everyone is running faster just to keep in the same place. No one is getting ahead, and everyone would be better off if they all stopped running. The pool of potential high-quality students is essentially fixed. If colleges and universities stop giving very attractive merit-based aid packages, these students would still go to college. They might attend the same colleges they would attend in a mature arms race. Not all institutional aid is merit based, so stopping this arms race does not mean that all institutional grants would disappear. Nevertheless, if merit-based awards disappeared, there would be a large list-price-tuition decrease at many institutions. And because of this tuition decrease, the amount of need-based aid required would be reduced as well. The benefits of stopping the merit-based grants arms race could be substantial. The losers would be the merit-based aid recipients. They could still afford to attend college, but they would have to pay more.

On balance then, society likely would benefit if schools could find a mechanism to curb the use of institutional grants aimed solely to affect the college choice of highly-sought-after students. More resources would be available to create access for needy students, and this would not close off access for any of the others who are currently recruited. But if the current process has all the properties of a maturing arms race, then there are few benefits to unilateral disarmament. A few schools have tried that tactic, but it only works in extreme situations in which the schools cannot fill their classes. And not all schools necessarily would choose to shut down the race even if such a mechanism existed. Richer schools benefit from accumulating talent in a national market, and schools trying to rise rapidly up the quality ladder would not want to be bound by any arms-control treaty. The status quo seems very durable. Institutions cannot or will not stop the process unilaterally, and without a change in the anti-trust laws they are legally bound not to use the standard remedy for a mature arms race.

11

Outside Financial Aid

This chapter completes our look at the relationship between the cost of higher education and the price that students and families actually pay. Higher education is a heavily subsidized activity, so the average student does not pay the full cost of his or her education. Universities also use tuition discounting to affect the composition of their incoming students, so the price paid by different students at the same university can vary substantially. The providers of outside financial aid supply the final part of the picture. The federal government, state governments, and various charities all offer grants to college and university students. As a result of both institutional grants provided by schools and these outside grants from governments and private groups, the actual amount many students or their parents have to finance is well below the list price charged by the college or university.

In addition to grants, loans play an important role in the financial aid system. But loans and the lending market will not play a significant role in our discussion here. We are interested in the final bill a student faces after he or she receives all grants. After a student (and the student's family) knows the final bill, they face a second decision about how to finance the expenditure. Loans allow the student and his or her parents to spread payments across time rather than paying the entire cost out of current funds. College students seldom have established credit ratings or collateral to offer lenders, so without some assistance many students who could succeed in college would be shut out of credit markets. Government loan guarantees solve this problem for students from low- and middle-income families, and having parents bear ultimate responsibility for repayment solves the problem for students from higher-income families. We will have more to say about loan programs later in the book, but for this chapter our focus will be on grants that reduce what students must pay for higher education.

The federal government is the largest source of outside grants to students. Until quite recently, nongovernmental charitable entities were not very important, but they have grown in importance and now give the second largest amount of outside grants. State governments are the smallest source of outside grant funding to students, though as we have seen they remain are a large provider of direct subsidies to schools. We will assess all three sources of outside aid to students. Once we have those facts in hand, we will be able to tackle the interesting question of how these multiple sources of grant aid interact to determine a student's final bill. Grant aid plays a crucial role in creating access to higher education for many families, and the complex interaction of aid programs affects the decisions of millions of families each year.

To preview our main results, the aid system is a complicated labyrinth for students and parents to navigate. A main thrust of reform efforts in financial aid is simplification, and we will use our discussion here as a springboard to talk about broader reforms of the financial aid system in chapter 14. We also show why the order in which donors provide aid to students is quite important. The fact that federal aid is doled out to students *before* schools themselves decide how much in institutional grants to offer is not a distinction without a difference. But before we embark on this discussion, we want to offer some perspective by giving a brief historical overview of the growth and development of federal financial aid.

A Brief History of Federal Financial Aid

Financial aid as we know it has not always been an important part of the higher education system. Grants and scholarships always have been available, but over much of the history of the American higher education experience, they were very limited, and often they were directed to students pursuing particular career tracks such as the ministry. Prior to World War II, in the minds of most observers the appropriate type of aid for needy students was work-study. Needy students should be given a chance to work their way through college. Aiding students with college expenses was certainly not one of government's responsibilities. This view was widespread even among those who had a very expansive notion of the role of government. As a prime example, in July 1939, Franklin D. Roosevelt said, "Just because a boy wants to go to college is no reason we should finance it."[1]

Four factors played an important role in changing views on the advisability of government-sponsored financial aid. First, the Servicemen's Readjustment Act of 1944, typically called the G.I. Bill, demonstrated that more people could take advantage of higher education than the prewar norms suggested. Many of the veterans who took advantage of the G.I. Bill's education benefits were not from the kind of families who had previously sent children to college. Despite its prominence, the G.I. Bill was not a financial aid program. Since it was tied to service, the bill's benefits were not widely available, and the program was scheduled to end when veterans exhausted their benefits. The G.I. Bill is better thought of as deferred compensation for veterans. Still, it demonstrated that a large fraction of the country's youth would take advantage of a college education if they could afford it.

Second, at a time when the federal government was doing little to redress inequalities in educational opportunity, in the early 1950s, a group of colleges and universities acting together as members of the College Entrance Examination Board made considerable progress. In 1954, the College Board formed the College Scholarship Service (CSS) as a clearinghouse for information on the financial need of college students. The CSS developed the first widely-used system for calculating financial need. A large number of institutions subsequently adopted the CSS approach. This needs-analysis methodology regularized what had been a fairly chaotic system and provided a pattern the federal government followed when it started its own financial aid programs over a decade later.

Third, the launch of the Sputnik satellite by the Soviet Union on October 4, 1957, shocked the United States. One of the reactions was the National Defense Education Act (NDEA) of 1958. This act created federal scholarships for students in particular fields, primarily the sciences. The NDEA was not a full-blown financial aid program, but it was a start. Most of the scholarships were for graduate students, but some were for undergraduates. The NDEA put the federal government in the higher education business in a way it had not been earlier. Since the founding of the country, education had been a state or private function. Many in Congress believed strongly that the federal government had absolutely no business getting involved in education, either at the K–12 level or in postsecondary schooling. The NDEA challenged this notion in a big way.

Finally, the landslide victory of Lyndon Johnson in the 1964 presidential election, along with large Democratic majorities in Congress, paved the way for important social legislation. One of the new laws was the Higher Education Act of 1965. This act set up the major components of the existing federal financial aid system: needs analysis, grants, work-study, and loan guarantees. The Higher Education Act clearly put the federal government in the business of trying to assure that all qualified students had sufficient funds to pursue some form of postsecondary education.

Since 1965, there have been many changes in federal financial aid programs, but most of them have been variations on themes and not wholesale changes. For example, in 1972 the Pell Grant replaced the basic grant that had previously been administered on campus. Pell Grants depend only on a family's ability to pay, not on any decision made on campus. Also, the original Higher Education Act gave more money directly to institutions than it did to students. Over time, direct aid to students grew in comparison to the amount allocated to institutions. Now the vast majority of the funding authorized by the Higher Education Act goes to students as need-based student aid. The one really dramatic change in federal financial aid since 1965 was the introduction of tuition tax credits in 1997. Tuition tax credits were discussed in 1964 and 1965, but they were not part of the financial aid landscape until 1997.

We will turn next to how needs analysis is done. Needs analysis is a critical part of many financial aid decisions made by federal, state, and private decision makers. We will discuss each of these aid givers in turn. The final part of the chapter takes up the complex interactions among financial aid programs. Because financial aid is an amalgam of programs administered by schools, the federal government, state governments, and private entities, the result is a bewildering maze of programs and options. Janet S. Hansen (1991) is too kind when she says the system is "not the result of a grand design." Charles T. Clotfelter (1991) is closer to the mark when he likens the financial aid system to "a Rube Goldberg machine." The lack of coordination and systemic planning in such a non-system is a serious issue for families and policy-makers alike.

The Needs-Analysis System

To be eligible for federal financial aid, a student has to demonstrate that he or she has financial need. Once the student's eligibility for federal financial aid has been established, this triggers eligibility for many other types of financial aid. The process starts with students and parents filling out the Free Application for Federal Student Aid (FAFSA). The FAFSA asks a series of questions about the family's income and assets. Typically, families cannot fill out the FAFSA until they have completed their federal income tax forms for the year. In what follows we will describe the way the federal government takes the information on the FAFSA and calculates the family's Expected Family Contribution. Do not despair if this seems quite complicated. It is.

The first piece of information is family income, typically the Adjusted Gross Income from the federal income tax form. The first deductions from family income account for taxes: federal income taxes, state taxes, and social security taxes. The second deduction is called the income-protection allowance. This allowance accounts for the costs of feeding, clothing, housing, and providing medical care and transportation for the family. The income-protection allowance varies with the size of the family. The final deduction is the employment-expense allowance, which is available to families with two wage-earners. The amount left over after making these deductions from family income is called the Parents' Available Income.

The second part of the process involves the family's assets, excluding the value of its home. It may also include a portion of the value of a business or farm. An asset-protection allowance is subtracted from the value of the family assets. The asset-protection allowance depends on the age of the parents. Older parents receive larger asset-protection allowances because they are closer to retirement. The Parents' Contribution from Assets is 12 percent of the difference between assets and the asset-protection allowance.

In the final step of the process, the Parents' Available Income and the Parents' Contribution from Assets are added together to get the Parents' Adjusted Available Income. The parents' portion of the Expected Family Contribution is then determined using a progressive scale in which the rates increase from 22 percent to 47 percent of Adjusted Available Income as the Adjusted Available Income increases.

The calculation of the Student's Contribution is done in a similar fashion. There are three differences. First, 35 percent of the student's assets, not 12 percent, are used to determine the Student's Contribution from Assets. Second, there is no asset-protection allowance for students. Third, the entire sum of the student's available income and contribution for assets are added together (i.e., there is no progressive scale applied to determine the student's contribution.) Finally, the total of the Parents' Contribution and the Student's Contribution is the Expected Family Contribution (EFC).

This basic strategy for calculating the EFC traces back to the first needs-analysis system developed by the College Scholarship Service in the 1950s. The system is generally sensible. Families are expected to contribute a fraction of their after-tax income and accumulated assets. The amount they are expected to contribute is sensitive to the age of the parents, the size of the family, and the number of workers. After deductions, families with greater income and/or assets are expected to shoulder more of the costs of college than less-well-to-do families. And lastly, students are expected to contribute more of their disposable income and accumulated assets than are their parents.

There are separate calculations for independent students without dependents other than a spouse and independent students with dependents other than a spouse. These calculations follow the basic pattern described above. The biggest difference is in the way assets are treated. The percentage of assets that are finally included in the EFC is 35 percent for independent students without dependents other than a spouse and 12 percent for independent students with dependents other than a spouse.

A major difficulty with the needs-analysis system is that to most parents and students the process is a black box. They submit their numbers, and out comes the amount that they are expected to pay for a college education. Parents have little sense of how the number is calculated, and they have few, if any, options if they feel the number is too high.

Also, the timing is unfortunate. Critical parts of the required information depend on entries on the income-tax forms the family submits for the tax year prior to the year for which the financial aid is to be awarded. For example, the 2008 income-tax information is needed for a family whose child is going to start college in the fall of 2009. The needed information, W-2 forms, 1099 forms, and so on, may not be available to the family until early February. Several important decisions are already made well before early February. Students applying for early decision have already applied and have been accepted or rejected by that time. Also, many regular-decision application deadlines have passed before the first of February. Students and their families are making a lot of decisions in a cloud of uncertainty over the cost consequences of their choices.

There are frequent calls to simplify the needs-analysis system. Many have proposed basing the EFC solely on income information. This makes the EFC something that could be calculated more easily and with much less information and documentation. Many families could estimate their EFC fairly accurately in the fall, many months before they fill out their form 1040 for the tax year. All of the uncertainty has not been resolved, since the actual EFC awaits the actual 1040. The only way to eliminate all uncertainty is to use the previous year's tax information (2007 income in 2009), but this is deeply problematic as well since a family's fortunes may have changed substantially and the financial aid system is trying to match aid with current need.

This kind of simplification is very appealing, but there are tradeoffs to consider. Basing the EFC only on income information could create some inequities. There are some families with low income and high assets. Some of these families can afford to pay quite a bit of their children's college education, so they might have no need for federal help. These families could qualify for a substantial amount of federal aid if the system were one based entirely on income. In essence, the determination of the EFC faces a tradeoff between simplicity and equity. The simpler the system, the more possible inequities it may contain. Adding complexity may eliminate some possible inequities, but it will make the system more cumbersome and harder to understand. It will also reduce the amount of information people have at the time they need to make important decisions.

The final difficulty with the needs-analysis system is that it determines the family's *Expected* Family Contribution. There is often a difference between what the federal government expects the family to pay and what it is willing to pay. Some families are willing to pay more, and other families are willing to pay less. There are few options other than private loan markets for students whose families are unwilling to pay as much as the government thinks they should pay. This is a problem without a solution. There is no way a family can be forced to contribute as much as the government expects. And adjusting the financial aid awards of students whose families were unwilling to pay the EFC would set up an obvious incentive problem.

Federal Financial Aid Programs

The broadly available federal financial aid programs come in four flavors: Pell Grants, campus-based programs, guaranteed student loans, and tuition tax credits.[2] Pell Grants are by a large margin the most important federal grant program. Pell Grants are based solely on the student's EFC. Each year, Congress sets the maximum Pell Grant. A student who has an EFC equal to zero receives a Pell Grant equal to this maximum. A student who has a positive EFC that is less than the maximum Pell Grant receives a Pell Grant sufficient to make his or her EFC plus the Pell Grant equal to the maximum. A student who has a positive EFC that is larger than the maximum does not qualify for a Pell Grant. Essentially, the Pell Grant program provides a minimum ability to pay college expenses for every student in the country. The Pell Grant is based solely on the EFC and not on the list-price tuition of institution the student decides to attend. The Pell program is about basic access to the higher education system, not choice within it. In almost all years, the amount guaranteed by the Pell Grant has exceeded the average tuition and fees at two-year institutions, but it only covers a fraction, and sometimes a very small fraction, of the tuition and fees at most four-year institutions.

The campus-based programs have three components: the Supplemental Economic Opportunity Grants (SEOG), Perkins Loans, and work-study. The federal funds for these programs are given to campuses to distribute. These programs are available to students with financial need. A student has financial need if the cost of attendance at his or her college or university exceeds the EFC (or EFC plus the student's Pell Grant). These federal funds are supposed to be distributed to the students with the most financial need. Often they are the students who have already received Pell Grants but who still have unmet need. As a result, a needy student frequently will get a financial aid package that contains money from several of these pots. Unlike Pell Grants, the campus-based programs are sensitive to the price of the institution the student attends. Students attending high-price institutions will have more unmet need than students attending low-price institutions.

The third federal program is the Guaranteed Student Loan Program. Prior to 2010 loans are either made by private lenders as Stafford Loans or directly by the federal government as William D. Ford Loans. Starting in July 2010 all federal student loans will be direct loans. The government pays any interest that accrues while the student is still in school, provides a loan guarantee to the private lender involved in a Stafford Loan, and pays subsidies to lenders so that the borrower is charged a below-market interest rate. These subsidized loans are available to students with unmet financial need, but there are limits on the size of the loans. These loan limits are larger for students in their third and fourth year as an undergraduate than they are for students in the first and second years of their undergraduate program.

As college costs have risen, the volume of federal loans has increased dramatically. Figure 11.1 gives the percentage of total federal financial aid given in the form of loans, grants, work-study, and tax benefits from 1970–71 to 2006–7.[3] Loans have grown in importance relative to grants with the exception of increases in the grant percentage in the years after the creation of Pell Grants in 1972. After 1980, loans accounted for the largest share, and by 2006–7, 70 percent of federal financial aid is in the form of loans. Work-study has never been a terribly significant program. The tuition tax credits, which first affect the 1998–99 data, were immediately more important than work-study, but they are not as large as either grants or loans.

The tuition tax credits are the final part of federal financial aid. There are two kinds of tuition tax credits. First, the Hope Credit, whose name was changed to the American Opportunity Credit in 2009, covers undergraduate education. It gives a tax credit of up to $2,500 for tuition payments for a dependent student who is enrolled at least half time in a degree-granting program. The tax credit is phased out for high-income

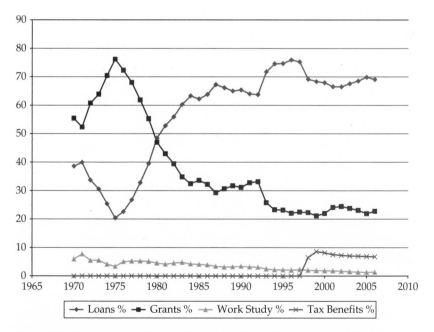

Figure 11.1 Percentage of Federal Financial Aid as Loans, Grants, Work Study, and Tax Benefits, 1970–2007

tax payers. The phase out starts for taxpayers filing single returns with incomes of $80,000 and joint returns with incomes of $160,000. Taxpayers filing single returns with incomes over $90,000 are completely ineligible for the tax credit. In like fashion, taxpayers filing joint returns with incomes over $180,000 are ineligible. The second tax credit is called the Lifetime Learning Credit. This credit is available for any kind of postsecondary education. It allows a credit of 20 percent for up to $10,000 of tuition payments. The Lifetime Learning Credit also has income limits. It is phased out for single filers starting at $50,000 of income, and single filers with incomes of over $60,000 are completely ineligible. The limits for joint filers are $100,000 and $120,000.

The argument that kept tuition tax credits out of the original Higher Education Act of 1965, and that kept them out of subsequent reauthorizations until 1997, is that they represent very poorly targeted financial aid. The lowest income families have no federal income tax liability, so they would receive no benefit from tax credits. Tuition tax credits are a much bigger benefit to the middle class. These families have an income-tax liability that the credit can reduce, but their incomes are below the upper limits beyond which the benefit disappears. Given the limits, up to $90,000 for single returns and $180,000 for joint returns, a broad stretch of the middle class is eligible for this financial aid. The American Recovery and Reinvestment Act of 2009 changed this somewhat. Starting in 2009, up to $1,000 of the American Opportunity Credit is refundable. That means that a family can still receive some of the credit even if the credit exceeds the family's total income-tax liability. Still, the vast majority of the tax credits go to families much further up the income distribution than the families whose children are eligible for Pell Grants and other federal financial aid.

State Financial Aid

States have always provided large general subsidies to state-supported colleges and universities. They also provide student-specific aid in the form of state-sponsored scholarships and other financial aid. For quite some time, state financial aid practices mimicked federal practice. In fact, many of the state programs were created in response to incentives in the form of federal matching funds. The resulting state financial aid systems were need-based systems that worked much like the campus-based federal programs.

More recently, quite a bit of state financial aid has shifted toward some measure of merit and away from a strict need-based formula. In 1993, Georgia jump-started this with its HOPE (Helping Outstanding Pupils Educationally) Scholarship Program. Any Georgia student who had a certain grade point average was eligible for a HOPE Scholarship covering full tuition at a state-supported college or university. Several states subsequently created programs like Georgia's HOPE Scholarship. Data from the National Association of State Student Grant and Aid Programs show that in the academic year 1996–97, 84.9 percent of state grants were need-based grants. That percentage declined to 71.7 percent in 2006–7.[4] In 1996–97, only six states (Alabama, Alaska, Florida, Georgia, Louisiana, and North Carolina) gave less in need-based grant aid than they offered in non-need-based grant aid. In 2006–7, the number of such states had grown to thirteen (Florida, Georgia, Idaho, Kentucky, Louisiana, Michigan, Mississippi, Missouri, Nevada, New Mexico, South Carolina, Tennessee, and West Virginia).

These merit-based scholarships are politically very popular. In some cases, the programs represent an expansion of financial aid, but in other cases they are squeezing out need-based financial aid. Michael McPherson and Morton Schapiro (2006) demonstrated that institutional aid seems to be more sensitive to measures of ability and less sensitive to measures of need than it used to be. Combined with the shift toward merit aid in state programs, this represents a serious retreat from the notion that financial aid should be based on need.

Private Financial Aid

The final source of financial aid comes from private sources not directly associated with a college or university. Many companies, private organizations, and secondary schools give scholarships of various sorts to college students. These organizations can be as well known as the National Merit Corporation or the Rotary Club and as little known as the WJCC Community Scholarship Fund. The latter is a private nonprofit organization that raises scholarship money for students from Lafayette, Jamestown, and Warhill, which are the three high schools in Williamsburg, Virginia, where we live. The private scholarships can be based on need, merit, a combination of both, or neither. The scholarships given by some companies to the sons and daughters of their employees explain the last category.

Figure 11.2 presents the data on grants awarded in constant dollars from 1970–71 to 2006–7.[5] The College Board only started presenting data on private grants in 1988–89. As the figure indicates, private grants have grown rapidly since that time. By the mid-1990s, private grants had surpassed state grants in total, and if their present trajectory continues, they might well surpass federal grants in the foreseeable future. This is part of a general shift of the responsibility for financial aid to the private sector. Adding private and institutional aid together, the government share of all grants clearly has been declining for most of the last twenty-five years. The dramatic increase in institutional grants and the less precipitous but nevertheless steady growth in private grants lead to this result.

This shift toward the private provision of financial aid represents an important evolution. In the 1970s and 1980s, when the federal government dominated the provision of grants, the resources of the country were being redistributed from the general tax base to students from low-income families. Financial aid was part of a progressive taxing-and-spending system designed to increase access to higher education for students with demonstrated financial constraints. More recently, the redistribution that takes place through the financial aid process is much

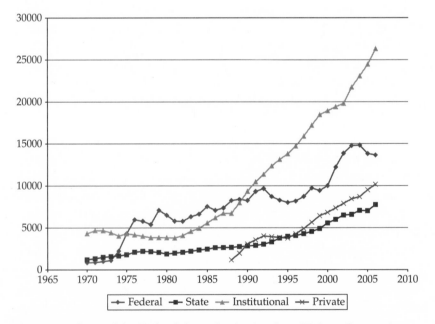

Figure 11.2 Grants from Federal, State, Institutional, and Private Sources in Constant 2006 Dollars, 1970–2006

less clearly progressive. Institutional aid offered by schools redistributes income from the general student body to students the school identifies as more talented or merit worthy about as much as it does from students of high-income backgrounds to students of low-income families. States also are reducing the progressivity of their aid systems by putting an increasing share of their financial aid dollars in merit-based programs. Private financial aid muddies the waters further. Many of the donors who support outside financial aid are very well-to-do, so this voluntary redistribution might be progressive. But many of the grants are based solely on merit, so the progressive nature of the redistribution is muted.

Interactions between Financial Aid Programs

This section completes our description of the financial aid system in the United States. As we have said, the use of the word "system" suggests more design than is really present. The system is a largely uncoordinated hodgepodge of programs that interact in many ways. Some of these interactions are well known, but many are poorly understood. The interaction between outside financial aid and institutional aid depends on the ordering of the decisions to award aid.

Determining who gets to go last is critical in the distribution of need-based aid. The entity that gets to go last faces the least amount of unmet need. Suppose a student has a $10,000 gap between the cost of attendance at the chosen school and his or her EFC. This need can be met by a variety of contributors. Suppose the student gets an SEOG grant of $2,000. This reduces the unmet need to $8,000. Next suppose the student receives an outside scholarship of $5,000. This reduces the unmet need to $3,000. Finally, the institution awards the student an institutional grant to complete his or her aid package. Further suppose that in the absence of the outside scholarship, the institution would have been willing to make a grant of $8,000 to the student. In this example, because it got to go last, the institution was able to reduce its contribution to the funds used to meet the student's need.

The difficulty this example illustrates is that awarding the privilege of going last to the institution undercuts the incentive for private organizations to award grants. In this example, the private grant reduced the student's institutional grant dollar for dollar. The motive of the donors who support outside scholarship programs is to benefit students, not institutions. A practice of allowing institutions to go last thwarts that intent since the school can essentially tax the private grant at a 100 percent rate. The alternative of allowing private scholarships to go last yields a different problem. Suppose the institution awarded an $8,000 institutional grant that met the entire remaining need, then the $5,000 outside scholarship would allow the student's family to contribute less than the Expected Family Contribution or it would allow the student to spend more lavishly than the typical student relying on need-based aid.

A common solution to this problem is for institutions to count only a portion of an outside scholarship as a contribution toward meeting need. For example, many schools only count 50 percent of outside scholarships in their calculations of remaining need. Using the same example, the institution would credit $2,500 of the $5,000 outside grant toward the unmet need. This leaves $5,500 in unmet need the institution would have to cover with a grant. In this way, the institution and the student and his or her family split the benefits of the outside scholarship. This eliminates some of the difficulty associated with going next to last for private donors, but it does not eliminate it entirely. With no central coordination, the problems of the ordering are very difficult to manage.

12

The College Affordability Crisis?

If tuition had doubled over the past decade but income tripled during that same time, the general public may not be nearly as concerned about the affordability of higher education. However, the fact is that by two common measures of income—median household income and per capita disposable income—college tuition increased faster than income.
—*National Commission on the Cost of Higher Education (1998)*

The crisis exists because for decades, tuitions have been rising at a rate much more rapid than family income or student aid can keep pace with, and a boiling point has been reached in which students and families are losing out on the opportunity for higher education.
—*John A. Boehner and Howard P. "Buck" McKeon (2003)*

Every year, the annual round of increases in college tuition and fees sparks a flurry of reports and editorials about the waning affordability of higher education in the United States, and about the dire economic and social consequences that will follow if young Americans cannot acquire the educational entry ticket to the twenty-first-century economy. The quotes above are fairly typical of the rhetoric of affordability today. The fact that higher education expenses eat up an increasing *percentage* of a person's or a family's income is taken as automatic and indisputable evidence that a college degree is becoming progressively less affordable. In the heated language of Boehner and McKeon's *College Cost Crisis*, these tuition increases are "pricing students and families out of the college market, and forcing prospective students to 'trade down' in their post-secondary educational choices because options that may have been affordable years ago have now been priced out of reach."

We have spent a lot of time and ink trying to understand the forces behind the long-term upward trend in higher education costs and why cost growth has accelerated over the past thirty years. We have also separated the concepts of cost and price, and we have distinguished between list price and net price. Changes in subsidy levels, for instance, can affect the net price to students even if cost increases are not part of the picture. The effects of changing subsidy levels are perhaps clearest in the context of public funding of state universities. We have documented a thirty-year retreat by the states that has significantly reduced the public portion of state-university budgets. In addition to its effects on the quality of public universities compared to their private counterparts, this retreat has put strong upward pressure on tuition at state universities. Lastly, we have also told the story of how universities influence access to higher education by using tuition discounting. This discounting itself pushes up sticker prices and makes discerning the net price the average family must pay somewhat difficult.

Now we need to tackle the thorny problem of affordability more directly. A quick look at the quotes above tells us that important public commissions have concluded two things. First, if tuition rises at a faster pace than family income—and this means that the family must spend a higher fraction of its income to purchase a year of college—then higher education must have become less affordable. The first conclusion is indisputable. The annual percentage rise in tuition does tend to be larger than the annual percentage increase in family incomes, so the fraction of a year's income required to purchase a year at college goes up. The second conclusion is not. The first "fact" does not tell us that college has become less affordable. And there is no reason to conclude that qualified students either get pushed out of the market entirely or are forced to trade down to worse postsecondary choices because options that once were "affordable" have been priced out of reach.

Although the topic of affordability is a minefield, we can offer a roadmap that will help an interested reader navigate through the explosive rhetoric to arrive at an understanding of the underlying issues. We will start by showing that the common measures of affordability that people use don't really tell us much about either affordability or about access to the higher education system. We will propose what we think is a better way to think about the concept of affordability. Secondly, we need to review the facts carefully. What are the things that *could* cause affordability problems and *who* is affected? Are cost pressures in the driver's seat as tuition supposedly careens out of control? How important are changing patterns of subsidization by governments and by the schools themselves?

To preview our results, we have spent much of this book showing that the same process of technological advancement that produces higher real income in the economy also generates increases in higher education cost. As a result, for most families, higher education actually is more affordable than it was in the past. This does *not* mean that affordability is a nonissue. Many families face real affordability problems today, but this is due primarily to changes in state budget priorities that have shrunk the higher education share of the state budget and to changes in the U.S. income distribution over the last thirty years that have favored the well educated. Reductions in the share of college cost covered by federal and state subsidies shifts more of the burden to families, and widening income differentials between people with a college degree and people who lack one means that the affordability question is still very pertinent for many families with below-average income. But true to the perspective we have taken all along, we see the causes of affordability problems in these broader economic trends more than in any growing inefficiencies in the provision of higher education itself.

How to Measure Affordability

The number that gets the lion's share of public scrutiny is the share of personal or family income that it takes to buy a year of college. This measure deserves a closer look. If your income is fixed, then a tuition increase must squeeze either higher education or something else out of the budget. This is the clearest case of a nasty tradeoff people face when a price goes up, and it is clearly a sign of an affordability problem. This is what people are thinking about when they hear the simple fact that a year in college eats up a bigger fraction of the average family's income than it did in the past. On the other hand, if personal or family income is growing, then there is no straightforward logic in calling an expansion of higher education's budget *share* an affordability problem. Nor is there any reason to say that an increase in the net cost of a college education "forces" anyone to change behavior or to trade down to worse alternatives.

A simple numerical example will show what is going on. Suppose that a family purchases two things: "higher education" and "other stuff." In the first year, the family has an income of $50,000 and they spend $8,000 on higher education and $42,000 on other stuff. In the following year, the price of the college education goes up to $10,000, the price of other stuff remains unchanged, and the family's income goes up to $52,500. The price of higher education has soared by 25 percent. Income has risen by a mere 5 percent. In the initial year, higher education spending consumed 16 percent of the family's budget. After the price change, it consumes 19 percent of the family's budget. By the typical definition, higher education has become less affordable because its budget share has increased. This is nonsense. The family previously could afford both the higher education and $42,000 in other expenditures. Now they can afford the same higher education and $42,500 in other expenditures. In fact, this family can afford to buy more *of everything* than they could before, so the language is being tortured to suggest that higher education has become less affordable.

In this numerical example, we simply assumed a particular increase in the cost of higher education together with the rise in family income. As you know by now, there is actually a very good theory that links the two. That theory is cost disease. To reiterate a little, productivity growth is not uniformly distributed across all industries within the economy. Productivity-enhancing technical change tends to be more rapid in industries that produce goods rather than services, and productivity growth is slowest in the personal services.

Another simple example will show how productivity growth in manufacturing makes services more expensive *without* making them less affordable. Suppose a "representative" worker can work either in the service sector or in manufacturing. Using a representative worker is obviously a simplification and an abstraction, but it allows us to focus on what is important. What happens to the average worker is what happens to the country as a whole.

Suppose technological change allows this representative worker to produce double the manufactured output for each hour worked, but the same worker's productivity if he or she works in the service sector is unaffected by the new technology. This technological progress has caused two things to happen. First, the service is now twice as "costly" to produce. Cost is what you have to give up when you make a choice to do something. To produce the service takes labor, and that labor could have worked in manufacturing. So society now gives up twice as much of the manufactured good as before when it chooses to produce the service.

Secondly, the country is clearly better off. If all of our workers continue to work just where they are, the country will have twice the amount of manufactured goods and the same amount of the service. So, has the service become less affordable? Indeed not. The productivity growth in manufacturing has produced more than enough extra income for the representative worker to buy the now more expensive service.

This is the explanation of rising college cost that we laid out in chapter 3. What we have done now is to use that idea to frame the question of affordability. This cost-disease explanation also gives us a completely different way to measure affordability. Instead of looking at how much the cost of a year of college eats up as a percentage of income, ask instead whether the amount *left over* after subtracting the cost of college is rising or falling over time.

Cost and Income

Is rising college cost (not price) creating an affordability crisis in America? If cost disease is the driving force behind rising higher education costs, we would not expect to see reduced affordability for the representative citizen. On the other hand, if prestige games and gold plating were the primary forces behind higher education cost increases, we could well see affordability issues even as we have defined them. These inefficiencies or mission changes would cause college-cost increases that are independent of any productivity gains in manufacturing. If rising inefficiency were the cause of cost increases, then to maintain the same consumption of higher education, families would have to cut their consumption of "other stuff." Higher education would indeed have become less affordable for the representative citizen.

We need to take a look at the data to sort out what actually has happened to affordability. Figures 12.1 and 12.2 show a thirty-year history (1970–2000) of the two alternate measures of affordability.[1] The first figure shows us that current fund expenditures at public four-year institutions have indeed risen from 37 percent of a worker's net real income in the United States to 45 percent. Evidence of this type is often used to make the case for a cost crisis that limits access to higher education. But if cost disease is a significant share of the explanation for rising college cost, then the rising income share allocated to college cost need not crowd out other spending.

Figure 12.2 shows the *difference* between net real domestic income per worker and current fund expenditures using the same data. This is our preferred measure of affordability. The difference rose from roughly $31,400 in 1970 to $39,000 in the year 2000 (in 2005 dollars). The mean income per worker available for things other than college costs rose by

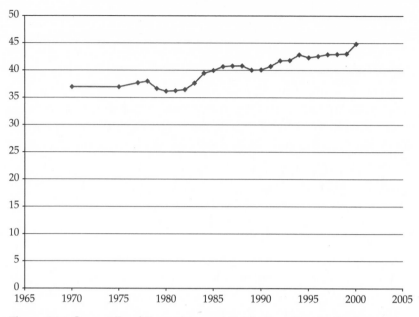

Figure 12.1 Current Fund Expenditures at Public Four-Year Institutions as a Percentage of Net Domestic Income Per Worker, 1970–2000

24 percent over that time span. There are indeed short periods in which affordability declined, and these are usually associated with downturns in overall economic activity. But over long stretches of time, overall productivity growth dominates the increase in higher education cost.

We have just shown something that is quite important. Over long stretches of time, college costs have been rising at a faster *pace* than income per worker, yet the average worker's actual dollar income has gone up by *more* than the costs, leaving more resources on the family table to spend on other things. This is another piece of circumstantial evidence that college costs may be driven upward by the same forces that cause economic growth in the economy. And if this were the only thing going on in the economy, we would be hard-pressed to call it an affordability crisis. But the representative worker doesn't pay the college's costs. Real families pay the college's price.

Family Income and Affordability

In this section, we shift our focus from the relationship between college costs and income per worker to the relationship between family income

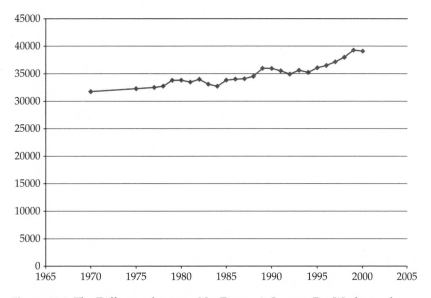

Figure 12.2 The Difference between Net Domestic Income Per Worker and Current Fund Expenditures at Public Four-Year Institutions, 2005 Dollars, 1970–2000

and student charges. This shift involves two changes. First, when we talked about cost disease, the individual worker was the primary unit of analysis. But the representative worker does not finance college expenses, families do. Families can include more than one worker, and the composition of families can change. Second, families do not face the full cost of higher education. A portion is covered by general subsidies from state governments, private giving, and endowment earnings. Also, individual students receive subsidies in the form of grants and scholarships. As we shift from workers to families and from costs to student charges, we move the discussion of affordability to its more traditional footing.

We are also not just interested in the average, or representative, family. A poorer family is not in the same economic world as a richer family. In order to tell an accurate story about how college affordability has changed for America's families over time, we need information about families at a variety of points on the income distribution. How much does a family at the 20th percentile of the income distribution earn, and how has that changed over time? This family is right at the dividing line between the poorest fifth of American families and the next-poorest fifth. A family at the 80th percentile, by contrast, is at the cusp of the richest fifth. The Census Bureau has good data on family income for families at the 20th, 40th, 60th, and 80th percentiles of the income distribution.

Income differences aren't the only differences that matter for college affordability. We also need information about the average cost of attendance, which is not the same as list-price tuition, and about how financial aid affects the net cost of attendance for families at these different points on the income distribution. Richer families, for instance, qualify for less need-based aid and tuition discounts than do poorer families. Lastly, the world looks very different if you or your family is contemplating a private four-year school, a public four-year school, or a two-year community college.

We have put together information about income, tuition, and student aid to tell the story of college affordability over the last twenty years at different types of school. We will start with the evidence about how need-based tuition assistance varies by where you are on the American income distribution and by what type of school you might choose to attend. Table 12.1 shows how the average tuition grant varies by family income and by what sort of school one attends.[2] The entries in the table give the multiple of the average grant given by the various institution types. Here is how you can read the table. The first entry in the table is 2.06. This number tells you that a student attending a public four-year institution and whose family income was centered at the 20th percentile of the income distribution got a grant that was 2.06 times the average grant for all students attending public four-year institutions.

The entries in table 12.1 tell an important story. First, grants are income sensitive for all types of school. Poorer families get more grant aid than richer families, and the richer the family the less aid they get. Second, the relationship between grants and income has been fairly stable across time, particularly at public institutions. But lastly, grants at

Table 12.1 Multiples of the Average Grant by Income

Percentile	1990			2004		
	Public 4-Year	Private 4-Year	Public 2-Year	Public 4-Year	Private 4-Year	Public 2-Year
20th	2.06	1.50	1.52	2.02	1.31	1.98
40th	1.01	1.28	0.83	0.99	1.13	0.86
60th	0.62	1.07	0.51	0.67	1.06	0.51
80th	0.41	0.79	0.19	0.57	0.88	0.33

private institutions are *not* as targeted to students from low-income families as are grants at public institutions, and the income sensitivity of grants at private institutions is lower in 2004 than it was in 1990. This last fact has implications for affordability over time.

Now we can move to table 12.2, which shows the impact on families of changes in net tuition and fees once we have adjusted for the different aid amounts offered to representative families at differing points on the national income distribution.[3] The table is divided into three parts: (a) for private four-year institutions, (b) for public four-year institutions, and (c) for public two-year institutions. We are comparing two time periods. The first is the three-year average for 1990–92 and the second is the three-year average for 2003–5. These are the two ends of the available data. The averaging of three years ensures that we avoid problems from picking a single year that may be an outlier, while the fifteen-year time span allows us to speak about longer-term trends. As in the previous section on cost, we compare our "income left over" measure of affordability with the usual "budget share" measure that gets all the press.

Before we unpack the numbers in the table, there are overarching changes in the U.S. income distribution to mention. We first touched this issue in chapter 4 when we explored both the causes and the effects of the growing chasm in earnings between those with a college degree and those whose formal education stopped at their high school graduation. Although families at all of the percentiles of the income distribution are better off at the end of the sample period, the income distribution has widened substantially. Real income in 2005 is only 4.87 percent higher than in 1990 for families at the 20th percentile of the income distribution. The comparable increases are 6.79 percent, 11.50 percent, and 14.64 percent for the 40th, 60th, and 80th percentiles.

Let's start with private four-year institutions. The percentage of income required to cover net tuition and fees has increased. This is why many people argue that a higher education has become *less* affordable over time. Yet the amount of income left over after paying net tuition and fees has increased more often than it has decreased. This suggests that a higher education has become *more* affordable. This is basically the same result we found earlier when we compared higher education costs to the average income of workers. Increases in the percentage of family income devoted to higher education need not translate into less money for other things. The one case where income left over actually declines tells us that the severe affordability problem is limited to the bottom of the income distribution, not the middle class.

Table 12.2   Affordability Results for Net Tuition and Fees

A. PRIVATE FOUR-YEAR Institutions

	1990–92	2003–05	Change
Budget Shares			
20th Percentile of Income	25.00%	39.20%	14.19%
40th Percentile of Income	17.32%	25.55%	8.23%
60th Percentile of Income	13.74%	17.65%	3.91%
80th Percentile of Income	11.12%	13.05%	1.93%
Income Left Over			
20th Percentile of Income	$17,735	$15,568	−$2,167
40th Percentile of Income	$33,120	$33,378	$259
60th Percentile of Income	$52,038	$56,355	$4,316
80th Percentile of Income	$78,346	$90,043	$11,697

B. PUBLIC FOUR-YEAR Institutions

	1990–92	2003–05	Change
Budget Shares			
20th Percentile of Income	−0.18%	−4.62%	−4.44%
40th Percentile of Income	3.73%	4.65%	0.93%
60th Percentile of Income	3.49%	4.55%	1.06%
80th Percentile of Income	2.76%	3.31%	0.53%
Income Left Over			
20th Percentile of Income	$23,693	$26,787	$3,309
40th Percentile of Income	$39,543	$42,745	$3,201
60th Percentile of Income	$58,221	$65,320	$7,100
80th Percentile of Income	$85,712	$100,122	$14,410

C. PUBLIC TWO-YEAR Institutions

	1990–92	2003–05	Change
Budget Shares			
20th Percentile of Income	1.43%	−6.12%	−7.55%
40th Percentile of Income	2.13%	1.13%	−1.00%
60th Percentile of Income	1.88%	1.70%	−0.18%
80th Percentile of Income	1.56%	1.45%	−0.11%
Income Left Over			
20th Percentile of Income	$23,312	$27,170	$3,858
40th Percentile of Income	$40,198	$44,327	$4,129
60th Percentile of Income	$59,195	$67,269	$8,073
80th Percentile of Income	$86,767	$102,046	$15,280

Part B repeats the exercise for public four-year institutions. There are a couple of unusual entries on the row for the 20th percentile of the income distribution. The negative entries in this row tell us that for the poorest families, the average grant is actually larger than list-price tuition and fees. This means that the average grant covers both tuition and fees and some of the room and board charges. The results in this table are similar to the private university results, but the numbers are all smaller since tuition and fees are much lower at public institutions. The budget share tends to increase, but there is also more income left over after paying for net tuition and fees.

Part C repeats the exercise for public two-year institutions. Here we see a different pattern. The two measures of affordability agree. However you measure affordability, public two-year institutions have become more affordable. Net tuition takes a smaller percentage of income in 2003–5 than it did in 1990–92, and there is more income left over in 2003–5 than there was in 1990–92.

We have argued that the "income left over" measure of affordability has more going for itself than the "budget share" measure. Using our preferred measure, the notion that college has become less affordable is only true for the poorest students attending private four-year colleges and universities. Families in the bottom fifth of the income distribution have less income left over after paying net tuition and fees at private four-year schools than they did fifteen years earlier. This is the only place with a negative entry for Income Left Over. The case for an affordability problem also has legs for families at the 40th percentile attending private universities, since this group sees almost the whole of their income gain eaten by increased net costs of attendance. But this affordability problem has little to do with rising college costs and much more to do with the broad economic forces that are widening the American income distribution in favor of the well educated.

Yet we can learn something from looking carefully at decisions taken within the academy itself. Going back to table 12.1, we see that students from families at the 20th percentile of the income distribution received grants at private four-year schools that were 1.50 times the average grant in 1990 but only 1.31 times the average grant in 2004. This information allows us to construct a simple counterfactual exercise. What if the multiple of the average grant had stayed the same? In that case, the change in income left over using net tuition for students from families at the 20th percentile of the income distribution attending private four-year institutions would change from –$2,167 to –$670. This indicates that a substantial part of the affordability problem faced by students at private four-year schools from families in the bottom of the income distribution had to do with changes in the distribution of grant aid at private institutions.

In recent years, a growing number of private universities have begun to offer more generous need-based aid that replace loans with grants in the financial aid packages for students from families with incomes below some specified level. This will probably redress the affordability problem at these institutions. Harvard, for instance, was the first university to offer free education to families making less than $60,000 per year and improved aid for those making less than $80,000 per year. These institutions, essentially the Ivy League and its competitors, are very well endowed. Less-well-endowed private institutions cannot easily follow the lead of these schools. Still, the emphasis that these institutions are putting on channeling aid to their poorest students is clearly a step in the right direction.

There is much more detail one can add to flesh out the affordability story. First, the composition of the family may evolve over time. Changes in the average number of workers in a family or in the number of dependents can influence affordability. We cannot measure these things by the 20th, 40th, 60th, and 80th percentiles of the income distribution. Nonetheless, we can say something about what is happening to the median family, and this will suggest the flavor of what this might mean for affordability.

The real income of the median family could change if the number of wage-earners in that family rose or fell. In our data, this is not an issue. Between 1990 and 2005, the average number of wage-earners per household remained steady at 1.46, so over our time period this is not likely to have had a big overall impact. On the other hand, even with a constant average number of wage-earners per family, the *spread* of family income could rise if the fraction of married couples with two wage-earners rose over time while the fraction of married couples in the population of families itself declined. This has indeed happened. In 1990, the fraction of all families composed of married couples was 78.6 percent. By 2005, the percentage had declined to 75.2 percent. Yet within the group of married couples, the percentage with two wage-earners rose from 58.1 percent of all married couples to 60.9 percent. Double-income families earned a median income of $78,755 in 2005, compared to $44,457 for married couples with only one wage-earner.

There has also been a small increase in the percentage of female-headed households, from 17 percent of all households in 1990 to

18.2 percent in 2005. Female-headed households have the lowest median family income ($27,244 in 2005) of all the reported subgroups. This is another factor that might work to reduce affordability for certain groups of people who are substantially poorer than average. Nonetheless, these effects seem rather small in comparison to the changes in the structure of the family that occurred in the 1970s and 1980s.

Conclusions

A year in college takes an increasing share of peoples' incomes. That is a fact in search of a story. The current narrative that gives fuel to congressional inquiries starts from the waste and inefficiency arguments we encountered in chapter 7. Prestige competition and gold plating needlessly push up costs and hence tuition and fees, which then chokes off access to higher education for the unprotected middle class. Cause meets effect. The rising budget share is the obvious statistic that supposedly nails down the case. We think this story is about as wrong as it is possible to be. We have argued that the difference between income and the cost of college is a better way to understand affordability, and by that criterion there is no national affordability problem. As a result, talk of a college-cost crisis is unnecessarily alarmist.

It is important to recognize that what we have discovered about the affordability of college is just the result one should expect based on the cost-disease explanation of the rapid rise in college costs. Rising college costs are driven by rapidly increasing productivity in other parts of the economy. This productivity growth also creates the income necessary to pay the higher college costs and have more left over to buy other goods and services.

But we also know that the rich are getting richer faster than the poor and that this has been going on since the late 1970s. This means that the amount of income left to spend on other things is growing more rapidly for families at the upper end of the income distribution. This is not a surprise, but it is not driven by any pathology in the higher education industry. The widening of the American income distribution and the "hollowing out" of the middle class are broad phenomena that go well beyond the scope of higher education policy. The causes include skill-biased technical change that increases the relative demand for skilled labor, changes in the composition of the family that leave more children in single-parent settings, immigration into the United States of a pool of labor with less formal education than the native-born population, and trade liberalization in the developing world that puts downward pressure on unskilled wages in developed nations. To the extent that this "rich getting richer" phenomenon is driven by technological progress that advantages the college educated, we would expect to see continued increases in demand for places at American universities. But since the demand reflects the increased value of the college degree, the fact that people are willing to pay a greater fraction of their income to attain a degree is not particularly surprising.

Lastly, the affordability story we are telling is about hypothetical families at different points of the U.S. income distribution. It is not about any particular family. There are surely families whose circumstances lead them to forego higher education for their children because of cost increases. And there are surely families who are forced by cost pressures to "trade down" to cheaper and perhaps less desirable educational alternatives. Not every family receives the "average" increase in income. Some families see their income fall. To some extent, the financial aid system cushions families in those circumstances, but in the time period for which we have data, the financial aid processes at private four-year universities have become slightly less progressive despite a stretching of the national income distribution. Nonetheless, we must be careful not to fault higher education policy for failing to act as a complete substitute for an effective national social safety net, or for things that result from broad economic and social trends in which higher education plays only a bit part in the drama.

If rising college cost is not the cause of a national affordability crisis, then policies built around forcing costs to rise less slowly are unlikely to do much good and may yield many undesirable and unintended consequences. If our policy goals are built around increasing access to higher education so that a greater fraction of the population can acquire the skills that come with a high quality education, then we must build those policies with a clear understanding of the broader social and economic forces that limit access.

PART IV
Policy

13

Federal Policy and
College Tuition

Federal policy on tuition is in its infancy. Tuition and fees are set by state institutions or by private institutions, not the federal government, so the lack of a long history of federal policies on tuition is not necessarily surprising. On the other hand, through the financial aid system the federal government has become a big tuition payer, so the incentives to regulate tuition certainly are present. In recent years, there have been rumblings in the halls of Congress that are clearly calls for federal regulation of tuition, and legislation passed in 2008 contains provisions that are arguably precursors of tuition regulation. In this chapter, we discuss tuition regulation, its rationale, its recent history, and its advisability.

We start the chapter by laying out two possible ways to think about the relationship between college tuition and federal policy. The first argument is well known. It was first articulated by Secretary of Education William Bennett in 1987. The "Bennett Hypothesis" is the claim that increases in federal financial aid create a climate that makes higher tuition more likely. The second possibility reverses the causality. In what we call the "Congressional Squeeze," increases in tuition raise the pressure on Congress to provide more-generous federal financial aid. In other words, past tuition increases raise the effectiveness of lobbying by colleges and universities on behalf of raising the amounts of aid available to each student.

In the first case, increases in federal financial aid cause increases in tuition. In the second case, increases in tuition cause increases in federal financial aid. In either story, there is a relationship between college tuition and federal policy. Given these seemingly plausible links, and given the history of tuition over the past thirty-five years, the political salience of tuition regulation is clear. The real surprise may be that Congress has not yet acted forcefully in this area. In the final part of the chapter, we look at the possibilities for tuition regulation. We explore the tuition provisions enacted in the College Opportunity and Affordability Act of 2008, and we evaluate the likely consequences of adopting more-thorough efforts to restrict tuition increases through price-control mechanisms.

The Bennett Hypothesis

In 1987, the then secretary of education William Bennett wrote an op-ed article in the *New York Times* titled "Our Greedy Colleges." Bennett argued that there was a link between the generosity of federal financial aid and the tuition charged by colleges and universities. Bennett's claim, which has become known as the Bennett Hypothesis, is that increases in government financial aid give institutions room to raise their charges. In Bennett's words, "Federal student aid policies do not cause college price inflation, but there is little doubt that they help make it possible."

This is a strong assertion about behavior. The federal government's aid policies supposedly enable colleges to behave in a way that contributes to tuition inflation. On the surface, Bennett's hypothesis seems quite plausible, though if you dig a little deeper, the causal pathways are not at all obvious. To analyze the Bennett Hypothesis, we will use our hundred-student college from chapter 10. Recall that in our simple example, the college has a budget of $2,000,000. It receives a general subsidy of $1,000,000 from state support and/or endowment earnings. In the case we want to consider, the school raises the other $1,000,000 that it needs in tuition revenue by setting a list-price tuition of $11,000 and discounting that tuition by $2,000 for fifty of its one hundred students. The tuition policy raises $550,000 by charging fifty students the list price and $450,000 by charging the fifty scholarship students $9,000. The students paying $9,000 receive institutionally supported grants. Further suppose that the fifty scholarships were need-based grants. To evaluate the Bennett Hypothesis, we need to ask what would happen if the federal government initiated a need-based scholarship program that awarded $2,000 in federal funds to the college's fifty scholarship students.

We discussed a very similar situation in chapter 10. There we assumed that the college received a new gift to create an endowment that yielded an additional $100,000 annually for the school. The new federal scholarship program has the same effect, and it presents the college with a lot of good options. First, the college could use the extra federal funds to give its scholarship students larger scholarships. In this case, it could double their scholarships to $4,000, half from the new federal program and the other half from its own institutional sources. Doing this would *not* change the list-price tuition. Second, it could decide to offer a $2,000 scholarship to every student. The fifty who qualify for the need-based scholarships would have their aid funded by the federal government, and the school would shift its own institutional grants to the other fifty. In this example, the school is taking advantage of the psychological ploy of offering all students a discount without changing the list-price tuition, but it is analytically the same as a list-price tuition reduction to $9,000. So the federal aid could easily lead to the opposite of what Bennett supposed. Third, the college could leave the tuition unchanged and take $100,000 less from its endowment. In this case, college funds previously used for scholarships would be added to the endowment, which would now grow by $100,000 per year. Again the list-price tuition would remain the same. Finally, the school could leave the list price at $11,000, replace its institutional grants dollar for dollar with federal money, and spend the extra $100,000 that it has just saved on things that improve the quality of its programming.

None of the examples we have offered yield a tuition increase as the Bennett Hypothesis suggests. In these four examples, the college had the opportunity to redirect the budget relief provided by the $100,000 in federal aid money toward other uses. The key insight from these examples is that no Bennett effect can occur as long as the schools redirect *no more than* the $100,000 they have received from the federal government. To give us a concrete case, suppose the federal government makes its grants more generous, and the college takes advantage of the situation to increase spending by more than the extra $100,000 that it receives. This would trigger a tuition increase, and it would be consistent with the Bennett Hypothesis. This is a fairly special case, and it is not at all obvious why the incentives would align to yield this sort of behavior.

Suppose we do observe tuition rising after increases in federal financial aid allocations. Is this the Bennett effect at work? Perhaps, but there is an added complexity to consider. We don't know what the university would have done in the absence of the federal program. To measure the true effect of the new federal aid, we would have to compare it to the counterfactual situation we do not actually observe (though we may be able to predict or forecast it). Suppose, for instance, that the institution had intended to increase its total spending by $150,000 in any event and to raise list-price tuition as a result. With the extra federal money in hand, the effect of the new federal grant is to decrease any tuition consequences of the increased spending. Clearly this is not what Secretary Bennett had in mind. On the other hand, suppose the increased spending was *not* something the institution had intended, and it only decided on the whole $150,000 spending increase after finding out about the $100,000 additional federal financial aid spending. This tuition increase could be pinned to the increase in federal financial aid spending. Perhaps a college would not have embarked on certain expenditures had they been required fully to fund them with a tuition increase. In this case, the new federal grants did not cause the tuition increase, but in Bennett's words, "they help make it possible."

This last notion is consistent with the title of Bennett's article, "Our Greedy Colleges." Colleges and universities are viewed as institutions that have unfulfilled desires to increase spending. In addition, the adjective "greedy" suggests that these desires are somehow self-centered and unrelated to quality. They reflect wasteful things that make working at the college or university more pleasant, not productive things that allow the college or university to provide a better education or to maintain quality in the face of rising input costs. As we explained in part II of the book, colleges and universities have faced strong cost pressures that have required significant revenue increases in order to maintain the quality of their offerings. Increases in federal financial aid funding have helped reduce the tuition consequences of responding to this cost pressure. For those who authorize increases in federal financial aid, the frustration is almost palpable as they watch rising tuition seemingly eat up the benefits. Yet it is a considerable stretch to say that increases in federal financial aid cause, or even contribute to, the increase in tuition that would naturally have happened anyway. These aid increases likely reduce the impact of rising cost on tuition.

Our analysis aside, many researchers have treated the Bennett Hypothesis simply as an empirical question about the statistical relationship between increases in federal financial aid and increases in tuition. In the end, these studies give contradictory results. Michael S. McPherson and Morton Owen Schapiro (1991) conclude, "we find that, at private four-year institutions, increases in SEOG and Pell expenditures do not cause schools to raise tuition and fees, although increases in federal financial aid do lead to higher tuition and fees at public four-year institutions." In a study of public institutions, Michael J. Rizzo and Ronald G. Ehrenberg (2004) find that increasing the maximum Pell Grant award will increase in-state tuition, but it will have no such effect on out-of-state tuition. Larry D. Singell and Joe A. Stone (2007) find no effect of increases in Pell Grants on in-state tuition at public institutions, but they find that increases in Pell Grants will increase tuition at private institutions and out-of-state tuition at public institutions. Finally, the Department of Education (2001) found no effect of federal financial aid on tuition at any type of institution.[1] You want a result; you pick your study. Clearly, the empirical literature on the Bennett Hypothesis is far from settled.

We do not want to muddy the waters any more than they are already, but still there seems a considerable gap in this literature that needs filling. None of these studies wrestles directly with the presence or absence of a causal relationship between tuition and aid. True causality cannot be discerned by a statistical test, but there is a basic statistical technique developed in the 1960s by Nobel Laureate Clive Granger that is consistent with how we think about causality. In Granger's approach, a variable such as the maximum authorized size of a Pell Grant "causes" changes in another variable, like the average level of tuition, if the current level of tuition is driven by the historical evolution of the maximum size of a Pell Grant. This is a sensible way of thinking about how to measure causality statistically. Cause is before effect, so past values of the causal variable should influence current values of things affected. If there is some deep but unmeasured process by which Pell Grants actually cause tuition to go up, as the Bennett Hypothesis asserts, you are likely to see in the data that increases in Pell Grant maximums in the past tend to push up tuition levels in the present. If "Granger causality" is not found, that does not disprove a causal relationship. The true causal process may be more complex than the statistical model can catch. But finding Granger causality is decent evidence that something of interest is going on.

We present the formal results of a Granger test in appendix 2. In brief, using data from 1973–74 to 2007–8, we find that there is indeed causality running from past increases in the Pell Grant maximum to changes in the average tuition charged at private universities. But contrary to Bennett's contention, these past increases in the federal Pell Grant maximum tend to *reduce* average tuition today. This is perfectly consistent with one of the basic facts of tuition discounting that we presented earlier. Private universities discount tuition heavily, and tuition discounting is one force that pushes up list-price tuition. If increased Pell support reduces the need for private schools to discount tuition as much, the result is lower pressure on list-price tuition. We find no significant pattern of causality running from Pell Grant support to list-price tuition changes for public universities, which are less heavily engaged in tuition discounting.

By no means do we expect that our test of the Bennett hypothesis will settle the issue. Our technique and our data are different than those used by previous investigators, and so are our results. Do the different findings just reflect the different techniques and the different data or have we found something that escaped others? These are difficult questions, and this is not the appropriate venue to thrash this all out. What we can say is that our results are consistent with a "Reverse Bennett Hypothesis." Increases in federal financial aid cause lower tuition increases. This is the type of behavior we would expect to see in a world in which institutions are heavily engaged in tuition discounting. At the very least, this brief look at the published research, as well as our new finding, should serve as a cautionary tale for anyone who wants to assert a simple and obvious relationship between federal financial aid and the tuition charged by colleges and universities.

The Congressional Squeeze

The second interaction we want to discuss is one that we think is a better description of the political process that links tuition and fees with federal financial aid. The Bennett Hypothesis suggests that increases in the generosity of financial aid cause or enable increases in college tuition. The Congressional Squeeze analysis reverses the process. Here, increases in college tuition ultimately build pressure for increases in spending on financial aid programs.

The Congressional Squeeze works as follows. For a myriad of reasons, the costs of providing a college education rise more rapidly than the overall inflation rate. This will mean that a given federal commitment to meeting the financial need of students attending college will be less and less effective over time. In these circumstances, when legislation to determine federal financial aid spending is before Congress, leaders of colleges and universities will lobby strongly in favor of financial aid spending increases. This is simple interest-group politics, and colleges and universities can easily illustrate their case with convincing data presentations.

Suppose that costs are going up, and suppose further that schools are increasing the size of their own institutional grants to try to cushion the blow to the students with the most financial need. Both of these forces, the rising costs and the schools' response with larger institutional grants, will push up list-price tuition. Under these circumstances, college presidents easily can show what is happening to the percentage of the cost of attendance covered by the maximum Pell Grant. And the fact that their schools have been setting aside more institutional aid (never mind that this too puts upward pressure on list price) demonstrates that colleges and universities understand the seriousness of the financial issues facing poorer families. Unless the maximum Pell Grant has been growing very rapidly, the percentage of the cost of attendance covered by a Pell Grant likely will be falling and perhaps falling substantially. This simplifies the lobbying task.

Yet the percentage of the cost of attendance covered by a maximum Pell Grant is not the best measure of whether there is a pressing need for additional federal financial aid spending. A better measure would look at the situation of a typical needy student. Many schools do not meet all demonstrated need, so families must raise more money than the contribution they are expected to make based on their financial resources. And many students either do not attend any school or may be under-placed because financial constraints force them to trade down to less expensive options. Sound policy judgments about the plight of needy students require a great deal of additional information. Nevertheless, in a political world in which sound bites and bumper stickers often substitute for analysis, a statement about the decline in the percentage of the cost of attendance covered by a maximum Pell Grant has a lot of power. Lobbyists for higher education can easily paint Congress into a corner: increase financial aid spending or look very bad. This is the Congressional Squeeze.

On the other hand, members of Congress know full well that annual increases in college costs are one of the driving forces behind the steady erosion in the percentage of the cost of attendance covered by the maximum Pell Grant. In addition to donor fatigue at ever-rising demands for federal support, resentment may build up over the years from being squeezed in this way by college and university presidents who continually suggest that the Congress is not keeping its commitment to ensure access to higher education. This kind of sentiment led to the National Commission on the Cost of Higher Education created by Congress in 1997, and it fueled *The College Cost Crisis* by Congressmen Boehner and McKeon that we have quoted frequently and liberally. Members of Congress have a strong suspicion they are being blamed for a "problem" they did not cause. And members of Congress who agree with Secretary Bennett's assessment that greedy colleges are the problem can be openly hostile to increases in financial aid spending.

From a policy perspective, the key question is whether the root causes of rising college costs are to be found in the broader forces we emphasized in part II or are instead a result of wasteful and excessive spending on campuses. If the major cost drivers are economy-wide forces largely beyond the control of a college or university, and the schools are only trying to preserve the quality of their offerings, then there is a lot of sense in their requests for Congress to continue to do its part. On the other hand, if prestige games and gold plating are the main drivers of college cost, then there is a lot of sense in Congress pushing back at schools that come asking for relief for their financially stressed students. The fact that colleges and universities have been meeting increasing resistance in Congress suggests that they have not been doing a good job of explaining the causes of the cost increases that are pushing up demands for federal support.

Congress versus the Education Lobby: The Chicken Game

We are clearly skeptics of the Bennett Hypothesis. The theory behind it is not well specified and there is no clear evidence that congressional aid appropriations actually *cause* rising tuition. There is even some evidence (ours) that it causes lower tuition. Nonetheless, the Bennett Hypothesis has some resonance in Congress since it offers support for members who want to resist increases in aid funding. We think the Congressional Squeeze, on the other hand, *is* a plausible description of the politics of higher education funding. Over time, as inflation and rising college cost erode the real value of existing aid programs, pressure builds for Congress to do something. Congress may resist for a while, and the Bennett Hypothesis offers intellectual support for the resistors, but over time resistance proves futile and gives way to the seemingly inevitable. This political process seems to fit the very simple framework of the chicken game.

Anyone of a certain generation will remember Jim (James Dean) and Buzz racing junk cars toward the cliff in *Rebel Without a Cause*. First one to jump out the door is a chicken. In the movie, Buzz accidentally catches his clothing in the door and is unable to jump before his car tumbles over the edge. Thus he "wins" the game at the cost of his life. A slight variation on this movie theme will help us understand how the chicken game between Congress and the advocates for higher education has played out over the last thirty-five years. In this variation, the two cars are driven toward each other down a straight highway. The first person to swerve is a chicken. The important twist here is that in this version of the game, each driver retains control over the car.

In the game between Congress and the higher education lobby, Congress would like colleges to control cost so that existing federal support retains its effectiveness. College presidents, on the other hand, face rising costs. They would like Congress to fund access by maintaining or raising the percentage of the college bill that a Pell Grant supports. A look at the history of the Pell Grant program suffices to show that Congress can hold the line for a while. But pressure ultimately builds and the Pell maximum is raised. In some years, the higher education lobby fails to achieve an increase in the size of a Pell Grant, but in the end Congress is the chicken and swerves. Colleges never swerve in the sense of actually controlling their costs to Congress's satisfaction. The debate between them is about the moral and economic high ground, and this is where competing claims bubble up for public attention. On one side, we have arguments about dysfunctional universities driving up costs needlessly and about federal aid increases that abet tuition increases, and on the other, we hear about a failure of federal policy to achieve the social goals of access. Our own arguments about the importance of cost disease and about cost-increasing (but quality improving) technical change may become additional ammunition in the struggle over public opinion.

This is a game that some in Congress would like to change. But in order to win a contest of nerves like the chicken game, you have to convince the other side that next time around you really won't swerve first. Expressions of concern and stern warnings that "this is the last time the wallet will be opened" lack credibility. Congress also seems particularly handicapped by its two-year election cycle. Yet in theory there is a way to win a chicken game. You have to show the other side that you really don't control the outcome any more. Go back to our adolescent dare story and imagine two cars coming at each other down a straight highway at a combined 120 miles per hour. Suppose now that one driver had loosened his steering wheel before the game began. As the cars head toward each other, that canny driver now takes the wheel and ostentatiously holds it out the window for all to see. He no longer has discretionary control over his car. The only car that *can* swerve is the one that will. The key to winning the chicken game is automaticity. Your response to the other side has to be on autopilot.

During the last reauthorization of the Higher Education Act, the resistance in Congress coalesced around a set of proposals that would cut off schools from federal aid programs if their tuition increased too fast. The proposal was mechanistic. A simple formula would determine if a school's behavior would cause it to lose eligibility to participate in federal aid programs. Turning policy decisions over to a formula is the key to winning the chicken game. But is it good policy?

Price Controls in Higher Education

The 1998 report of the National Commission on the Cost of Higher Education starts by noting the public's concern with rapidly rising tuition and fees at colleges and universities. Following that discussion the report contains the following language: "Members of the Commission are equally convinced that if this public concern continues, and if colleges and universities do not take steps to reduce their costs, policymakers at the Federal and state levels will intervene and take up the task for them."[2] This is not an explicit threat of price controls, but one does not have to have a wild imagination to see them or some similar policy lurking in the background.

As time passed, in the eyes of many in Congress the Commission's report had little if any effect on the behavior of colleges and universities. As a result, proposals designed to make good on the threat started to surface. In 2003, Representative Howard P. McKeon (R-CA), the chair of the House Subcommittee on Postsecondary Education, Training, and Life-Long Learning and one of the people responsible for creating the presidential commission, wrote an article in the *Chronicle of Higher Education* explaining his proposal to control the cost of attendance:

> Each year, just as they do now, colleges that take federal money would report the annual cost that students must pay to attend— tuition, fees, room-and-board charges, and miscellaneous other expenses—to the U.S. Department of Education. If a college's price exceeded the new affordability index, or more than two times the CPI, then that institution would have to explain why and present a plan to hold down future price increases. If the college did not reduce the rate of increase, it would trigger various sanctions. As a last resort, the institution would be declared ineligible for federal financial assistance.[3]

This is a type of price control plain and simple. If an institution's tuition, fees, and room and board increased by more than twice the rate of increase of the Consumer Price Index, sanctions would ensue. At the extreme, the federal government could use the biggest club it holds over a college or university. It could cut off eligibility for federal financial aid funds.

Not surprisingly, this proposal created quite a stir in higher education circles. Two objections surfaced immediately. First, the proposal appeared to trigger sanctions based on what is happening to list-price tuition. As we have demonstrated, list-price tuition depends on, among other things, the generosity of institutional grants offered by the college or university. Under this proposal's rigid criteria, an institution that is in the process of making its need-based grants more generous could end up raising list-price tuition enough to trigger the sanctions. In essence, a school could be punished for improving access for low-income students. Clearly, this is not what Representative McKeon intended.

Second, the proposal's extreme penalties could lead to other perverse results. At public universities, repeated state budget crises have forced most schools to choose between rapid tuition increases or declines in the quality and availability of their programming. Federal sanctions could tip more schools toward allowing quality to fall in ways that push real costs onto students. As one example, time to graduation likely would rise, and that is a substantial cost to students. Another unintended consequence of mechanistic federal penalties is potentially even more sinister. States can hold down the pace of tuition growth at their state universities if they transfer money from the state's own financial aid budget directly into appropriations for the operating budget of public universities. Federal penalties for tuition growth could induce states to sacrifice access for poorer students on the altar of a federal formula that is completely arbitrary.

Institutions that raise tuition substantially usually are institutions in financial jeopardy. They are having difficulty making ends meet. A school in financial straits needs as much outside subsidy as it can put its hands on, yet this sort of school would be punished instead by having an extraordinarily important source of financial aid removed. If rising tuition were always and everywhere a sign of bad decision making and gross inefficiency, cutting federal support might be a reasonable incentive to improve behavior, but colleges and universities are not in complete control of all of the factors that determine tuition and fees. The vagaries of state governments and financial markets can influence the amount of tuition revenue an institution needs to raise. For a school facing a budget crunch, a rapid increase in tuition may have been the best of a bad set of options. Adding the potential loss of federal financial aid to their woes likely would force a college or university to choose an even worse option.

Representative McKeon's proposal did not see its way into law, but similar ideas were part of the College Opportunity and Affordability Act of 2008. Previous reauthorizations of the Higher Education Act of 1965 had kept the focus on college access, the "college opportunity" part of the current title. The focus on affordability is new.

The affordability provisions are contained in Section 109 of Title 1. In this section, the Secretary of Education is required to create lists of institutions with high and rapidly growing tuition and fees. These lists are to be published by the Department of Education on the Internet. Separate lists will be published for list-price tuition and fees, and for net tuition and fees. The lists would include all schools in the top 5 percent of price raisers. The department will keep separate rankings for each pricing concept (list price and net price) and for various types of institutions (public, private nonprofit, and private for-profit four-year institutions; public, private nonprofit, and private for-profit two-year institutions; and public, private nonprofit, and private for-profit less-than-two-year institutions). In addition to being on these lists, each offending school is required to report to the Department of Education on their plans to reduce the rate of increase in tuition and fees. The schools on the lists face no further sanctions.

Essentially, the act institutes a form of public shaming for schools that misbehave. This is a lot like being put in the stocks on the village green in colonial times. And the act imposes additional reporting requirements for the institutions with the highest tuition increases. Neither of these actions, however, is likely to restrain rising college costs, and the law of unintended consequences suggests that the impact on tuition setting is as likely to be perverse as helpful.

First, the public relations staff at any college or university likely will have little difficulty deflecting any short-term harm to the school's reputation that might follow its placement on an obscure website. The public shame may go largely unnoticed, so unlike the original McKeon proposal that had financial teeth, the sanctions in the current law are relatively light.

Second, the current act attempts to shame schools that raise tuition more than their peers, not the ones who raise tuition more rapidly than some clear and absolute standard. Twice the inflation rate is a very clear (if arbitrary) standard. Under Representative McKeon's first proposal, if every institution were able to keep the rate of increase of its cost of attendance below twice the rate of increase in the Consumer Price Index, no institution would have been liable for sanctions. Remember the data on cost from the 1970s. In that decade most schools would have been free of any fears of losing federal support. There is no such absolute standard under the 2008 act. There will always be a group of schools in "the worst 5 percent," even in a decade like the 1970s when real costs were constant or falling. The lists are created under the presumption that those with the largest rates of increase deserve shame, no matter how rapidly *or slowly* their tuition and fees happen to rise.

If, as we suspect, the proposals in the 2008 act have little noticeable effect on university pricing behavior, Congress's enthusiasm for price controls with sharper teeth may grow. The rapid increase in tuition and fees in recent years is a great concern to many families. It is also an issue that lends itself to polemics based on compelling anecdotes and head-line-quality statements. University of X increased its tuition 20 percent last year! The cost of attendance at College of Y just passed $70,000! The issue will not go away as long as Congress, college leaders, and the American public lack common ground in their understanding of the underlying processes that are pushing up college cost. Without that common ground, they cannot easily forge a compromise that eliminates the destructive chicken game. Readers should stay tuned for future developments in this relationship. Congress has put a toe into the waters of tuition control. Perhaps cooler heads will prevail. A core of elected officials, college and university leaders, and higher education scholars may develop a shared understanding of the causal forces behind rising costs and tuition. A shared perspective could change the competitive "if I win, you lose" chicken game into something far more cooperative, stable, and mutually beneficial for all parties involved. In this case, the momentum toward federal tuition regulation may be halted. The toe will be withdrawn. If the climate of cost increases begins to abate, we may see a similar outcome. This could happen if the forces for rising income inequality begin to reverse. On the other hand, if the politically divisive squeeze continues, federal interference in basic price setting may grow. Price controls with real teeth could be in the future of colleges and uni-versities. If our analysis is correct, these price controls could well do real damage to the quality of education.

14

Financial Aid Policy

The basic federal financial aid programs have been in place since 1965. Any set of federal programs creates interest groups, and any time there are interest groups, there is political jockeying. As a result of the political jockeying, the structure and funding levels of the federal programs has evolved over time and programs have proliferated. In response to federal incentives, state governments also have gotten into the financial aid business with varying degrees of enthusiasm. In addition, private entities of various sorts have expanded their own financial aid offerings. Finally, and most importantly, colleges and universities themselves have become the largest providers of grant aid by giving institutional grants to selected students. As a result of the large number of players and the uncoordinated way in which policies have changed over time, the resulting financial aid "system" is complex to say the least. Most scholars and policy-makers agree that it needs to be changed, but forging an agreement among them about just what to change and how the change should occur is difficult. The webs of interests that benefit from the current programs further complicate the process of pushing changes through the political system.

Beyond the problems of managing incremental reforms, forging a consensus about the shape of an ideal aid system is elusive as well. In this chapter, we will frame the discussion of what to do about financial aid as a continuum of policy choices. The continuum ranges from extreme simplification of the process at one end, to extremely fine targeting of who receives aid at the other end. As we will show, there is an inherent tradeoff between simplification and targeting. At present, federal aid targets benefits toward families of lesser means. But efficient targeting requires a lot of information, hence the complexity of the current system. Most calls for reform today advocate some form of simplification while not abandoning targeting as an overarching goal. We will make the case for a radical makeover of the program by suggesting reasons why complete simplification may be the most desirable alternative.

As we write, there is a lively discussion underway about how to reform the financial aid system. The conversation is taking place within a growing consensus that the United States should increase its college-going and college-completion rates. Any look at the data reveals that the college-going and college-completion rates of students from high-income families are not the problem. Students from high-income families are going to college and completing college at quite high rates. Students from low-income families are another story. Since the current financial aid system is designed to provide aid so low-income students can succeed, the data are telling us that the financial aid system needs to be fixed.

What Is Wrong with the Financial Aid System?

The basic strategy behind offering financial aid is to lower the price that low-income students have to pay, so the first question we need to ask is whether or not price matters in the college-going decision. In 1987, Larry Leslie and Paul Brinkman summarized a large number of studies measuring the effect of price differences on college attendance. They found that the college-going rate would decrease by roughly 5 percent for a $1,000 (1990 dollars) increase in college cost. Several later studies came to very similar conclusions. Students are sensitive to price differences, so financial aid that reduces the price for low-income students should increase college-going rates among that group.

On the other hand, using data from before and after the initiation of the Pell Grant program, studies by Lee Hansen in 1983, Charles Manski in 1993, and Thomas Kane in 1994 found that the initiation of the Pell program yielded no significant growth in the enrollment of low-income students. The initiation of the Pell grants in 1972 represented a significant change in the most important federal grant program for low-income students. Given the evidence that students are price sensitive, the finding about the early years of the Pell program at first may seem quite surprising.

To understand why Pell Grants had no effect on college-going rates of low-income students, we have to understand the process that leads a high school student to college. First, the student must take a college preparatory curriculum and must succeed at that curriculum. Note that we did not use terms like "excel." Many students with less-than-stellar high school records are admitted to college. Next the student has to gather a substantial amount of information and take some important preliminary steps to prepare for college. Usually this involves visiting some colleges. Students often must register for and take tests like the SAT or ACT. Finally, they must fill out a college application that includes writing one or more general or college-specific essays. A careful study done by Christopher Avery and Thomas Kane in 2004 of a group of low-income students in Boston high schools demonstrates that low-income students can trip over each one of these preliminary steps. The financial aid system only comes into play after an application is successfully completed. Many low-income students, even among those who had expected to go to a four-year college, have fallen by the wayside well before they have had any dealings with the financial aid system.

A 1999 study done for the U.S. Department of Education provided a detailed look at data from the National Educational Longitudinal Study (NELS), which is a nationally representative sample of high school seniors who were graduated in 1992.[1] The study classifies family income in three categories: low (family income less than $25,000), middle (family income between $25,000 and $75,000), and high (family income greater than $75,000). Income clearly affects the college-going rate. Only 28 percent of the students from low-income families were enrolled in a four-year college by 1994 (two years after completing high school) compared to 42 percent of the students from medium-income families and 71 percent of students from high-income families.

Part of this difference reflects the fact that a smaller percentage of the lower-income students were "college qualified." The study used an index of high school grade point average, senior class rank, the results of an aptitude test given to NELS participants, SAT and ACT scores, and curricular rigor to determine whether a student was college qualified. Only 53 percent of the low-income students were college qualified, compared to 68 percent of the middle-income students, and 86 percent of the high-income students. A host of sociological factors such as parent's attitude toward education, absence of role models, and general health probably explain these differences. To look at the impact of financial aid programs, we need to restrict our sample to the college-qualified students. Restricting the sample to the college qualified does change the results. The probability of being enrolled in a four-year college conditional on being college qualified rises to 52 percent for the low-income group, 62 percent for the middle-income group, and 83 percent for the high-income group. The effect of income is not as pronounced as it is in the entire sample, but it still is strong.

The Department of Education study broke down the steps students must take to successfully enroll in a four-year college. First, students have to think that college is a real possibility for them. Not as many low-income students expect to have a bachelor's degree. Only 74 percent of low-income college-qualified students expected to have a bachelor's degree compared to 84 percent of the middle-income group and 96 percent in the high-income group. The effect of being in the low-income group only disappears if we limit the sample to college-qualified students who expect to go to college *and* who have taken steps toward admission to a four-year college. Of these students, 84 percent of the low-income group actually attended a four-year college compared to 85 percent for the middle-income group and 91 percent of the high-income group. The impact of income is not eliminated, but the low-income group is brought to rough equality with the middle-income group.

Once a student gets involved with the college application process and takes steps toward admission to a four-year college, the low-income students find that their low income is no greater a hurdle for them to overcome than is the middle income of the students in that income group. When students get some solid evidence about the actual costs revealed by financial offers, the financial aid system does the job it is intended to do. On one hand, this is evidence of a successful program. When students know about the financial aid programs, the programs tend to work. On the other hand, it suggests a difficulty. The helpfulness of the financial aid program is not apparent to students until they have some direct experience working the system.

Why does the financial aid system seem to affect the behavior of students who have direct experience and not others? On its face this seems to be a perverse result. The financial aid programs are not a secret. High school counselors certainly know about these programs, and they should be getting out the word to college-qualified students. At least the Pell Grant program should be easy to explain. Word-of-mouth advertising should also work. The success of older students from families of similar means should be compelling to some students. Still, financial aid that depends on family income is difficult to advertise. It is based on confidential data. The information that last year Joe Smith got this amount of aid or Jane Jones got that amount of aid may not be useful to a student this year. The only way to know about your particular case is to get your parents to fill out the forms and go through the application process.

Many analysts argue that the complexity of the financial aid system is the problem. Filling out the Free Application for Federal Student Aid (FAFSA) is a daunting task for many families. As we described in chapter 11, understanding how the FAFSA information translates into an Expected Family Contribution is not a trivial exercise. And even then, a student does not know whether his or her family will be willing to contribute as much as the federal government judges they should be expected to pay. The evidence suggests that the complex multi-step application and aid process takes a considerable amount of explaining, and it only gets explained well enough to change behavior when a student becomes actively involved in the process and sees how financial aid affects his or her particular circumstances. The programs are too complex to impact behavior as long as they are just abstractions.

If the United States is serious about raising the level of college attainment of its citizens, we have to change the financial aid process. Several countries now have surpassed the United States in the percentage of citizens with college degrees. Among older adults between the ages of thirty-five and sixty-four, the United States and Canada still lead the world in the percentage that hold at least a college degree. But among younger adults between twenty-five and thirty-four, the United States is significantly behind major partners like Canada, Japan, and Korea. College attainment among this group of Americans is now closer to that of Spain, France, and the United Kingdom. We have to be very careful how we interpret this information. We are not necessarily hurt by rising educational attainment abroad. The global economy is not a pie of fixed size in which if they eat more, we eat less, and it is inappropriate to think we are engaged in a race that we are somehow losing. Rather, we should look at the success of other countries as a challenge. If other countries can raise their college-attainment rates, why can't we?

Education has long been an engine of economic growth. One important reason for the U.S. surge to economic primacy in the twentieth century was the early spread of secondary schooling to an overwhelming majority of the population. American primacy in innovation is at least partially attributable to the early spread of university education to a large fraction of the labor force. But that early success has given way to a period of stagnation and retrogression. This stagnation is caused by our poor performance at getting students from low-income families through postsecondary education. If all U.S. students had the college-going rates and the college-completion rates of our high-income students, the United States would once again be at the top of the lists. To achieve this requires a better financial aid system.

Copy Success

One of the advantages of a federal system of government is that states often adopt very different solutions to problems. At times, the fifty states in the United States are running fifty simultaneous experiments about how to deal with a particular problem. Adding the federal government often gives us a fifty-first experiment. Therefore, one interesting place to start looking for a way to overhaul the financial aid system might be the various state experiments. Which state program is the most successful? Can its success be copied at the federal level?

We will make the case for the Georgia HOPE Scholarship Program as perhaps the most successful state scholarship initiative.[2] This suggestion will create a knee-jerk reaction of horror from many financial aid experts. The Georgia HOPE Scholarship Program is a merit-based program, and many experts argue that the shift toward merit-based aid is one of the most disturbing trends in the current financial aid system. We recognize this, but give us a few paragraphs. First, if nothing else, the Georgia HOPE Scholarship is clearly one of the most copied financial aid programs. After the Georgia HOPE Scholarship Program was founded in 1993, broad-based merit-aid programs similar to it have been created in fourteen other states. The list comprises Alaska, Florida, Kentucky, Louisiana, Massachusetts, Michigan, Mississippi, Missouri, Nevada, New Mexico, North Carolina, South Carolina, Tennessee, and West Virginia. Other states clearly think that Georgia is on to something.

The term HOPE is an acronym for Helping Outstanding Pupils Educationally. Essentially, the HOPE program offers grants to all students who are residents of Georgia and who earn a B average in high school. The grant covers tuition, approved mandatory fees, and a book allowance for students attending public colleges and universities in Georgia. Also, students attending private colleges and universities in Georgia are eligible for grants of $3,500 per academic year. To keep their grants, students have to maintain a B average in college. Initially, students from families with incomes in excess of $66,000 were ineligible for HOPE scholarships, but the income cap was raised to $100,000 in 1994 and eliminated completely in 1995. There are other details. For example, home-schooled students can be granted a HOPE scholarship retroactively if they earn a B average in their first year in college, and nontraditional students (those who graduated from high school before 1993) can earn a HOPE scholarship after their sophomore year if they maintain a B average. Still, the backbone of the program is the simple promise that if you have a B average in high school, you get the scholarship, and if you keep a B average in college, you keep the scholarship.

The two big advantages of the HOPE scholarship program are its *simplicity* and its *universality*. Simplicity is important. To succeed, a program has to be easy for people to understand. A randomly selected set of high school students in any state likely could not describe the federal Pell Grant program with any accuracy, but students in Georgia know about the HOPE Scholarship Program. In a survey reported by Gary T. Henry, Steve Harkreader, Philo A. Hutcheson, and Craig Gordon (1998), over 70 percent of Georgia high school students could name the Georgia HOPE Scholarship, and even when unaided over 58 percent of them named the 3.0 grade point average as a requirement for HOPE eligibility. Also, the survey showed that the parents of Georgia high school students had an even greater awareness of the scholarship program and its requirements than did the students. If we want to encourage people to take advantage of programs that help them pay for college, they have to know about the programs and understand their options. We have already seen that complexity is a barrier that reduces the enrollment rate of college-prepared lower income students. A simple program whose rules are easily understood by aspiring students and their parents will be better than a complex program that leaves parents and students partially in the dark until late in the decision-making process.

The second important idea is universality. A large number of Georgia families benefit from the HOPE Scholarship Program. Every Georgia resident, even ones who are neither college students nor their parents, likely knows many HOPE scholarship recipients. Some of these recipients probably are part of his or her extended family. Universal programs like this have a much more solid political base than narrowly targeted programs. Social Security provides the standard example. The target population of the Social Security program is the low-income elderly, yet Social Security is not just a program for them. It supports all retirees. Political support for broad-based programs like Social Security is much stronger than the support for a means-tested welfare program of any sort, including for the elderly, because everyone anticipates being a Social Security beneficiary if they can reach a certain age. By contrast, many people would never qualify for means-tested benefits, and they know it. Critics of universal programs argue that much of the money spent on them is wasted. High-income retired people don't need the social security checks, and students from wealthy families don't need HOPE scholarships. Still, when the budget gets tight, universal programs fare much better than more narrowly based programs. The sociologists William Julius Wilson (1987) and Theda Skocpol (1995) have called this "targeting within universalism."

The B-average requirement makes the HOPE Scholarship Program less than completely universal, but this is not a big problem. Maintaining a B average should be within the reach of all high school students who aspire to go to college. And if a student does not maintain the B average, the fault largely lies with the student. People understand that the incentives are aligned correctly, particularly when compared to the incentives in means-tested programs like the ones sponsored by the federal government. The incentives in the HOPE Scholarship Program are to succeed in school. The incentives in means-tested programs are to be poor or to find a way to look poor.

Finally, studies of the HOPE Scholarship Program indicate that this kind of financial aid spending does increase enrollments. For example, Susan Dynarski (2000) studied the difference in enrollment rates for youths in Georgia relative to youths in other Southern states. According to her estimates, the HOPE Scholarship Program increased the enrollment rates of 18–19 year olds by 7.0 to 7.9 percentage points. A study by Christopher Cornwell, David B. Mustard, and Deepa J. Sridhar in 2006 gets similar results. Also, Dynarski's 2008 study that looks at both the Arkansas and Georgia state merit-based programs finds that these programs affect college-completion rates as well as college-enrollment rates. These results are quite different from the results of no effect for Pell Grants found by Hansen, Manski, and Kane.

Another study by Dynarski (2003) used the 1992 termination of the Social Security Student Benefit Program as a natural experiment to test the impact of a non-means-tested program on college-attendance rates of students who would have been eligible for the program had it continued. She found that the elimination of the program reduced attendance probabilities by more than one third. She also found that an offer of $1,000 in aid increases the probability of attending college by around 3.6 percent and that aid eligibility also increased college completion. Both the Georgia HOPE Scholarship and the Social Security Student Benefit program are (or were, in the case of the terminated Social Security Student Benefit) outside of the means-testing system. No FAFSAs have to be filled out to obtain the funds in the two programs, both of which have had a positive effect on college-going rates.

Are the characteristics of the Georgia HOPE Scholarship Program that make it such a success easily transferred to the federal level? First, consider simplicity. The complexity of our current federal aid system is a common target of criticism. Almost any policy analyst who has crafted a financial aid reform proposal calls for the program to be simplified. A good example comes from the 2008 report of the Rethinking Student Aid Study Group headed by Sandy Baum of the College Board and Michael McPherson of the Spencer Foundation. The Rethinking Group's first recommendation is to "make federal financial aid simple, clear, and transparent." Similarly, the 2009 report from the study group organized by the National Association of Student Financial Aid Administrators (NASFAA) says, "The current financial aid process depends on an exceptionally complex application and delivery system that is intimidating to families. It can, in itself, discourage students from pursuing college."[3] The NASFAA group also has a series of proposals to simplify the process of applying for financial aid.

Most of the simplification proposals target the needs-analysis system described in chapter 11. The FAFSA requires families to provide information on income and assets. The government runs this information through complicated formulae to determine the expected family contribution. A college or university that admits this student then uses the Expected Family Contribution information to design a financial aid package consisting of a combination of grants, loans, and work-study. If the expected family contribution is below a certain limit, the financial aid package will include a Pell Grant no matter which college is composing the financial aid package. Other parts of the financial aid package will vary by institution. There are two strikes against this system. The process is complex, and it is not transparent to the student and his or her family.

Both the Rethinking Group and the NASFAA group propose to simplify the process by dropping the asset information from the calculation of the Expected Family Contribution. By ignoring assets, information from the federal income tax forms alone could be used to determine the Expected Family Contribution. Since a student will qualify for the same Pell Grant at any college he or she attends, the amount of the Pell Grant the students would receive could be known after the family files its federal income tax forms. This simplifies the process by eliminating one complex federal form.

This suggested simplification is not cost free. Some families with low incomes but high asset levels will appear to be needy when they are not. Yet the benefits of simplifying the system seem large compared with this hypothetical risk of unfairness. In addition, with a system based only on income, the parents of eighth graders could be notified of the Pell Grant their child would qualify for if he or she were older in much the same way that every participant in the Social Security system is currently notified annually of their retirement benefits at their estimated time of retirement. With this kind of notification, the size of potential aid packages from the federal government would be more common knowledge.

There are families who do not file federal income tax because their income does not reach certain thresholds. Often these families qualify for other federal programs such as food stamps or free and reduced-price school lunches. Children from these families would automatically qualify for the maximum Pell Grants, and they could be made aware of this benefit through the federal agencies that provide their other benefits.

These proposals are indeed sensible, and they are good as far as they go. Eliminating the FASFA form will make many a parent of a college student very happy. Notifying people of their eligibility for Pell Grants early and often also is a very good idea. Low-income families often are headed by individuals with no college experience and therefore no knowledge of the possibilities for financial aid. Unfortunately, Pell Grants are the only kind of federal assistance whose generosity can be estimated based solely on the Expected Family Contribution. The eligibility for SEOG grants, work-study, and subsidized loans depend on financial need, and financial need depends on a combination of the costs of attendance and the Expected Family Contribution. There is no way of determining this prior to knowing which institution the student wants to attend.

In conclusion, the existing federal model can be simplified up to a point, but by its very nature it cannot be made really simple. Can it be universalized? As a means-tested approach, it is certainly not universal. It is explicitly targeted toward children from low-income families.

A large number of students do not receive a federal grant of any kind. The only truly universal part of the financial aid system is the tax-advantaged college savings programs. This program has no income caps, but these savings programs are of negligible use to families who do not pay income tax.

A Proposal to Chew On

Making a program universal requires taking away its income sensitivity. This is a radical idea, and it clearly has a cost. Financial aid funds would flow to families who do not need them. This is perhaps undesirable, but is this all that unusual? In fact it is not. The federal government clearly gives Social Security payments to lots of elderly people who do not need the money. Closer to home, consider the way states provide funds to state-supported colleges and universities. Virginia gives appropriations to schools like the College of William and Mary and the University of Virginia, and these appropriations allow the institutions to charge in-state tuition that is well below the cost of the education provided. Students receive the benefits of low in-state tuition without regard to family income. Many of these students could afford to pay out-of-state tuition, but as Virginia residents they do not have to. As a result, this kind of government assistance flows to many people who do not need it. This sort of universal benefit is an easy target of criticism. The late Milton Friedman once remarked "Why should families in Watts pay taxes to subsidize families in Beverly Hills who send their children to UCLA?"[4] This is a good question, and it explains the desirability of targeted programs. To argue for universal benefits, you must believe that extreme simplification is valuable, and that the political support that comes from universality is important.

Before we go further, let us put a specific proposal on the table. We have taken our idea from the Rethinking Group's third proposal. They propose to create a federal savings account for low-income families that could be used for college expenses. In their plan, the federal government would make a deposit in an account for each child in any family whose income was low enough that a child from that family would qualify for a Pell Grant if the child had been in college. Each year the family income remained below this threshold, the account of each child would be credited, and any balance in the account would earn interest. Funds from this savings account could only be used to meet expenses associated with attending college.

And the funds would stay in the account until the account was completely exhausted. This would allow a student to start college at any time in his or her life. The suggestion we want to consider is taking away the income cap on these savings accounts. Make them universal.

More specifically, the proposal is to make the savings accounts the sole basis of federal financial aid. It should replace all the grant programs and the tax benefits. The amount of the deposit in the savings account should be calibrated so that by year eighteen, the deposits and interest would be sufficient to cover the Pell Grant maximum for four years. The actual savings accounts would not have to exist; rather, this language would be used to describe a commitment the federal government was making. In actual practice, it would be a pay-as-you-go system much like the Social Security system.

A similar proposal was made by Jonathan Grayer, the former chairman and CEO of Kaplan Inc. Grayer's proposal would give every sixth grader a 529 savings plan worth $10,000. James J. Dunderstadt, president emeritus of the University of Michigan, has offered a similar idea.[5] He proposed what he calls "Learn Grants for the Millennium Generation." These grants would go to each student upon entering kindergarten.

> Each year students (and their parents) would receive a state-ment of the accumulation in their account, with a reminder that this is their money, but it can only be used for their college edu-cation (or other postsecondary education). An initial contribu-tion of say $10,000 (say, a $5,000 federal grant with a state $5,000 match) would accumulate over their K–12 education to an amount that when coupled with other financial aid would likely be sufficient for their college education at a public college or university.

Both of these proposals are in the spirit of our idea.

The purpose of the Pell Grant is to provide a guaranteed minimum available for college expenses. It does so in a very opaque and compli-cated way by using information from the FAFSA (or the income tax system under the reform proposals) to determine the grants that make up the difference between what the family is expected to contribute and the Pell Grant maximum. The universal savings account can accomplish this same goal in a much simpler way. Every student would know that they could draw down their savings account by an amount equivalent to the Pell Grant maximum.

In touting their savings program plan for low-income families, the Rethinking Group says,

> We believe that these accounts, explicitly targeted by the federal government to make money for college available to low-income children, have the potential to change significantly the way parents view their children's prospects for education...Today most affluent families see a college education for their children as a natural part of the growing-up process, something like a birthright. The program we propose here can help weave the expectation of college into the fabric of growing up in America, not just for affluent families but for all families.[6]

This is a laudable goal, but it is one that we think the universal savings accounts would accomplish more effectively. We acknowledge that our suggestion, and those of Grayer and Dunderstadt, would be more costly than a means-tested savings account targeted at the poor, but our proposal would be more easily understood. Under the means-tested savings program, families would see deposits in their accounts in some years, but if their income expanded, not in others. As a result, similar to other means-tested programs, families are penalized for increasing family income. In addition, the drawdown from the savings account would be part of the Expected Family Contribution, so the family would lose aid. If this is the case, the means-tested savings account would not be a benefit at all.

As proposed, the universal savings accounts would have a significant price tag. Only 37.6 percent of the full-time-equivalent students received Pell Grants in the 2006–7 academic year, and by no means did all of these students receive the maximum Pell Grant. To build a system that gave all students the equivalent of a maximum Pell Grant would cost substantially more than current Pell appropriations.

We can come to a rough estimate of the cost of the program by estimating the size of the student body under the assumption that we achieved the current target of 60 percent college completion set by the current administration.[7] Census data allows us to estimate the number of people in a four-year age span. If 60 percent of these people would tap a savings account for $5,350, which is the 2009–10 Pell Grant maximum, the total annual costs of the program would be roughly $50 billion. This is a high-end calculation, and one that assumes considerable educational success. We assumed the country reached its goal of enrolling 60 percent of its students in four years of higher education. This is a long-run goal that is quite unlikely to be met in the near term, so the costs of the program could be quite a bit less than this biggest-case estimate.

The dollar cost is not completely new money since the proposal is partially self-funding. This savings account program would replace all existing federal grant programs. The elimination of the current Pell Grants, SEOG grants, LEAP program, ACG grants, SMART grants, federal work-study, and educational tax benefits offsets roughly $24 billion in 2007–8.[8] There would be additional savings from dismantling the bureaucratic apparatus currently required to implement means testing. Nonetheless, the program could require the federal government to double its commitment for student aid. We are proposing to create a federal entitlement, and such things are not cheap.

There is another offset through the schools themselves. Many middle-income families currently receive tuition discounts from the schools they attend, and this broad entitlement proposal would reduce the need for tuition discounting. As we have shown, this would put downward pressure on list-price tuition, so some of the people whose taxes might rise to pay for the entitlement might have their disposable income increased because list-price tuition grows less rapidly.

The question comes down to this. Does the United States want to do what it has to do to increase the college attainment of its citizens? The universal college-savings proposal might well be what we have to do. Such a program has a lot going for it. It is *simple*. The government savings account provides a minimum amount for each child in the country to spend on college expenses. There are no complicated forms one has to fill out to see how much federal aid a child is going to receive. As they approach college-going age, it would be easy to see how much money would be available from the federal government. It is also *universal*. Every child living in the United States would automatically qualify for a savings account. Since parents would receive notifications of the amount in their child's savings account every year, the program would be common knowledge. College-qualified students would know that they had a college savings fund even if they came from very low-income families. Also, families could be encouraged to add to the savings account, and doing so would only increase the money available to meet college expenses. This program does not penalize families who save extra for college expenses.

Another advantage of these savings accounts is that the bargain struck between the government and students and their families is very clear. Under our proposal, a student has a limited account that can be tapped for higher education expenses that amounts to four years' worth of grant support, and only four years' worth. Currently, if your income is sufficiently low, you can obtain full federal assistance for five, six, or seven years. Similarly, an in-state student in a state-supported college receives the benefits of in-state tuition for as long as he or she is enrolled. Our proposal says that the government has done its bit by giving an amount equivalent to four years' worth of assistance. If you want to go to school longer than four years, it is your right to determine which of the four years you receive the assistance for, or you can only take partial assistance in some years. You have a fixed amount of government assistance for your undergraduate education, and it is up to you to determine how you use it.

The simple program should overcome many of the problems and perverse incentives that plague the complex system that we currently have. Students from low-income families would know about the program well before they start high school. If students know there is money available targeted for their college expenses, they will see more value in trying the college preparatory curriculum in high school. They will also have a greater incentive to work hard to succeed in mastering that curriculum. The high-income students are already doing this because they know the money will be there. Giving the low-income students the same awareness that the money will be there may change their behavior, and the evidence suggests that on average it would. And this change in behavior should happen well before they get to the college application process.

There are other advantages. The current system is based on determining the Expected Family Contribution, but there is no way of knowing whether the family is willing actually to contribute that much. In some cases, families are willing to contribute more, and this benefits the students. In other cases, families are willing to contribute less. In this case, if the student still wants to go to college, he or she faces financial constraints beyond what was used to determine the financial aid offer. Students in this situation often decide not go to college. The universal savings program eliminates this issue. The funds in the savings account can only be used for college expenses, and these funds do not depend on the willingness of the family to provide a federally calculated down payment called the Expected Family Contribution.

Another advantage of this program, one that it shares with proposals to base means testing solely on family income, is that it would eliminate the perverse incentives of the current means-testing rules. Consider the case of two families with similar incomes living side-by-side. One family diligently saves for their children's education while the other always has new cars, goes on expensive vacations, and puts a swimming pool in its back yard. When it comes time for the children to go to college, because of means testing that includes a family's financial assets, the family that had saved will have to pay more for college than the spendthrift family. These stories would no longer be true. The universal federal savings plan eliminates the incentives to arrange your finances to maximize the amount of financial aid you may receive.

In a similar vein, currently parents who do understand the federal financial aid rules recognize that the value of their house does not count as an asset in the federal calculations. If such a family is likely to qualify for federal financial aid, it makes sense for them to accumulate equity in their house rather than to increase their holdings of financial assets. This changes incentives in a way that increases investments in housing as opposed to other assets, and this can lead to unbalanced portfolios. Given the tax rates on assets implicit in the Expected Family Contribution formulae, this effect can be quite large.

We can anticipate many critiques of our proposal. It spends a great deal of money, and that money could do a world of good if it were simply added to the existing means-tested programs. The seeming ineffectiveness of the current programs may result from low funding more than any design flaws. This is a position that many serious higher education analysts would support. The current system has helped a large number of students, and increases in the available funding could be used to increase the maximum Pell Grant substantially if the current means testing were maintained. And we do not need universality to achieve some simplification. Changing the application process by eliminating the FAFSA and replacing it with IRS information should make the system simpler. And additional funds could be used to increase outreach efforts to make talented students aware of the existence of federal financial aid both earlier and more often. If the current system works well enough when students are aware of it, wouldn't making more students aware of it and making it even more generous be the better option?

The questions we have just posed are not ones for which we have ready answers, but the research we have cited is quite clear. The current means-tested financial aid system does not have the intended effect on college attendance and college completion among lower income students. One approach is to try to tinker with the system by simplifying the means testing and better targeting the subsidies that go to loan recipients. This approach is based on the idea that we understand the critical flaws in the current system. Our alternative approach is based on the idea that means testing itself is the problem, so no amount of tinkering will work. The means-tested benefits should be replaced by universal ones. The first approach has the clear advantage that it is less expensive, and it requires fewer changes. The second approach is more expensive, and it has not been tried on a national level. Still, the evidence on the state level suggests that it does work. The choice is not an easy one, but one thing is very clear. If we want to increase the college-going and college-completion rates, we have to change the financial aid system. The status quo is not desirable.

Loans

In their 1991 book, *Keeping College Affordable*, Michael McPherson and Morton Owen Schapiro made the point that paying for college can be done in two basic ways. The first way is for parents to pay for the education costs of their children by accumulating savings in anticipation of the student going to college. The second way is for students to pay for the costs of their own college education. Students can do this by borrowing and paying off the loans after completing their education. Any way you cut it, one generation has to reduce its consumption to pay for the college education. These two approaches aren't mutually exclusive. Students can get some help from their parents and do the rest using loans.

The existing Pell Grant program does not cover the full cost of attendance at most four-year programs. Universal savings accounts of the sort we have proposed will put a specified minimum amount on the table equal to the maximum Pell Grant times four, but this too will not cover the full college cost for most students. Depending on the cost of the chosen education, under either system federal support plus family assets may be insufficient to meet all college expenses. Unless the family is willing and able to cut back by enough on consumption from its current income, some form of student loan program still will be needed.

The federal government currently plays two roles in the student loan process. The first is as a guarantor of loans made to students by banks. The guarantor role remains a vital component of an efficient student loan program. Without loan guarantees, many students would be shut out of financing for their undergraduate education. Most students have no credit history and have no collateral to offer. Without a credit history and collateral, private lenders are understandably reluctant to lend for something as risky as undergraduate training, even if the average student does well. The default risk is too high. The private market does not work well at providing education loans to undergraduates in part because banks cannot truly assess the individual risks of lending to any particular student, and one reason for this is because students cannot sign contracts that commit them to choosing the most lucrative or stable career tracks.

The second role government currently plays in the student loan process is in subsidizing the interest costs of student borrowing. Currently, the vast majority of the government funding for loan programs goes to subsidize students who have financial need *at the time they are in college*. The subsidy pays the interest on their loans while they are in college and reduces the interest they have to pay after they leave. Only students whose financial need is apparent while they are in college receive these subsidies. This is not a particularly sensible approach.

First, interest subsidization encourages borrowing for college as opposed to saving for it in advance. We have already seen that the FAFSA process acts to discourage saving since the savings translate into a higher Expected Family Contribution. Saving for college is essentially taxed. One might wonder why the federal government has any reason to tilt the incentives one way or the other in the borrowing versus savings decision. Also, the government is on both sides of this issue. Offering tax advantages to 529 college savings plans tilts in the other direction.

Second, it is not at all clear that basing the subsidy on the income of the student at the time he or she takes out the loans is either efficient or equitable. First consider Susan, a low-income student who qualified for an interest-subsidized loan. She graduates from four years of college and gets a job that pays a large salary and generous benefits. She will have no difficulty repaying her subsidized loans. Next consider Arnold, an upper-middle-income student who takes out an unsubsidized loan. He graduates from four years of college, but the only job he can find has a very low salary and no benefits. Arnold will have considerable difficulty repaying his *unsubsidized* student loans. Arguably, an equitable allocation of government help would favor Arnold and not Susan. Susan's low income at the time she was a student does not insure that she will have a low income when she is a graduate, and Arnold's family's upper-middle income when he was a student does not insure that he will be upper-middle income when he is a graduate. Current practice does not treat similar people alike after they finish their studies. Two graduates can have the same income ex-post and yet be repaying very different amounts on the same level of borrowing.

In addition, since subsidizing the interest on loans encourages students to take on more debt than they otherwise would have chosen, that debt may affect what they choose to study in ways that are not necessarily optimal either for the student or for society as a whole. The larger the debt burden a student takes on, the more likely he or she is to pursue fields of study, and job categories within those fields, that pay a lot. While we are not averse to students earning large salaries, distorting the incentives is not a good idea. The Susan in our example might have had a love of inner-city teaching, and she might have been very good at it. Instead, she chooses investment banking because it's the only way to pay off her debt burden. Enough students face this issue anyway. There is no good reason for federal policy to exacerbate it.

The Rethinking Group has put forward very sensible proposals to reform how the federal government subsidizes student loans. The federal moneys should be redirected away from interest subsidization and targeted instead to help students with repayment after they graduate. A college education generally is a sound financial investment. On average, a college-educated individual will make sufficient income to pay off college loans without any great difficulty. The "on average" part of the last sentence is important. There are instances in which students have below-average success in the post-college job market, and these students often find repaying their loans to be a considerable burden. This burden often leads to bankruptcy that is undesirable for the individual and for the government.

The Rethinking Group proposes to eliminate interest subsidies, retain the important federal role in guaranteeing unsubsidized loans or lending directly to students, and shift subsidy funds to the Income-Based Repayment option that was introduced in the College Cost Reduction and Access Act of 2007. This program allows former students who cannot afford the regular repayment to pay instead a percentage of their income. The goal of the Rethinking Group is to strengthen this program so that no former student has to use more than 15 percent of his or her income to repay college loans. This is a version of an income-contingent repayment option that has been proposed by many analysts in the past. It is still a very good idea.

This proposal does not remove the government from the loan *initiation* business altogether, since the government will still be a major guarantor. But it gets the government out of the business of directly subsidizing loan interest. The government would continue to provide loan guarantees as long as the current practice of using private lenders is maintained. With the recent legislation, the federal government will become a the only lender to students. In this case there is no need for explicit guarantees since the government is self-insured. The proposal is to shift the subsidies away from the loan-initiation phase to the loan-repayment phase.

Summary and Conclusions

The best policy proposals generally find ways of accomplishing a particular objective with the smallest fiscal footprint. The strength of the cost drivers at colleges and universities suggest the fiscal footprint of an effective financial aid program is going to have to grow. The only way to keep expenditures down is to narrowly target the money so that no financial aid dollars go to students who do not need them. In order to accomplish this minimal fiscal footprint, additional information would have to be gathered about each student's finances. In other words, laser-like targeting requires lots of information that intrudes on privacy. Currently, the information gathered by the government from the FAFSA form does not include, for example, any assistance that a student's grandparents are intending to give or the value of home equity parents could tap. A more well- targeted system would try to find out this information, because we know that grandparents often provide assistance to students, and housing wealth can be tapped to meet college expenses. To reduce waste in the financial aid system, we would have to be unrelenting in targeting the funds where they are needed most.

The policy proposals we have discussed, both the simplification proposals of the Rethinking and NAFSAA groups and the universal savings account proposal we put forward, move in exactly the opposite direction. They are proposals to streamline the system. The Rethinking Group and the NAFSAA group would ask for less information about student finances. As a result, federal programs would be less precisely targeted. With a simplified income-based needs-analysis system, aid accidentally could go to students with ample assets with which they could finance a college education. With our universal savings accounts, aid would go to every student regardless of income and assets. There is a considerable difference in the amount of potential "waste" or "excess spending" that these two options advocate, so the plans are quite different. Still, they are similar in the sense that they are based on the notion that a less narrowly targeted financial aid system may be a more effective one if the goal is to increase the college-going rate.

The policy tradeoff in this situation is between optimal targeting and simplicity. If we are really serious about increasing the college-going and college-completion rates in the United States, we need a more effective financial aid system. How much targeting will we have to give up? We have discussed two options, the moderate option presented by two research groups brought together to suggest changes in financial aid and our more radical universal savings account proposal. One suggests that we can create a more effective system and still keep some targeting. The other suggests that any targeting is inherently counterproductive. The first option clearly is less expensive, and that is a great advantage. Still, it maintains the basic structures of the current system, and that may well be a critical flaw.

Reasonable people disagree about many issues involving financial aid. First, the entire discussion about financial aid reform takes as given a need to increase the college-going and college-completion rates in the United States. Some might not see the need for such an increase. Second, even given the desire for an increase, people could well disagree about where to place that desire in the hierarchy of needs for federal funds. Third, even among those who think it should have a very high priority, there is no reason to spend more money than needed. This gets us to the issue we have presented. Do we take the lesson from the Georgia HOPE Scholarship Program that a simple universal system will be effective, and then try to blow it up to the national level? Or do we think that we can take a less expensive route by simplifying the needs-analysis system but keeping the basic structure of the existing financial aid system that has not been as effective as we would like? These are not easy questions, but we think there is ample evidence to suggest that a significant move toward simplification and universality will pay large social dividends that justify the increased levels of federal spending such an approach would require.

15

Rewriting the Relationship between States and Their Public Universities

This chapter takes a slightly different tack than chapter 14. In chapter 14, we presented a proposal to distribute federal financial aid as an across-the-board payment to all students. This proposal was presented as an alternative to other proposals to reform federal financial aid. We were not engaged in advocacy. We are not sure just how a full evaluation of our proposal to make aid universal and proposals of others to simplify the process of distributing aid would come out. We are sure that the current financial aid system needs to be changed, but we do not know just how radical a change is required. Our proposal in chapter 14 was designed to help illustrate the tradeoffs involved in federal financial aid. Things are different in this chapter. Here we suggest a radical change in the way states finance higher education. Again there are tradeoffs, but we think we know how an analysis of the alternatives would turn out. We have been convinced for quite some time that this radical change is necessary. We will engage in advocacy in this chapter.

The basic funding scheme for public higher education—with states funding a portion of institutional operating expenses and partial or complete funding of capital projects—has been in place since the first state-supported college was founded in the United States in the eighteenth century. Until the 1970s, state appropriations were large enough that most public colleges and universities could offer residents access to high-quality, four-year degree programs at very low tuition. In recent years, rising operating costs and a declining share of higher education appropriations in state budgets have combined to break this implicit financing contract.

Despite soaring list-price tuition, spending per full-time student at public institutions has fallen further behind their private counterparts during the past quarter century. This has caused some to ask if the old implicit contract can be replaced with a new system that preserves high-quality programs and maintains a sufficient number of places for state residents, but that recognizes the shrinking role of the state.

For us, this is not an abstract question. In the fall of 2002, we sat down with the brain trust at the College of William and Mary, where we teach, to pitch a new proposal that we had immodestly titled "A New Compact for Higher Education in Virginia."[1] Like most states, Virginia was in the midst of a major budget crisis. State appropriations were being slashed, and we faced potentially years of financial retrenchment. As we noted in our presentation to the administration at the time, the college had been in this situation before. And as we draft this chapter, we are in the midst of yet another round of state retrenchment. Our proposal was motivated in part by the frustration of watching the slow-motion financial roller-coaster ride endured by our university. Back in chapter 9 (figure 9.2), we showed this rolling, but overall downward slide in the share of William and Mary's operating expenses covered by the state of Virginia. This is a pattern that is hardly unique to our school. Most state-supported universities have faced much the same story over the past thirty years.

State support falls during and immediately after economic recessions and then begins to rise later in the economic expansion as the state's coffers begin to fill up again. Yet the surge in funding that takes place in the good times always falls short of the prior peak level of state effort, and the result is a downward ratchet of state relevance. This pattern is not evidence of malice, or even of intent. It reflects instead the combination of four forces: (1) periodic declines in state revenues; (2) legitimate demands on state revenues for purposes other than supporting higher education; (3) a requirement to balance the state budget; and (4) the fact that increases in college tuition have become politically more palatable than increases in taxes. In a paper in the *Journal of Higher Education* in 2006, we showed that these forces are particularly strong in states that have passed some form of tax and expenditure constraints, such as requirements for a super-majority to increase taxes or explicit limits on the rate at which taxes or spending can increase. Figure 9.2 shows clearly how our college has become progressively more dependent on direct charges to students and on support from private donors. The data in table 9.1 show that this is also true for the average public institution.

The forces driving this change are not likely to stop. In 2002 we thought that the parties involved should recognize this and work to manage the changes these forces imply. Nothing has happened in the intervening years to change our minds. The consequences of inaction are fairly clear. In 1980, public universities spent roughly seventy cents per full-time equivalent student for every dollar that private schools spent. By the middle of the 1990s, that figure had fallen to fifty-three cents per dollar. These changes have consequences.

Colleges and universities operate in markets that mix private and public institutions. These markets have little respect for state boundaries, and they are very dependent on easily transferred human talent. People who work for public colleges and universities can teach, do research, or serve as administrators at private institutions and at state-supported institutions in other states. Our publicly supported institutions also compete with major corporations, banks, law firms, and a myriad other private- and public-sector employers. Talented individuals are mobile, and when state budget necessities keep salaries fixed and facilities in disrepair, these people are more likely to move. A particular state's budget problems often coincide with fiscal difficulties in other states, but they are not shared evenly, and private colleges and universities often are exempt from many of the problems.

We are not particular fans of university rankings, but a twenty-year evolution within one ranking scheme can offer some insights into how public higher education has fallen behind its private counterpart. In the inaugural edition of the *U.S. News and World Report* rankings that came out in 1987, eight public universities were in the top twenty-five. The University of California at Berkeley was fifth and Michigan was eighth. In the second ten, the University of North Carolina held the eleventh spot, Virginia was fifteenth, and Illinois was twentieth. Rounding out the list were William and Mary (22), Wisconsin (23) and Texas (25). As of this writing, the most recent *U.S. News* rankings (2010) list no public universities in the top twenty. Berkeley now is ranked twenty-first while University of California at Los Angeles and the University of Virginia are tied for twenty-fourth.

The formula that produces these rankings hasn't remained constant over time. Some movement in the rankings can't help but generate interest, after all. For this reason alone, we should interpret rankings like these with caution. Yet this systematic disappearance of public institutions from the top ranks may be telling us something. Moreover, if we look at some of the subcomponents that U.S. News uses to produce its overall rankings, we get a richer picture of why quality is clearly declining at the top public institutions relative to their private counterparts.

One of the important variables that U.S. News uses to create its overall ranking is a measure of each school's financial resources. With this, each school is ranked according to its available resources. There were 120 schools in the top half of the 2007 rankings for which U.S. News also calculated the same financial information in 1990. The group contained 57 private universities and 63 public ones. The average private school's financial resources rank rose by over four places over that time span, while the average public university's rank fell by more than six. Other information collected by U.S. News helps us to see how this comparative financial deterioration at public universities has an impact on quality. The 1990 and 2007 data both have information on the student-faculty ratio. There are 121 universities in the top half of the U.S. News rankings with data for this variable in both years. For 40 of the 58 private institutions, the student-faculty ratio declined over time. The average *decrease* in the student-faculty ratio for these private institutions was 1.84. The evidence is very different for public institutions. The average *increase* in the student faculty ratio for these 63 public institutions was 1.70. Lastly, the clustering of high achieving students (those in the top 10 percent of their high school class) is much more pronounced at the best private universities than at the best public universities.

The Elements of a New Compact

Our "New Compact" proposal joined together two major reform ideas for restructuring the relationship between states and their public colleges and universities. The first idea was that state universities needed to be operationally much more self-sustaining than in the past. Schools needed to control their own financial future independent of the state's boom-and-bust budget cycle, and they needed decision-making independence from the state over the thousands of processes that required expensive and often-delayed state approvals. Perhaps most importantly, for financial independence, the schools needed to own the tuition revenue they generated instead of having the funds flow into the state revenue stream. Second, the tuition decision needed to be firmly in the hands of the schools and their governing boards.

A few years ago at a dinner honoring the outgoing members of William and Mary's governing board, one of the honorees recounted how he had been instructed by the governor to "Go down there to William and Mary and get a handle on the cost problem." After his term on the board, he came to the conclusion that William and Mary did *not* have a cost problem. It had a revenue problem. The first part of our proposal was designed to solve this revenue problem.

The second key component of our proposal was perhaps even more daring. We argued that the state should get out of the business of writing appropriations directly to its public colleges and universities. Instead, the state should develop a program of direct subsidies to students. As we will argue below, this idea could change the politics and economics of public higher education in many positive ways. State universities would shift from being state-supported to state-affiliated or state-allied. This is not a mere semantic distinction. As state-affiliated institutions, they would still serve a public purpose and face some public constraints, but as decision makers, state universities would behave much more like private universities. They would have all the benefits that go with control, and they would also face the full winds of competition.

This is a new model of a college or university as a public-private partnership. Each state likely would create the legal entity a bit differently, based on its needs and influenced by the past evolution of its governing institutions and its universities. But we can envision some common properties of a new arrangement. In particular, state-allied public universities likely would have a governing board that was more self-sustaining, less politicized, and capable of taking a longer view. These boards likely would be chosen partially by the governor and partially by the institution itself. The boards would oversee institutions that were legally entitled to make a set of decisions that are currently encumbered or second-guessed by state agencies and elected officials.

At the time we were pitching our proposal to anyone in Virginia who might listen, similar ideas were percolating elsewhere. Perhaps the most well known of these efforts is the system-wide voucher proposal developed by Colorado's Blue Ribbon Panel on Higher Education for the 21st Century.[2] An amended version of this proposal was adopted, and starting in the fall of 2005 most of the state appropriation—which formerly went to Colorado colleges and universities—began to fund direct grants to students. A similar approach was adopted unilaterally by Miami University of Ohio. Miami pledged to return all of its state appropriation directly to its Ohio-resident students in the form of across-the-board grants and specific scholarships. All students thus would face the same list-price tuition. James Garland, the president of Miami of Ohio at the time, recently proposed a direct-funding idea much like ours in his new book, *Saving Alma Mater* (2009). Lastly, the State University of New York at Buffalo is the latest university to propose some sort of decision making divorce from its state.

The Mechanics of Direct Tuition Grants

When we talk to people about zeroing out colleges and universities from the state budget and replacing that system with direct tuition grants to students, the reaction is a predictable gasp. For starters, people often confuse direct tuition grants with the politically very contentious debate about school vouchers for K–12 students. The heart of the K–12 voucher debate is about school choice and the portability of public funding between public and private institutions. While a need may exist for more school choice in K–12 education, we believe there already is ample school choice in higher education. Our focus is on the funding mechanism of *public* institutions. If states wish to allow full or partial portability of their tuition grants between public and private institutions, they may choose to do so. But that kind of portability is not inherent in our proposal.

When we lay out the numbers, the reaction often changes from a gasp to narrowed eyebrows and a skeptical look. While direct tuition grants may sound like a radical departure from traditional funding practices, at first glance they can look more like an exercise in manipulating smoke and mirrors. Table 15.1 contains a simple comparison of a traditional state appropriation process to a direct-funding scheme. The example ignores the added complexity of out-of-state students, and all numbers are on a per-student basis. The major changes associated with a

Table 15.1 A Comparison of Funding Schemes

	Traditional Funding	Direct Funding
In-state tuition	$10,000	$18,000
State appropriation	8,000	0
Tuition grants to students	0	8,000
Net tuition expense	10,000	10,000
Revenue to the school	18,000	18,000
Cost to the state	8,000	8,000

shift to the direct-funding model are the elimination of state appropriations to institutions, an increase in list-price tuition, and the creation of a tuition grant that goes directly to every in-state student.

The accusation that these changes are an illusion or are only cosmetic has strong initial appeal. The amount of money involved remains the same. From the student's perspective in this example, $8,000 is added to the tuition bill, but he or she is unharmed because $8,000 is given to each student as a tuition grant. From the institution's perspective, it loses $8,000 in state appropriation, but it also is unharmed because it gains an additional $8,000 in tuition revenue from each of its students. Likewise, the state is unaffected; its checks are routed to the institutions through the students. Since all parties apparently wind up in the same place, what is the big deal? Although the numbers seem unchanged, the incentives within a tuition grant system prove quite different than the ones that motivate the current state appropriation process. Combined with genuine control over their revenue stream, a system of direct grants to students has the potential to remake public universities for the better.

The Case for Radical Change

The Planning Horizon

The rationale for colleges and universities controlling their revenues is fairly clear and straightforward. As long as state appropriations remain a meaningful part of an institution's educational and general (E&G) budget, the volatility of that appropriation means that any plans a college or university makes are speculative. And the fact that colleges and universities are so dependent on people with mobile talents makes life at a state-supported institution as bumpy as the financial roller coaster of state support would indicate. When state resources are flowing, institutions can build new programs, hire very talented faculty and administrators, and increase educational opportunities for their students. When resource flows slow or reverse, programs have to be eliminated, the faculty and administrators the institution most wants to keep may leave, and the educational opportunities for students dry up. The uncertainty the state budget process introduces, combined with the fact that state money often has to be used in one year or it is lost, makes long-range planning difficult. This greatly complicates the institution's problems in maintaining or increasing the quality of its programs. The financial roller-coaster ride of state support thus shortens a state university's planning horizon compared to its private counterparts.

By contrast, an institution's auxiliary enterprises face no such problem. If the college or university sets its own dormitory fees, the school can embark on a multi-year plan to finance renovations of the dormitories and follow that plan precisely. The reason for the difference in planning possibilities between E&G activities and auxiliary enterprise activities is easy to spot. Auxiliary enterprises are entirely funded by fees controlled by the college or university, while the E&G budget is funded by tuition and state appropriation. Universities do not control the state appropriation, and in many cases, they do not control tuition. If an institution has little control over its revenue, it cannot make reliable plans.

As long as tuition payments remain part of the state's revenue, the state can control tuition levels for political reasons. Tuition should be viewed as a price, and it is not usually a good idea to set prices politically. Central control of tuition, through freezes and reductions, is a relatively new phenomenon in our own state of Virginia. And yet in its short history, central control already has created problems. State budget procedures call for institutions to submit a set of new initiatives for possible state funding. If institutions controlled their own tuition, they could plan ahead to ensure that sufficient revenues were available to incorporate any state-funded new initiatives without having to constrain core activities. After tuition was frozen, however, most incremental funding was tied to new initiatives. The result of a few years of this practice is a quite-predictable shortfall in funds needed to carry out the basic mission of the state-supported institutions. In the language used in Virginia, this is called the "base budget adequacy" problem.

This planning problem could be mitigated somewhat if a public institution could save a portion of its state appropriation in a rainy-day fund. But in the usual state budgeting process, money can't be moved easily from one budget year to another. Often there are legal limits on the amount that can be shifted out of any one budget. Some budget officers avoid any savings for fear the state will take these savings for other purposes. Any state agency that reveals it can save has revealed to those who control funding, and revealed to competing agencies, that it apparently can get by on a smaller budget. This creates a use-it or lose-it mentality among state agencies.

This brings us to the first clear incentive effect of direct tuition grants. With direct funding of students, a college or university has no reason to avoid saving since no direct appropriation exists for the state to cut the following year. If savings allow the institution to improve its allocation of E&G expenditures across years, it can store some of its tuition revenue for future needs. The incentive for individual universities to take a longer view is reinforced if the direct tuition grant is system-wide or by tiers of schools. In that case, the state is unlikely to change the size of the grant except for general fiscal reasons. The fact that a few schools in any given year choose to save a portion of their current revenues for future use is unlikely to set off alarm bells in the state capital.

This suggests some political limits on the usefulness of direct-grant proposals. To receive the planning benefits, an institution must be able to set its own tuition, and tuition has to be considered institutional revenue instead of just another line on the revenue side of the state's accounts. The fact that many state legislatures either directly set tuition or put severe constraints on what university boards or regents can do clearly limits the number of state-supported institutions that could easily use this model. This highlights the need to think of these two reform ideas as partners instead of alternatives.

Effects on Fundraising

Another result of direct funding of students is that state-supported institutions would approach fundraising more like private institutions. At present, most state-supported institutions have active private fundraising ventures that augment the school's lobbying activities in the state's capital. Moving to a direct-funding model would make the private fundraising process more effective for these schools.

For instance, when a state-supported college or university president asks for support, potential donors may wonder whether the president is asking them to bail out the state. Successful fundraising may affect a state's future willingness to fund an institution. After all, if an entity has demonstrated that it can rustle up external support, the state may legitimately conclude that it can shift spending at the margin toward worthwhile activities that bring political support, but which do not have the ability to generate their own funding. With all due respect to the difficult task college presidents face in convincing donors that their gifts will not affect the level of state support the college may receive, they are not always convincing, and they are not always correct. States can effectively tax private donations by reducing an institution's annual E&G appropriation. This induces informed donors to be very specific about what their contributions will fund and to steer their donations toward new projects—projects that may be of less use to the university than gifts that would fund ongoing needs. A simple sobering number helps frame this issue. If a school draws 5 percent annually from a $1,000,000 endowment gift, then that gift yields $50,000 per year in revenues. A cut of $50,000 from the annual state appropriation is thus like taxing away $1,000,000 in the college's endowment.

Furthermore, while public college and university presidents currently are selected for their political expertise and reputation in the legislature as much as for their educational leadership abilities, the direct-funding model could change this. Since direct-student-funding proposals usually involve operating expenses only, a public-sector president's ability to lobby the legislature for capital projects would certainly remain important. However, the amount of time a college president and his or her staff would need to spend in the state capital likely would diminish considerably. This is a good thing, since much of this expensive lobbying is a socially unproductive exercise in protecting a university's existing budget from legislators who have other priorities and from other public institutions that might encroach on its share of the higher education pie. This lobbying by institutions diverts a considerable amount of time, effort, and talent from other activities that would contribute more to the school's long-range success.

State Responsibilities

Although the direct-funding model grants more decision-making power to colleges and universities, certain responsibilities should remain with the state. Most importantly, the state must be able to control the number of in-state students attending its public institutions. If states allowed institutions to determine their own size, legislatures would be making open-ended commitments. A state also has a responsibility to provide sufficient funding to maintain the physical plant necessary to accommodate the educational programs at its institutions. For these reasons, there should be binding long-range plans negotiated between the state and each institution that govern the size of the institution. If a plan calls for an increase in the student body, this should be coordinated with a process to increase teaching and research space for the institution.

Another advantage of the direct-funding model is that it allows a state to gain control of the amount of state subsidy for which each student can qualify. Within the current system, an in-state student can receive subsidized tuition for his or her third master's degree. While education is a good thing, there is no particular social need that is served by offering an open-ended subsidy for multiple degrees at a particular level. A state may wish to limit the number of semester hours for which a particular student is eligible to receive a tuition grant. While these limits should be liberal, leaving room for mistakes and experimentation, it is sensible to have limits.

Lastly, we think the direct-funding model should be limited to four-year institutions. These are the schools that have an interest in controlling the size of their enrollment. On the other hand, part of the mission of two-year institutions is to serve as a second chance for students whose high school records do not forecast immediate success in college. Because students mature at different rates or change educational interests after gaining experience, by taking advantage of the education offered at a two-year institution, many students with less-than-stellar high school careers eventually become college graduates. Because of their different mission, two-year institutions should not be selective. By contrast, most four-year institutions should be selective, with spaces reserved for individuals whose high school records or whose prior performance at two-year schools forecast success in selective four-year colleges and universities.

Institutional Accountability

A system of direct student funding gives considerable independence to colleges and universities. For starters, it relieves them of the responsibility to go to the legislature every year to justify an increase in the school's state appropriation. And with control of their own tuition revenues, schools become independent financial entities within their states. Without the government's power of the purse, schools may seem less accountable to elected officials and to the public, but we think this accountability deficit is more apparent than real.

A state and its public higher education institutions often have disputes about size or programming. Within a traditional funding mechanism, schools can play games with a legislature by expanding enrollments and then clamoring for more support because of a decrease in per-student funding. This is the state-level counterpart to the Congressional Squeeze we discussed earlier. On the other side, legislators may think that institutions are not doing their part in advancing the economic development of the state. Legislators may urge universities to initiate or to expand particular programs. The legislative hearing on an institution's state appropriation currently is an important venue for these and similar concerns. A direct-funding model would eliminate these regular hearings and so would appear to diminish legislative control, but this is not as large a concern as it might first seem.

With tuition grants, states would have a direct policy lever with which to influence the size of their public colleges and universities. In consultation with schools, a state would set the number of tuition grants it would fund. Little incentive exists for an institution to admit students without tuition grants, especially if the institution is mandated to meet financial need for state residents. Discussions about the number of tuition grants also provide a collaborative way to address state desires and/or university goals for new or expanded programs.

If a state's governor and legislature have specific programmatic goals that they believe are not currently being met by any of the state's institutions, the state has great power to craft incentives for schools to meet the perceived state need. A state could, for instance, offer to construct and equip a building to house an institute, school, or laboratory if a university commits to developing and staffing the program desired by the state. Competition among a state's universities would help clarify the costs and benefits of various sites for the program. These incentives are fully compatible with the ongoing support provided by a system of direct tuition grants to students.

Accountability often is equated with careful monitoring of spending undertaken by public agencies. State control of public universities typically includes rules that guide the way state money can be spent (i.e., only this much for lunch, never to buy alcohol, and only this much for a hotel room). States often have other oversight rules. On the College of William and Mary campus, we once needed formal state permission to erect a tent. Ten tents required ten separate permissions. For the most part, this external micromanagement is inefficient and redundant. Our proposal for a direct-funding model envisions many of these controls disappearing, since colleges and universities would become financially independent agencies within their state. Instead, colleges and universities should then accept the responsibility of strict post audits.

Clear thinking about what public institutions of higher education are supposed to produce is far more important than micromanaging spending, and less intrusive approaches are more likely to generate better outcomes in this dimension as well. No regulatory apparatus can ensure that talented and motivated students leave a university better trained than when they entered. A state government that adopts a very hands-on approach to managing what universities must do risks politicizing higher education in ways that are unlikely to attract talented faculty and administrators to its public institutions.

A state can enhance institutional accountability by acting as a clearinghouse for information about university performance. This is important, because institutions of higher education operate in a very competitive environment. In most states, a number of public and private institutions compete for students, and public and private institutions in other states provide additional competition. Unlike competition in many industries, the object of this competition is not to expand sales, but to increase the quality of programs. Many advantages accrue to an institution that attracts very able students. This competitive setting provides an important source of accountability. If an institution sees the quality of its student body declining, it receives a strong signal that it should change its behavior.

Fear of Shifting Risk

When we talk to people about the direct-funding model, one common reaction is a fear that risk will be shifted from universities and placed squarely on students and their families. Within the traditional funding scheme, the risk of a shortfall in state revenues is borne by the university. With direct funding, a state's budget shortfall cannot adversely affect an institution's revenue, because institutions do not receive a state appropriation. Students, on the other hand, do receive funds directly from the state in the form of tuition grants. These grants could be cut to help the state deal with a budget shortfall. Since the net tuition to families is list price minus the grant, lower grants mean higher net tuition unless schools choose to lower the list price.

The change here is less real than it may appear. For the most part, the difference is a one- or two-year change in timing. With the traditional funding scheme, when a state budget shortfall occurs, colleges and universities take budget cuts along with other state agencies. Since colleges and universities have the ability to recoup some of any budget reduction by raising tuition, they often face larger budget cuts than most other state agencies. The pattern of large tuition increases following budget shortfalls is evident in almost every state. The result is that the students end up paying in the form of higher tuition. Because institutions are at times unable to change tuition rapidly, these higher tuition payments are likely to be in the years following the actual budget shortfall.

If the state legislature does not allow public colleges and universities to raise tuition, families still bear the risk of budget cuts, but the consequences are measured in reduced quality instead of tuition dollars. In the short run, lower state appropriations mean larger class sizes, fewer courses, deteriorating facilities, and less capable faculties. In the long run, institutions that together form one of the state's important public assets are weakened, and the value of the diplomas those institutions grant are debased.

Two additional factors are worth noting. First, the political nature of a tuition grant would seem quite different from the political nature of a state appropriation to a college or university. Although we have no experience to guide us, tuition grants may end up being so popular that they would take a smaller hit during budget shortfalls than appropriations to state-supported colleges and universities traditionally do. If true, this would moderate the increase in net tuition that students usually experience during times of state budget duress.

Second, the direct-funding model dramatically changes the relationship between recessions and the list tuition charged by state-supported institutions. With the direct-funding model, no reason exists for large tuition increases to accompany recessions. If a state is forced to reduce the tuition grant, institutions may well respond by moderating tuition increases. Because a school realizes that its competitive position depends in part on its net tuition, if the net tuition is increasing because of a cut in the tuition grant, the institution has an incentive to reduce any planned tuition increase. Some institutions actually may choose to decrease list tuition during a recession.

Financial Aid Incentives

Most state legislatures currently face a tradeoff between funding institutions and funding financial aid for needy or talented students. Some portion of the state allocation for higher education already goes to students as financial aid, though the bulk of it is appropriated for colleges and universities. Within the direct-funding model, the moneys that currently are directly allocated to colleges and universities are redeployed as across-the-board tuition grants. States could opt instead to enrich their aid budgets and do away with the entire across-the-board component. In an important sense, the states face a choice that bears a strong resemblance to the one faced by the federal government as it ponders aid reform. And the tuition-grant component of our "New Compact" idea is an extension of the financial aid discussion in the last chapter.

Across-the-board tuition grants are simple to understand, and that improves the likelihood that college-qualified high school students will have the incentive to embrace a college-preparatory curriculum and that they will begin the process of applying to universities. Getting these students into the application pipeline is the easiest way to increase attendance rates and completion rates within the state's public higher education system. And political support for the grant program is likely to be much stronger the wider the program's reach. If college grants are seen as just another anti-poverty program, they are less likely to elicit wide and deep political support. On the other hand, these across-the-board grants are not well targeted. The rich receive them as well as the poor. Therefore the program is more expensive than an alternative that targets access among the groups in the population that cannot easily afford high-quality undergraduate training. The state winds up paying families whose children could have attended any institution they pleased.

States have always subsidized their resident students using across-the-board grants. This is why in-state students face a lower list price than non-residents. Our "New Compact" makes this discount explicit instead of implicit. Once the discount is made explicit, states will face a similar tradeoff between simplicity and targeting that the federal government faces in determining how to allocate its financial aid.

As a general rule, college and university presidents favor a well-funded state financial aid system. Yet a college president may very well oppose increased financial aid funding if that extra aid money comes at the expense of funding for his or her institution. A direct system of tuition grants changes the incentives. Because the college or university has no state appropriation to protect, its leadership can support increases in funding for the state financial aid system. This is true whether that aid is need-based or offered as across-the-board tuition grants. Their support for increased financial aid might well be the case even if the increased aid is financed by decreases in the size of across-the-board tuition grants. For universities that control their tuition revenue, cuts in the tuition grant don't change the school's revenue the way that cuts to E&G appropriations do today. In this regard, it is perfectly sensible for the schools themselves to favor increased need-based financial aid as well as increased across-the-board tuition grants. Nonetheless, there is a strong argument for across-the-board tuition grants based on the virtues of extreme simplicity and the broad political support that comes from universality.

The Road Ahead

Our New Compact proposal got good hearing at the college, and leaders in state government read it as well. Yet ultimately the proposal didn't bear fruit. The reasons are many. First we have the often-told frog story used quite recently in James Garland's *Saving Alma Mater*.Toss a frog into hot water and it will immediately jump out. If you put it into tepid water and slowly turn up the heat, the creature may allow itself to be cooked. This is an apocryphal tale, to be sure, but one that captures the essence of what has happened to public universities over the last forty years. The public role in financing a student's education has moved downward repeatedly in sudden budget-crisis induced jerks. Each jolt by itself is not enough to kill the university, and after each shock there is some time to adjust and accommodate. After several shocks, however, the environment becomes hostile enough that quality is degraded in increasingly obvious ways. If you had told administrators in 1980 that the percentage of their educational costs the state would cover in 2009 would be less than half of the percentage covered in 1980, many of them might have looked for the exits immediately.

Yet reform efforts often lack the support of the two groups most needed for any meaningful change, first the public officials who control decision making, and then the universities who would supposedly benefit! For governors and state legislators, influence over higher education institutions is one source of their power. Relinquishing that power is a cost to them. The benefits of reform are an abstraction in comparison to the immediate reduction in the scope of their authority. This is why we have attempted to enumerate the specific benefits to the state of letting go, in a sense, of the levers of control traditionally used to fund and to regulate public higher education institutions.

Reluctance from the schools themselves may seem at first glance like more of a puzzle. But like many large bureaucratic organizations, public universities tend to be conservative in their outlook. They are run and managed mostly by people whose careers and ideas have been formed within the system. College presidents and their governing boards look to state capitals and to state legislators as their key interlocutors and as their primary pillar of support. This is a description, not a criticism. But given this orientation, we should not be surprised that many thoughtful people see the decline in the financial relevance of the state as primarily a political failure. Politics has lost higher education its place in the fiscal hierarchy of importance, and so the answer is to find better arguments to persuade elected officials to restore our vital public institutions to their prior place at the fiscal table. This notion that better politics can restore what worse politics has taken away is one of the fundamental and enduring stumbling blocks to meaningful reform. We do not see any reasonable prospect that the halcyon days of high state effort and low list-price tuition could return.

Even so, for most public universities the tug of the status quo remains powerful. The public umbilical remains a vital part of their self-definition even if not of their revenue base, and short of fiscal catastrophe, most are too risk averse to chance a move to genuine fiscal independence from the state. Yet the de facto privatization of public universities has proceeded apace, and the time has come for people to think meaningfully about paradigm shifts in our industry. Proposals like our New Compact are meant to stimulate a reasoned discussion of alternatives that go beyond tinkering at the margins. A great number of state-specific details would need to be worked out before an actual proposal to decouple public colleges and universities from the state appropriation process could be put in front of a state legislature. However, the benefits of doing so should prompt those involved to determine how such a system would best work with their state's existing institutions and history. Any resulting proposal likely would contain flaws and compromises. Still, a system of direct tuition grants paired with functionally independent state-allied institutions need not be perfect. It just needs to be better than the existing system. We think it could be a whole lot better.

16

A Few Final Observations

Is our higher education system in an end-stage crisis of its own making? After working diligently through the prior fifteen chapters, you know that we are skeptical of apocalyptic claims about a crisis in higher education and a collapse of opportunity for the next generation. Yet this is the sort of talk that permeates current discussion of our higher education system. In telling the story of how cost and price have evolved over the last sixty years, we have adopted an aerial view of this important industry. Our storyline has emphasized slow processes that operate broadly in the entire economy. These forces have an impact on everyone and on all industries. Our holistic view of higher education fits it into the wider economic history of the nation rather than holding the industry under the microscope for closer inspection. Our approach naturally focuses attention on more impersonal things, like changing technology and the economic returns to schooling, and less on particular deficiencies in the higher education market and bad decision making within colleges and universities.

Our approach also informs the policy recommendations we have made. We have joined forces with others who have advanced some very ambitious suggestions for reforming the financial aid system and for transforming the relationship between state governments and their public four-year colleges and universities. A simplified universal aid plan is a radical departure from the current complex targeted aid process, and the proposal to switch state funding away from universities and toward students is an equally audacious departure from the status quo. Yet as ambitious as these ideas may be, they are also very modest in scope. The reason is that they too are rooted in our aerial view of the higher education landscape. Our aerial view narrows the range of policy options because it reduces the root causes of higher education's apparent "problems" to things that are more difficult to control or to affect with public policy. In plain language, our understanding of the higher education landscape is devoid of bad guys to slap down.

Thus we will take our leave after offering you the reader two final thoughts. The first is that a productive approach to solving the problems of higher education facing twenty-first-century America requires a ratcheting down of the rhetoric. The second is that we need to fix what *can* be fixed. These two observations clearly are related. Overheated rhetoric about the supposed ills of higher education often leads to counterproductive policy ideas that confuse symptoms with causes and which overestimate what government can do.

Ratchet Down the Rhetoric

With the exception of the 1970s, over the past sixty years college cost and tuition charges generally have increased faster than the overall inflation rate in the economy. This is a plain fact that is not in dispute. We recognize that the causes and consequences of this basic fact are the subject of much debate. Some people are inclined to use phrases like "cost crisis" or "affordability crisis" in describing the consequences of this fact. This crisis sentiment winds up generating titles like "Our Greedy Colleges," *The University in Ruins*, and *Going Broke By Degree*. Rising cost is a problem and someone must be to blame. Yet nothing that we have found suggests to us that the word "crisis" should be used. This inflammatory rhetoric is neither warranted nor helpful. College costs are rising, but they are not spiraling out of control. Increasing numbers of young people have sought and obtained postsecondary training even as cost and tuition have increased. And as we saw in chapter 12, amid the affordability problems that we do indeed face, over the broad course of time, college has become more affordable for a student from the median-income household.

The reasons for overheated rhetoric are many. Some stem from simple confusion. Newspapers often publish increases in list-price tuition without factoring in the aid that the vast majority of students receive from outside sources and from tuition discounting by schools themselves. Articles that focus on tuition at the most expensive schools are counterproductive as well. Very few students attend elite schools that sport a stratospheric list price, and few of those that do actually pay the full list-price tuition. This set of schools is quite an unrepresentative sample of where most people earn a degree. Allegorical tales of higher education's woes woven from the experiences of Harvard or Bard give us a false idea of the real problems that need to be solved in order to improve the delivery of higher education services to a greater fraction of the American population than we serve today.

Simple confusion is not the only reason for overheated rhetoric. In this book, we have argued that more fundamental misunderstandings of the causes of rising cost contribute greatly to the climate of anger and recrimination that permeates the politics of higher education. In chapters 3 through 5, we constructed a three-legged stool that we think firmly supports our story of why costs in higher education rise more rapidly than inflation. Each leg of the stool outlines a reason why technological forces have an effect on higher education costs and on the costs of a set of similar industries.

We don't need to repeat the case here. Instead we will leave you with two observations about these fundamental factors. First, in the main the technological gains that have rippled through the economy, and which have tended to push up college costs as a by-product, are not malignant forces. Cost disease, for instance, is caused by the massive increase in labor productivity in manufacturing that has transformed living standards over the last century. In other words, the increased labor productivity at the national level pays the larger college bill that cost disease indirectly generates. And second, where the effect of these technological forces is potentially undesirable—such as the widening income gap between those with more education and those with less—there is very little that a public policy directed at supposed inefficiencies in higher education can do about it.

By contrast, much of the current commentary on higher education puts the industry under a microscope to examine it in fine detail. This view tends to magnify flaws and it misses common factors that link higher education to broader forces at work in the economy. We have called this view the "new orthodoxy" and the "dysfunctionality narrative." In this view, prestige games, gold plating and other socially wasteful practices are endemic in American universities, and the problem is growing over time. In chapter 7, we lay out this view in some detail. Our aerial view suggests that the features uncovered by the close-up view are not the driving engine of college cost. There are indeed inefficiencies and incentive problems in higher education, as there are in many firms and industries, but stories that presume increasingly pathological inefficiency within the higher education industry do not do a very good job of explaining the evidence. If we are correct, this is hopeful. Perhaps we can begin to move away from shrill rhetoric and finger pointing and toward meaningful solutions to the real problems that exist.

Fix What Can Be Fixed

In November of 2009, a CEO summit convened by the *Wall Street Journal* pegged education as one of the most critical issues facing the United States today.[1] The summary of the report concludes that "[e]ducation is an urgent national priority—well ahead of health care, climate change and financial regulatory reform—and government and business policies need to reflect that. If we don't address this, we endanger our children, economy, businesses and national security." While the Obama administration may not be in full agreement with the prioritization, it apparently agrees with the urgency. On the education portion of the White House webpage one could read,

> The President believes that regardless of educational path after high school, all Americans should be prepared to enroll in at least one year of higher education or job training to better prepare our workforce for a 21st century economy. To accomplish these overarching goals, the President is committed to increasing higher education access and success by restructuring and dramatically expanding college financial aid, while making federal programs simpler, more reliable, and more efficient for students.

If the Obama administration and the *Wall Street Journal's* collected CEOs can share a perspective, then the middle ground seems wide enough to forge productive alliances for policy reform.

While we think it is unproductive to talk about a cost *crisis* or an affordability *crisis*, a university education is indeed becoming less affordable for people at the bottom of the income distribution, and far too many high school students who could succeed at some form of post-secondary education fail to enter the higher education track. The percentage of our young people who are acquiring the skills that a higher education provides is stagnant, and it is falling behind both demand and the achievement rates of many other nations. The current generation may be the first in U.S. history to have less economic opportunity on average than did their parents. For anyone who buys into the goals expressed by the CEOs or the Obama administration, this is clearly a problem.

Affordability problems clearly reflect the combination of rising tuition (price) and falling or stagnant incomes. You did not need to read this book to understand that claim. One major cause of this affordability problem is the stretching of the income distribution that has increased income inequality so significantly since the 1970s. This has happened in large part because the economic returns to acquiring extra years of schooling have increased. As we stressed in chapter 4, broad economic forces are behind this trend. The growing income disparity between college degree holders and the less well educated is driven by the race between technology and educational attainment. Technological factors that raise the demand for skill have outraced educational attainment since the late 1970s.

Since colleges and universities rely on a highly educated workforce, the same technological processes that have pushed up the returns to education also have forced up higher education costs. What we hope reading the book has shown you is that changes in the distribution of income and the fact that college costs are rising are *not* two completely separate trends. One of the major underlying forces that has depressed income growth among the less educated, and these are the people who are experiencing affordability problems, is also a force pushing up costs and eventually prices at colleges and universities. Again, this is not a sudden or immediate crisis. It is a deep-seated and slow-moving process. Our society would be healthier if we could reverse the affordability problems that this process has spawned.

How best can we accomplish this? First, don't try to fix the unfixable. We have no magic policy bullet that will change the way that technological innovation and high levels of educational attainment currently interact. Technology-skill complementarity has been a factor in the economic landscape for over a century, and there is no evidence that this fact is about to change. Our focus should be on educational attainment. We need to address the high dropout rates in high schools. We need to ensure that more high school students take the requisite curriculum to succeed in college. And we need to address the fact that most of the people who begin some form of college program don't finish. The hollowing out of the middle class was not inevitable, and it need not be permanent. We need to set a national priority to increase educational attainment and to identify policies that will promote this goal effectively and efficiently.

Increasing educational attainment requires better performance out of our K–12 programs as well as from colleges and universities. We have focused our attention on higher education because it is what we have studied, not because it is necessarily more important. There are two changes needed in higher education. First, students have to be convinced that an education beyond high school is academically attainable and desirable. To do this, colleges and universities have to have sufficient resources to provide the classes and the support systems required for a larger percentage of students to thrive in college. Second, we have to make it financially possible for students to obtain that higher education without imposing an unsustainable financial burden on them or their families. This is the motivation for the two reform proposals we have outlined in this book.

Our nation's community colleges solve part of these two problems quite well. Community colleges are almost all open-enrollment institutions, so students, even students who were not very successful in high school, can take advantage of a community college education. And the education is available at low cost. Our analysis in chapter 12 showed that no matter how one measures the change in affordability between 1990–92 and 2003–5, public two-year institutions have become more affordable for students from families at all parts of the income distribution. Also, these institutions focus much of their curriculum on job-related skills. All students should know that a community college education is a real possibility for them.

Community college systems do labor under some handicaps. First, they are clearly a distant second in prestige, and this stigma may reduce the number of students who take advantage of their programming. Second, their costs are subject to the same pressures that drive up costs at four-year schools. Third, they often have the least political clout among the colleges and universities in a state, and this means they often are underfunded relative to their mission. Fourth, because they will take anyone and everyone, these institutions have to spend a considerable amount of time and effort in remediation. Fifth, many of their students are part-time students with full-time jobs. Often, these students find it difficult to fit their education around job and family responsibilities. One of the advantages of reforming the financial aid system is that a simpler and more generous aid process should make students less likely to postpone their education so late that other entanglements make it difficult for them to complete a degree.

Now let us turn to four-year schools. Before we get to the problems, we have to recognize that the current system offers many advantages. First, the options are quite diverse. There are all sorts of colleges and universities: public and private, small and large, church-related and non-church-related, research-intensive institutions and programs that specialize in intensive faculty-student relationships, and ones with very competitive admissions and ones that are less competitive. This is a real strength of the U.S. higher education system. Second, by almost any measure, the top tier of U.S. colleges and universities contains some of the very best institutions in the world. Students from all over the world flock to U.S. universities, and this is particularly true for the opportunity to do graduate work. Highly talented professors, again from all over the world, are attracted to faculty positions in U.S. colleges and universities. The U.S. higher education system is a magnet that attracts talented people to the country. Third, the research conducted at colleges and universities in the U.S. has been critical to the economic development of the country. Research universities undertake most of the basic research that advances the frontier of knowledge, and this makes the research done by corporations that much more productive. Fourth, a college or university experience often provides a bridge between living with one's parents and living in the world on one's own. There are benefits from gaining independence in steps, and traditional colleges and universities provide one important step. Finally, colleges and universities provide a wide array of public service, cultural, and entertainment activities whose importance extends well beyond the confines of the campus.

While there is much to admire about colleges and universities in the United States, all is not well. Providing a high-quality four-year education is quite expensive. There are two parts of this problem: the costs themselves and the choice of who pays for it. Regarding costs, as we discussed in chapter 8, the jury is still out on whether or not distance learning is a technological fix that can provide a way to deliver high-quality higher education at lower costs. In most situations, high-quality higher education still requires face-to-face interactions in relatively small groups led by teacher/scholars. Economizing on labor input has many undesirable consequences. And the highly educated people needed to provide the service have other options. If salaries in higher education do not keep up, talented people will move elsewhere and less qualified people will take their place. This cost-disease process is one of the important reasons that costs have risen in the past and are likely to continue rising for the foreseeable future. This is not something we can fix, nor should we want to. Also, a modern education has to stay on the technological frontier, and this takes expensive equipment and facilities as well as the talented people who manage them. The cost problem is a difficult problem. There are no quick fixes other than ones that diminish quality.

If college costs will continue to rise, someone is going to have to pay them. The costs are divided among students and their families, private donors, state governments, and the federal government. Nothing is going to change here. These four will be the entities that will share the costs in the future. We have not tried to argue that one or the other of the four payers should pay a larger share of the costs. This is a thorny issue that is likely to lead us into unproductive arguments. Let us just say that all four have reasons to play their part.

The rationale for students and their families to contribute to the cost of higher education is fairly clear. They are the ones who benefit the most. The rationale for government support of higher education is to create a productive educated citizenry. The nation as a whole benefits if the pace of innovation and economic growth is enhanced when a larger percentage of its citizens take advantage of the opportunities offered by the higher education sector. The nation as a whole also may benefit from the effects of equalizing opportunity. Without any government role in funding higher education, college-going and college-completion rates would be lower than is desirable. Given this, the citizenry at large as represented by the government has a significant interest in paying some of the bill. Our recommendations about how the government should do its part focus on the *way* these payments can lead to the desired objectives. The government part of the payment should be made in a way that encourages college attendance and college completion.

Unfortunately, government support of higher education is not as effective as it might be because much of the support is hidden behind layers of complexity. We have argued that the portion of the costs paid by the government should be paid in a much more transparent way. At present, state government subsidies come in the form of lowered in-state tuition, while federal subsidies to students are individual grants that require families to navigate a lengthy and complex bureaucratic process to determine their eligibility. If you add in government research grants of various sources, taxpayers actually pay quite a bit of the bill. But because of the complex and often opaque processes by which the payments are distributed, much of the government support is difficult to see. Therefore the incentives are not always right.

Our proposal in chapter 15 to redirect state subsidies away from schools and into direct tuition grants to students was motivated in part by the idea that hidden subsidies are less effective than transparent ones. The discussion in chapter 14 of the current efforts to reform federal financial aid by simplifying the eligibility process, as well as the more radical suggestion to turn Pell Grants into an entitlement, are both attempts to overcome the fact that not enough students utilize the federal financial aid system. If we can find a way of simplifying the delivery of federal financial aid, the aid will be more effective at increasing attendance and completion. The college-going and college-completion rates of students from well-to-do families already are quite high. This follows in large part because these students know from a very early age that funds will be available for them to go to college, and they are expected to go to college. With their parents' help they prepare themselves, and this usually leads them to and through college. Children from less-well-to-do families do not have the same expectations. They do not expect to go to college, and in many cases their behaviors live up to the expectation. There are many cultural issues and other factors that reinforce behaviors that make college going a remote possibility for many of these children. Fixing the financial aid system will not fix everything. Yet there is a growing body of evidence that if students and their parents know from the very start that the government is going to cover a meaningfully large part of the bill for a college education, then reaching for a college degree becomes a real possibility for many more students.

The Last Word

Encouraging a greater fraction of the American population to seek out and to complete degree programs past high school should be a national priority. Two arguments for this are well known. Education and innovation are related, and innovation is a key to rising living standards. Second, educational opportunity is important for social mobility. We have added a third idea. Raising educational achievement in the United States can help to stop or reverse the process that has led to the hollowing out of the middle class. To achieve this, we should be ready to increase total spending on higher education as long as the process by which these resources are dispersed is transparent and sends the message to families that achieving a higher education is within their grasp. Federal financial aid policy can be reformed so that it does its job better.

Lastly, most students attend public institutions so the availability of good-quality public education is critical to achieving a good outcome from increasing the numbers of students who attend these schools. The funding base of public institutions has been under budget pressure for the last thirty years. Ultimately, the quality of our public higher education institutions is at stake. We have suggested ways to reform the financial relationship between states and their four-year colleges and universities. States should fund students directly instead of sending appropriations to schools, and schools should be given ownership of their revenue base. Both of these changes should produce very salutary incentives for all parties, including the state.

Unfortunately, if we do not attend to these problems this year or next year, we will still get by. College costs are rising rapidly because they are driven by strong underlying economic trends. Some of these trends can be reversed, but doing so will require a concerted policy effort over a long time. We wish we could use the word "crisis" in good conscience. If there really were a crisis, it could more easily focus attention on the things that must be fixed.

Appendix 1

Data on Costs and Prices

We are telling a story about college cost, so ideally we should have clear data on college cost to use in the story. The broadest measure of costs calculated for the entire higher education sector over a long time span is called "Education and General Expenses," or E&G for short. These expenses cover the bulk of the costs involved in the academic side of what colleges and universities do, including the costs of instruction, research, public service, academic support (which includes things like libraries), institutional support (which includes most administrative costs), student services (such as the admissions office or the registrar), maintenance and operations (which includes buildings and grounds), and scholarships and fellowships. Unfortunately, the data on E&G expenses are only available every other year until 1965, and the data series ends in 1995. The series stops in 1995 because the Department of Education changed the definitions of some of the variables, and the later information cannot be compared to earlier data. On the other hand, data for higher education prices (tuition and fees) are available annually from 1947 on a continuing basis.

Here is the problem. Our objective is to explain what has happened to higher education *costs*, but the most comprehensive data source covers higher education *prices* instead. Prices and costs are not the same in higher education because of the subsidies available from government support and from endowment income. If patterns of subsidization change, then price and cost do not have to move together. This is an important issue, and we will explore the role of subsidization in detail in Part III of the book.

In addition, although E&G expenses represent the most important costs covered by tuition and fees, they do not represent all of the costs. Some activities classified as auxiliary services, which are excluded from E&G expenses, are covered by mandatory fees. Auxiliary services are the self-supporting operations of the institution that provide a service to students or faculty and that charge a fee that is directly related to what they provide. Auxiliary services include things like residence halls and food services, student health facilities, parking services, and intercollegiate athletics (if not self-supporting). The auxiliary services covered by mandatory fees, such as student health facilities, student counseling services, and intramural sports, are included in tuition and fees but are not part of E&G costs.

The bottom line of this discussion is that we would prefer to have a more complete set of cost data, one that includes the parts of auxiliary services covered by mandatory fees. Unfortunately, the available cost data are incomplete, both in what they cover and the time period they cover. Yet all is not lost. We may be able to use the more comprehensive price data to build our facts about higher education. We have to make

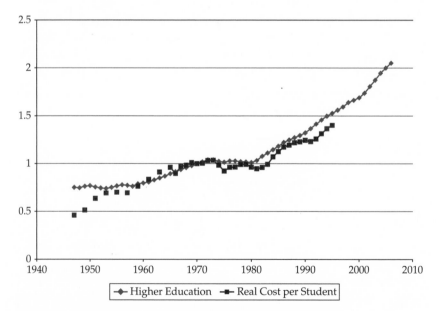

Appendix 1 Figure 1 A Comparison of the Real Cost of Higher Education and Real Higher Education Prices, (1970=1)

two assumptions to use these data. First, we have to assume that E&G costs behave similarly to the costs of auxiliary services covered by mandatory fees. Second, we have to assume that the price series follows the same basic path as E&G costs. There is no way to check the validity of the first assumption, but we can take a look at the available evidence for the second assumption.

Appendix 1 figure 1 compares the behavior of costs and prices. It clearly shows us that prices and costs do not behave identically over the time period of overlap, yet the behavior is broadly similar. Costs rose more rapidly than prices in the early years, but starting in the late 1950s, the two time series behave very similarly. Both series are rising through the late 1960s and both flatten out during the 1970s. Both series then start to rise again quite strongly in the 1980s. So, although the details of each series do differ, they share a basic pattern. Since our analysis does not require us to make fine comparisons, we think the similarity of the two series provides sufficient justification for us to say that the price series that we use in the analysis represents the basic behavior of both prices and costs.

Appendix 2

Granger Causality Tests of the Bennett Hypothesis

This appendix presents the results of our test of the Bennett Hypothesis. This causality test, first proposed by Clive Granger in 1969, is based on time-series evidence. Basically, the question is whether or not lagged information on a variable X provides any statistically significant information about a variable Y given the lagged values of Y. If the lagged values of the X variables do provide statistically significant information, it is said that "X Granger-causes Y." In our case, the X variable is the first difference of (or change in) the Authorized Maximum Pell Grant (PellFD) and the Y variable is the first difference of average published tuition at private four-year institutions (PrivFD). Data come from the 2008 editions of *Trends in Student Pricing* and *Trends in Student Aid* published by the College Board. The data are available for the 1973–74 academic year to the 2007–8 academic year. Since we measure the variables in first differences and include lagged values, our estimated equations do not cover the full time span.

The table contains the results for equations containing one, two, three, and four lags. The t-statistics for the estimated coefficients are included in parentheses. We have included the F-test for the joint significance of the coefficients of the various lagged values of the PellFD variables below the estimated equations. These tests confirm that changes in

Appendix 2 Table 1   Regression Results (t-statistics in parentheses)

Coefficients	Equations			
	(1)	(2)	(3)	(4)
PrivFDL1	−.1913	−.2579	−4.118	−.3634
	(0.99)	(1.37)	(1.89)	(1.53)
PrivFDL2		−.0178	−.0389	.0374
		(0.09)	(0.18)	(0.14)
PrivFDL3			.1494	.1393
			(0.76)	(0.63)
PrivFDL4				−.0769
				(0.37)
PellFDL1	−.2079	−.1798	−.2249	−.1917
	(1.12)	(1.06)	(1.29)	(0.99)
PellFDL2		−.5151	−.5212	−.5000
		(2.96)	(2.96)	(2.69)
PellFDL3			−.2845	−.2615
			(1.39)	(1.20)
PellFDL4				.2045
				(0.87)
Time	34.3985	38.5852	40.9854	37.0153
	(5.56)	(4.37)	(3.30)	(2.19)
Constant	181.74	226.06	254.54	2.65.20
	(2.57)	(2.91)	(2.68)	(2.23)
R^2	0.74	0.79	0.71	0.80
Granger F		5.16	3.98	3.26
	Prob > F	0.01	0.02	0.03

the authorized Pell Grant maximum Granger-cause changes in tuition at private four-year institutions. Since all but one of the coefficients on the PellFD variables are negative, our result is that larger changes in Pell Grants cause decreases in tuition changes. This is exactly the opposite of the prediction made by Secretary Bennett. For Secretary Bennett's prediction to be correct, all of the signs on the coefficients on the PellFD variables would have had to be positive.

We conducted the same analysis for average published tuition at four-year public institutions. These tests are inconsistent with Granger-causality. The comparable F statistics for 2, 3, and 4 lags are: 0.33 (Prob > F = 0.72), 0.35 (Prob > F = 0.79), and 0.98 (Prob > F = 0.44). Not only are the estimates of the effects of changes in Pell Grants maxima on public tuition statistically imprecise, they are much smaller than the coefficients for private universities. We can conclude that changes in the Pell Grant maximum have no effect on changes in public tuition.

Our results are not encouraging for the conjecture known as the Bennett Hypothesis. We find no such effect for public universities, and we find the exact opposite effect for private universities. This opposite effect for private institutions does not surprise us. These institutions are the ones most heavily engaged in tuition discounting. And, as we suggested in the text, additional funding of federal financial aid allow an institution to reduce tuition discounting. This allows the institution to pass some of the benefits to its existing students in the form of lower tuition. Far from being the greedy colleges that Bennett envisioned, these institutions set tuition with two things in mind: doing the best job of expanding knowledge they can and providing an education to the best set of students they can attract. When the federal government increases financial aid, this reduces the pressure on tuition that previously existed because some of the best students the institution could attract had demonstrated financial need.

Notes

Part I

We would like to thank John McPherson for giving us permission to reprint his *Close to Home* cartoon.

Chapter 1

The quotation is from Boehner and McKeon (2003, 1).

1. The data for the College of William and Mary come from college catalogs.

2. Data for tuition and fees for public and private four-year institutions come from *Trends in College Pricing* 2008 published by the College Board.

3. For an example of public opinion surveys, see Ikenberry and Hartle (1998).

4. Gross Domestic Product data for figure 1.1 come from the Bureau of Economic Analysis. Data for tuition and fees at public universities come from table 320 of the 2007 *Digest of Educational Statistics*. These data are deflated by the Consumer Price Index.

5. Both the quotations from *The College Cost Crisis* are from page 2.

6. The quotation from Breneman (2001, 13).

Chapter 2

1. The data for prices we use extensively in the figures in this chapter can be found in table 2.4.4 on the Bureau of Economic Analysis website.

2. We make a much more technical presentation and detailed analysis of the data for industries whose price behavior is similar to higher education in Archibald and Feldman (2008).

3. The Motley Fool interview can be found at http://www.fool.com/investing/general/2009/10/29/why-does-college-cost-so-much.aspx?source=ihpsitmpa0000001. See Archibald and Feldman (2009) for the *Alumni Magazine* article.

4. The quotation is from Lewis and Dundar (2001, 172).

Chapter 3

1. The quotation is from Ricardo (1821, chapter 7, paragraph 35).

2. The quotation is from Baumol (1967, 416).

3. Baumol made the connection between cost disease and higher education. See Baumol and Blackman (1995).

4. Apparently, in 1897 a cousin of Mark Twain's (James Ross Clemens) was seriously ill, and though the relative eventually recovered, the story got around that it was Mark Twain who was ill and that he eventually died. Mr. Twain enjoyed setting people straight.

5. The quotation is from Triplett and Bosworth (2004, 17).

Chapter 4

1. The data for table 4.1 were taken from the EU KLEMS website. Workers are classified as either high skilled, medium skilled, or low skilled.

2. The data for table 4.2 were taken from the Bureau of Labor Statistics Occupational Employment Statistics website.

3. See Goldin and Katz (2008, 84) for the data for figure 4.1.

4. The data for figure 4.2 come from the Economic Policy Institute Datazone.

5. See Binfield (2004) for a detailed history of the Luddites.

6. Figure 4.3 repeats figure 1.4 in Goldin and Katz (2008, 20). It gives the average years of schooling achieved by each birth cohort by age 35. In other words, the 1950 birth cohort had reached an average of 13.6 years of schooling by 1985. Since most of that total is completed well before age 35, the turning point for the labor force as a whole likely occurred in the late 1970s. We would like to thank Claudia Goldin for providing these data and Harvard University Press for allowing us to include this figure.

7. Figure 4.4 repeats figure 7.1 in Goldin and Katz (2008, 249). Again we would like to thank Claudia Goldin for providing these data and Harvard University Press for allowing us to include this figure.

Chapter 5

1. In figures 5.1 and 5.2, the data for higher education come from the *Digest of Educational Statistics* 2005 (table 350). The higher education data ends in 1994, and we matched the other data to that ending point. The data for the other industries come from the U.S. Department of Commerce's Bureau of Economic Analysis data on Net Capital Stock of Private Non-Residential Fixed Assets. To construct real values, we used price indexes from the BEA on non-residential structures to crease a time series for buildings and on equipment and software to create a time series for equipment.

2. The data for the stock of computers come from the U.S. Department of Commerce's Bureau of Economic Analysis data on Private Fixed Assets by Type.

3. For figure 5.3, the data for all three years for higher education come from the *Digest of Educational Statistics* 2005 (table 222). The data for health care less hospitals and legal services for 1978 come from Bureau of Labor Statistics (1981). The data for hospitals come from, Bureau of Labor Statistics (1984), and data for 2004 come from the Bureau of Labor Statistics website (http://bls/oes/current/oessrci.htm).

4. The quotation of Michael Brostek is in Fletcher (2000, A33).

5. Estimates of multifactor productivity in Triplett and Bosworth (2004, 19) show that productivity in health services declined by 0.5 percent from 1995 to 2001 and productivity in educational services declined 0.8 percent over the same time period.

6. The quotation is from Fong (2005, 44).

7. The titles of a number of these books on higher education are revealing; for example, see D'Souza, *Illiberal Education: The Politics of Race and Sex on Campus* (1991); Readings, *The University in Ruins* (1990); Wilshire, *The Moral Collapse of the University: Professionalism, Purity, and Alienation* (1990); Kimball, *Tenured Radicals: How Politics Has Corrupted Higher Education* (1990); Shaw, *The War Against the Intellect: Episodes in the Decline of Discourse* (1989); Anderson, *Imposter in the Temple: American Intellectuals Are Destroying Our Universities and Cheating Our Students of their Future* (1992); P. Smith, *Killing the Spirit: Higher Education in America* (1990); Hersh and Merrow, eds., *Declining by Degrees: Higher Education at Risk* (2005); and Massy, *Honoring the Trust: Quality and Cost Containment in Higher Education* (2003).

8. The quotation is from Bok (2006, 29).

9. We gathered data for thirty-seven institutions in the same tier of the 2000 *U.S. News and World Report* rankings as St. John's. Between 1996 and 2007, the increase in spending on instruction per student at St. John's Annapolis campus was the fourth fastest, and the increase in spending per student at St. John's Santa Fe campus was eleventh fastest. On average, instruction spending per full time equivalent student increased 1.53 times at the thirty-seven institutions. The comparable figure for St. John's (Annapolis) was 1.97 and for St. John's (Santa Fe) it was 1.66. Data come from the Integrated Post-Secondary Data System of the Department of Education.

Chapter 6

1. The productivity growth figures come from the Bureau of Labor Statistics, "Superseded Historical SIC Measures for Manufacturing, Durable Manufacturing, and Nondurable Manufacturing Sectors, 1949–2003."

2. The faculty salary data are in Kane (1999, 75).

3. The data for the weights for the price index come from "Table 2.4.5—Personal Consumption Expenditure by Type of Product" and "Table 2.4.4—Price Indexes for Personal Consumption Expenditure by Type of Product" on the Bureau of Economic Analysis website. The industries included in the special index were: 1. Physicians, 2. Dentists, 3. Other Professional Services, 4. Hospitals and Nursing Homes, 5. Bank Service Charges, Trust Services, and Safe Deposit Box Rental, 6. Services Furnished Without Payment by Financial Intermediaries Except Life Insurance Carriers, 7. Expense of Handling Life Insurance and Pension Plans, 8. Legal Services, 9. Nursery, Elementary, and Secondary Schools, 10. Other Educational Services, and 11. Religious and Welfare Activities.

Chapter 7

1. The quotation is from Winston (2000, 2).

2. See Zemsky, Wegner, and Massy (2005, 34) for the use of "mutually assured destruction."

3. The quotation is from Zemsky, Wenger, and Massy (2005, 23).

4. The data for the percent of employment classified as executive and administrative/managerial come from the *Digest of Educational Statistics* 2006, table 222.

5. The quotation is from Bowen (1980, 19).

6. The probabilities in this example are calculated using the hypergeometric distribution.

7. In table 7.1, the data for the for-profit institutions come from the IPEDS database. The nonprofit-sector data was for tuition and fees from the College Board's *Trends in College Pricing* 2007 (table 3a).

8. The source of the data in figure 7.2 is the *Digest of Educational Statistics* 2007, table 346. The data series begins in the 1971–72 academic year and goes through 2001–2. Current fund expenditures include basically everything that schools spend that is not part of the capital budget.

9. The data for figure 7.3 come from the *Digest of Educational Statistics* 2006, table 320.

10. Ehrenberg's data suggest that advertising expenses amount to 5 to 10 percent of gross revenue from first-year students. If each college class had the same size, we could just divide these figures by four to determine advertising-to-sales ratios of 1.25 percent to 2.5 percent. Since sophomore, junior, and senior classes tend to be smaller than freshman classes, we adjusted our estimates.

11. The source for the data on advertising-to-sales ratios is Waldman and Jensen (2006).

Chapter 8

1. The data on the percentage of instructional faculty who are full-time come from *Digest of Educational Statistics* 2008, table 248.

2. The quotation is from Vedder (2004, xv–xvi).

3. It is easy to find listings of online institutions, for example, the Distance-Learning College Guide can be found at http://www.distance-learning-college-guide.com/online-bachelor-degrees.html (accessed August 5, 2009).

4. The survey is reported in Allen and Seaman (2008). For this survey, an online course is defined as one in which at least 80 percent of the course content is delivered online.

5. The faculty survey results are reported in Seaman (2009).

6. The "Evaluation of Evidence-Based Practices in Online Learning: A Meta-Analysis and Review of Online Learning Studies" is from the U.S. Department of Education (2009).

7. See the website of the Center for Academic Transformation at Rensselear Polytechnic Institute (http://www.center.rpi.edu/).

8. For a report on the studies discussed, see Twigg (2003).

9. The MIT Open Course Ware site is http://ocw.mit.edu/OcwWeb/web/home/home/index.htm.

10. The Carnegie Mellon Open Learning Initiative site is http://oli.web.cmu.edu/openlearning/.

11. The *Chronicle of Higher Education* piece is Perry (2009).

Chapter 9

1. The data for figure 9.2 come from the Virginia State Council of Higher Education.

2. The data for figure 9.3 come from the Grapevine project at Illinois State University, http://www.grapevine.ilstu.edu/historical/index.htm (accessed December 10, 2009).

3. For more information on the effects of the tax revolt on public higher education, see Archibald and Feldman (2006).

4. The data for table 9.1 come from the Delta Cost Project website.

5. The data are from Winston (1999, 19).

Chapter 10

1. Hubbell and Lapovsky (2005) provide data about the practice of giving tuition discounts to 100 percent of students.

2. The data for private four-year institutions in table 10.1 come from two sources: first, *Trends in College Pricing* 2006 published by the College Board. *Trends* has information on list-price tuition, tuition minus grants, and tuition tax credits. The second source is Baum and Lapovsky (2008). Baum and Lapovsky give data that allows us to distinguish between institutional grants (tuition discounts) and grants and tax credits from outside sources. The tuition-discounting information is for 2003–4, which explains why we used the data for this academic year.

3. The data are from Hoxby (1997).

4. The quotation is from McPherson and Schapiro (1999, A48).

Chapter 11

1. The quotation of Roosevelt can be found in Blum (1965, 42).

2. Our discussion of federal financial aid programs leaves out the two newest programs: Academic Competitiveness Grants and National Science and Mathematics Access to Retain Talent (National SMART Grants). These grant programs started in 2006. We have left them out of the discussion because they are not available to all college students. Academic Competitiveness Grants are for first- and second-year college students who completed a very rigorous high school curriculum, and National SMART Grants are for the third and fourth years of college and are aimed at students specializing in particular courses of study. For details, see http://www.ed.gov/about/offices/list/ope/ac-smart-families.html (accessed October 14, 2009).

3. The data for figure 11.1 come from *Trends in Student Aid 2007* published by the College Board.

4. The data on state grants come from the National Association of State Student Grant and Aid Programs, *NASSGAP 38th Annual Survey Report on State-Sponsored Financial Aid 2006–07 Academic Year*.

5. The data for figure 11.2 come from *Trends in Student Aid 2007* published by the College Board.

Chapter 12

The first quotation is from the National Commission on the Cost of Higher Education (1998, 7).

The second quotation is from Boehner and McKeon (2003, 6).

1. The data in figures 12.1 and 12.2 combined data from three sources: Current Fund Expenditures of Public Four-Year Institutions is from table 346 of the 2007 *Digest of Educational Statistics*; Net Domestic Income is from table 1.76 on the Bureau of Economic Analysis website; and Civilian Employment is from the Bureau of Labor Statistics website. Unfortunately, the data for higher education costs are not available in a comparable fashion after 2000.

2. The data for table 12.1 come from U.S. Department of Education, *National Post-Secondary Student Aid Survey* (2009).

3. The data for table 12.2 come from the College Board, *Trends in College Pricing 2007*, and the U.S. Department of the Census.

Chapter 13

1. See Cunningham, Wellman, Clinedinst, Merisotis, and Carrol (2001) for the Department of Education study.

2. The quotation is from National Commission on the Cost of Higher Education (1998, 1).

3. The quotation is from McKeon (2003, B20).

Chapter 14

1. See Choy (1999) for the Department of Education study.

2. The Georgia HOPE Scholarships were not the first state merit-based program. That honor goes to Arkansas that initiated its program in 1991. The Arkansas program was a hybrid program mixing grade-average requirements and test-score requirements in an overall program that also was subject to income caps. We focus on the Georgia HOPE program because it is the much better known of the two early merit-based programs.

3. The quotation is from Day (2009, 9).

4. The quotation is from Friedman (1968, 108).

5. Grayer's plan is discussed in Zemsky (2009). Dunderstadt's proposal is discussed in Dunderstadt (2007).

6. The quotation is from Baum and McPherson (2008, 8).

7. We obtained the data for our cost estimate in the following way: data on the population from www.census.gov show 21,514,358 people aged 15, 16, 17, 18,or 19 years old. A 4-year span would be 17,211,486 students. If 60 percent of this age cohort were in college, there would be 10,326,892 students. This is a considerable increase over 2007 in which there were 6,490,499 full time undergraduates (See *Digest of Educational Statistics 2008*, "Table 191—Total Fall Enrollment in Degree-Granting Institutions, by Level of Enrollment, Sex, Age, and Attendance Status of Student: 2007"). We completed the estimate by multiplying the number of students by the Pell Grant maximum.

8. Data for the expenditures on grants come from the College Board's *Trends in Student Aid 2008*.

Chapter 15

1. A shorter version of the new compact argument can be found in Archibald and Feldman (2004).

2. For details of the Colorado Plan, see *Governor's Blue Ribbon Panel on Higher Education for the 21st Century* (2003). For details of the Miami of Ohio plan, see *Chronicle of Higher Education* (2003). For details of the University of Buffalo, see Carlson (2009).

Chapter 16

1. See *Wall Street Journal* (2009) for the story on the CEO's priorities.

Bibliography

Allen, I. Elaine, and Jeff Seaman. 2008. "Staying the Course: Online Education in the United States, 2008." Sloan Consortium. http://www.sloanconsortium.org/publications/survey/staying_course (accessed September 1, 2009).

Altman, Stuart H., and Robert Blendon, eds. 1979. *Medical Technology: The Culprit Behind Health Care Costs?* U.S. Department of Health, Education, and Welfare Publication Number (PHS) 79.3216.

Anderson, Martin. 1992. *Imposter in the Temple: American Intellectuals Are Destroying Our Universities and Cheating Our Students of Their Future.* New York: Simon & Schuster.

Archibald, Robert B., and David H. Feldman. 2002. "A New Compact for Higher Education in Virginia." http://faculty.wm.edu/dhfeld/NewCompact.pdf.

———. 2004. "Funding Students Instead of Institutions." *NACUBO Business Officer* 38 (October): 27–32.

———. 2006. "State Higher Education Spending and the Tax Revolt." *Journal of Higher Education* 77 (July/August): 618–44.

———. 2008. "Explaining Increases in Higher Education Costs." *Journal of Higher Education* 79 (May/June): 268–95.

———. 2009. "Why College Costs So Much." *William and Mary Alumni Magazine* 75 (Fall): 17.

Avery, Christopher, and Thomas J. Kane. 2004. "Student Perceptions of College Opportunities: The Boston COACH Program." In *College Choices: The Economics of Where to Go, When to Go, and How to Pay for It*, ed. Caroline M. Hoxby, 355–94. Chicago: University of Chicago Press.

Baum, Sandy, and Lucie Lapovsky. 2008. "Tuition Discounting: Not Just a Private College Practice." The College Board. http://www.collegeboard/prod_downloads/press/tution-discounting.pdf (accessed September 11, 2008).

———, and Michael McPherson. 2008. *Fulfilling the Commitment: Recommendations for Reforming Financial Aid: The Report of the Rethinking Student Aid Study Group.* http://professionals.collegeboard.com/profdownload/rethinking-stu-aid-fulfilling-commitment-recommendations.pdf.

Baumol,William J. 1967. "Macroeconomics of Unbalanced Growth: The Anatomy of an Urban Crisis." *American Economics Review* 57 (June): 415–26.

———, and S. A. Blackman. 1995. "How to Think About Rising College Costs. *Planning for Higher Education* 23 (Summer): 1–7.

———, and William G. Bowen. 1966. *Performing Arts: The Economic Dilemma.* New York: Twentieth Century Fund.

Bennett, William. 1987. "Our Greedy Colleges." *New York Times*, February 18, A27.

Binfield, Kevin. 2004. *Writings of the Luddites.* Baltimore: Johns Hopkins University Press.

Bloom, Allan. 1987. *The Closing of the American Mind.* New York: Simon & Schuster.

Blum, John Morton. 1965. *From the Morgenthau Diaries: Years of Urgency 1938–1941.* Boston: Houghton Mifflin.

Boehner, John A., and Howard P. "Buck" McKeon. 2003. *The College Cost Crisis; A Congressional Analysis of College Costs and Implications for America's Higher Education System.* http://cssp.us/pdf/CollegeCostCrisisReport.pdf (accessed October 15, 2009).

Bok, Derek. 2006. *Our Underachieving Colleges: A Candid Look at How Much Students Learn and Why They Should be Learning More.* Princeton, N.J.: Princeton University Press.

Bowen, Howard. 1980. *The Costs of Higher Education: How Much Do Colleges and Universities Spend Per Student and How Much Should They Spend?* San Francisco: Jossey-Bass.

Breneman, David. 2001. "An Essay on College Costs." In *Study of College Costs and Prices, 1988–89 to 1997–98*. Vol. 2, *Commissioned Papers*. National Center for Educational Statistics, NCES 2002-158.

Bulger, Daniel T., Gary T. Henry, and Ross Rubenstein. 1999. "An Evaluation of Georgia's HOPE Scholarship Program: Effects of HOPE on Grade Inflation, Academic Performance, and College Enrollment." Georgia State University. http://aysps.gsu.edu/publications/arc/csp/DownLoad/HOPE991.pdf (accessed December 9, 2009).

Carlson, Scott. 2009. "In a Shrinking City, a University Offers a Bold, and Chancy, Vision of Growth." *Chronicle of Higher Education*, August 3. http://chronicle.com/article/In-a-Shrinking-City-a-Bold/47531/ (accessed January 6, 2010).

Choy, Susan P. 1999. "College Access and Affordability." U.S. Department of Education, Office of Educational Research and Improvement, NCES 1999-108.

Chronicle of Higher Education. 2003. "Miami U. of Ohio Weighs Equal Tuition for State Residents and Outsiders Alike." http://chronicle.com/article/Miami-U-of-Ohio-Weighs-Equ/22403/.

Clotfelter, Charles T. 1991. "Financial Aid and Public Policy." In *Economic Challenges in Higher Education*, ed. Charles T. Clotfelter, Ronald G. Ehrenberg, Malcom Getz, and John J. Siegfried. Chicago: University of Chicago Press.

College Board. various years. *Trends in College Pricing.*

———. various years. *Trends in Student Aid.*

Cornwell, Christopher, David B. Mustard, and Deepa J. Sridhar. 2006. "The Enrollment Effects of Merit-Based Financial Aid: Evidence from Georgia's HOPE Scholarship." *Journal of Labor Economics* 24 (October): 761–86.

Cunningham, Alisa F., Jane V. Wellman, Melissa E. Clinedinst, Jamie P. Merisotis, and C. Dennis Carrol. 2001. "Study of College Costs and Prices, 1988–89 to 1997–98." U.S. Department of Education, NCES 2002-157.

Day, Philip R. 2009. *Preliminary Recommendations for the National Association of Student Financial Aid Administrators*. Washington, D.C.: NASFAA.

Delta Cost Project. http://www.deltacostproject.org/ (accessed December 10, 2009).

D'souza, Dinesh. 1991. *Illiberal Education: The Politics of Race and Sex on Campus*. New York: Free Press.

Dunderstadt, James J. 2007. "Raising the Bar: America's Challenge to Higher Education." Millennium Project papers, Ann Arbor, Michigan, January 12, 2007. http://milproj.dc.umich.edu/publications/raising_the_bar/index.html (accessed August 4, 2009).

Dynarski, Susan. 2000. "Hope for Whom? Financial Aid for the Middle Class and Its Impact on College Attendance." *National Tax Journal* 118 (September): 602–35.

———. 2003. "Does Aid Matter? Measuring the Effect of Student Aid on College Attendance and Completion." *American Economic Review* 93 (March): 279–88.

———. 2008. "Building the Stock of College-Educated Labor." *Journal of Human Resources* 43 (Summer): 576–610.

Economic Policy Institute Datazone. http://www.epi.org/page/-/old/datazone/06/wagebyed_a.xls (accessed May 20, 2009).

Ehrenberg, Ronald. 2000. *Tuition Rising: Why College Costs So Much*. Cambridge, Mass.: Harvard University Press.

———and Liang Zhang. 2005. "Do Tenured and Tenure-Track Faculty Matter?" *Journal of Human Resources* 40 (Summer): 647–59.

EU KLEMS website. http://www.euklems.net (accessed May 19, 2008).

Fletcher, Michael A. 2000. "A Sea Change in the Secretarial Pool; Clerical Ranks Shrink as the Jobs Evolve." *Washington Post*, May 11, A33.

Fong, Bobby. 2005. "The Economics of Higher Education." *Liberal Education* 91 (Winter): 42–47.

Friedman, Milton. 1968. "The Higher Schooling in America. *Public Interest* 11 (Spring): 108–12.

Garland, James C. 2009. *Saving Alma Mater: A Rescue Plan for America's Public Universities*. Chicago: University of Chicago Press.

Goldin, Claudia, and Lawrence Katz. 1999. "The Returns to Skill Across the Twentieth Century United States." NBER Working Paper no. 7126 (May).

———. 2008. *The Race Between Education and Technology*. Cambridge, Mass.: Harvard University Press.

———, and Robert Margo. 1992. "The Great Compression: The Wage Structure in the United States at Mid-Century." *Quarterly Journal of Economics* 107 (February): 1–34.

Governor's Blue-Ribbon Panel on Higher Education for the 21st Century. 2003. "Final Report" http://highered.colorado.gov/Publications/Studies/Taskforce/BlueRibbon/final/report.pdf. (accessed May 21, 2010).

Hansen, Janet S. 1991. "The Roots of Federal Student Aid Policy." *New Directions in Higher Education: The Changing Dimensions of Financial Aid* 74 (Summer): 3–19.

Hansen, W. Lee. 1983. "Impact of Student Financial Aid on Access." In *The Crisis in Higher Education*, ed. Joseph Froomkin. New York: Academy of Political Science.

Henry, Gary T., Steve Harkreader, Philo A. Hutcheson, and Craig S. Gordon. 1998. "HOPE Longitudinal Study First Year—Results." Council for School

Performance, Georgia State University. http://aysps.gsu.edu/publications/
acr/csp/DownLoad/HOPE_yr1.PDF (accessed October 1, 2009).

Hersh, Richard H., and John Merrow, eds. 2005. *Declining by Degrees: Higher Education at Risk*. New York: Palgrave Macmillan.

Hoxby, Caroline. 1997. "How the Changing Market Structure of U.S. Higher Education Explains College Tuition." National Bureau of Economics Research, Working Paper 6323 (December).

Hubbell, Loren Lumis, and Lucie Lapovosky. 2005. "Tuition Discounting: A 15-Year Retrospective and Current Issues." *NACUBO Business Officer*. Online feature article at http://www.NACUBO.org, July 2005. http://www.nacubo.org/Business_Officer_Magazine/Business_Officer_Plus/Tuition_Discounting_15_Years_in_Perspective.html (accessed October 15, 2009).

Ikenberry, Stanely O., and Terry W. Hartle. 1998. *Too Little Knowledge is a Dangerous Thing: What the Public Thinks and Knows About Paying for College*. Washington, D.C.: American Council on Education.

Illinois State University. Grapevine Project. www.grapevine.ilstu.edu.

Kane, Thomas J. 1994. "College Attendance by Blacks Since 1970: The Role of College Cost, Family Background, and the Returns to Education." *Journal of Political Economy* 102 (August): 878–911.

———. 1999. *The Price of Admission: Rethinking How Americans Pay for College*. Washington, D.C.: Brookings Institution.

Kimball, Roger. 1990. *Tenured Radicals: How Politics Has Corrupted Higher Education*. New York: Harper & Row.

Leslie, David. 2006. "Redistribution of Faculty Career Opportunity: 1988–2004." Paper presented at the Association for the Study of Higher Education (November 3), Anaheim, Calif.

Leslie, Larry, and Paul T. Brinkman. 1987. "Student Price Response in Higher Education: The Student Demand Studies." *Journal of Higher Education* 58 (March/April): 181–204.

Lewis, Darrell R., and Halil Dundary. 2001. "Costs and Productivity in Higher Education: Theory, Evidence, and Policy Implications." In *The Finance of Higher Education: Theory, Research, Policy and Practice*, ed. Michael B. Paulsen and John C. Smart, 133–188. New York: Agathon.

Manski, Charles F. 1993. "Income and Higher Education." *Focus* 14 (Summer/Fall): 14–19.

Massy, William. 2003. *Honoring the Trust: Quality and Cost Containment in Higher Education*. Bolton, Mass.: Anker Publishing Company.

———, and Andrea K. Wilger. 1992. "Productivity in Postsecondary Education: A New Approach." *Educational Evaluation and Policy Analysis* 14 (Winter): 361–76.

McKeon, Howard P. 2003. "Controlling the Price of College." *The Chronicle of Higher Education* 49 (July 11): B20.

McPherson, Michael S., and Morton Owen Schapiro. 1991. *Keeping College Affordable: Government and Educational Opportunity*. Washington, D.C.: Brookings Institution.

———. 1999. "Gaining Control of the Free-for-All in Financial Aid." *Chronicle of Higher Education* (July 2): A48.

———. 2006. "Watch What We Do Not What We Say: How Student Aid Awards Vary with Financial Need and Academic Merit." In *College Access: Opportunity or Privilege,* ed. Michael S. McPherson and Morton Owen Schapiro, 49–73. Washington, D.C.: College Board.

National Association of State Student Grant and Aid Programs. *NASSGAP 38th Annual Survey Report on State-Sponsored Financial Aid 2006–07 Academic Year.* http://www.nassgap.org/viewrepository.aspx?categoryID=3# (accessed October 14, 2009).

National Commission on the Cost of Higher Education. 1998. *Straight Talk About College Cost and Prices.* Phoenix: Oryx Press.

Perry, Marc. 2009. "Obama's Great Course Giveaway." *The Chronicle of Higher Education* (August 3).

Readings, Bill. 1990. *The University in Ruins.* Cambridge, Mass.: Harvard University Press.

Ricardo, David. 1821. *On the Principles of Political Economy and Taxation.* London: John Murray.

Rizzo, Michael J., and Ronald G. Ehrenberg. 2004. "Resident and Nonresident Tuition and Enrollment at Flagship State Universities." In *College Choices: The Economics of Where to Go, When to Go, and How to Pay for It,* ed. Caroline M. Hoxby, 303–53. Chicago: University of Chicago Press.

Seaman, Jeff. 2009. "Online Learning as a Strategic Asset—Volume II: The Paradox of Faculty Voices: Views and Experiences with Online Learning." Association of Public Land-Grant Universities (August).

Shaw, Peter. 1989. *The War against the Intellect: Episodes in the Decline of Discourse.* Iowa City: Iowa University Press.

Single, Larry D., Jr., and Joe A. Stone. 2007. "For whom the Pell Tolls: The Response of University Tuition to Federal Grants-in-Aid." *Economics of Education Review* 26 (June): 285–95.

Skocpol, T. 1995. "Targeting Within Universalism, Politically Viable Policies to Combat Poverty in the United States." Chapter 8 of *Social Policy in the United States: Future Possibilities in Historical Perspective.* Princeton, N.J.: Princeton University Press.

Smith, Marshall S. 2009. "Opening Education." *Science* 323 (January 2): 80–93.

Smith, Page. 1990. *Killing the Spirit: Higher Education in America.* New York: Viking.

Sykes, Charles J. 1988. *ProfScam: Professors and the Decline of Higher Education.* Washington, D.C.: Regency Gateway.

Triplett, Jack E., and Barry P. Bosworth. 2004. *Productivity in the U.S. Services Sector: New Sources of Economic Growth.* Washington, D.C.: Brookings Institution.

Twigg, Carol A. 2003. "Improving Quality and Reducing Costs: Designs for Effective Learning." *Change Magazine* (July/August): 22–29.

U.S. Department of Commerce, Bureau of Economic Analysis. "National Economic Accounts." various tables. http://www.bea.gov/national/nipaweb/SelectTable.asp?Selected=N——. "Data on Net Capital Stock of Private Non-Residential Fixed Assets." http://www.bea.gov/national/FA2004/Details/xls/detailnonres_stk1.xls (accessed May 20, 2009).

———. "Private Fixed Assets by Type." http://www.bea.gov/national/FA2004/SelectTable.asp#S2 (accessed May 20, 2008).

U.S. Department of Education, Office of Planning, Evaluation, and Policy Development. 2009. "Evaluation of Evidence-Based Practices in Online Learning: A Meta-Analysis and Review of Online Learning Studies." Washington, D.C.

U.S. Department of Education. *National Post-Secondary Student Aid Survey*. http://
    nces.ed.gov/surveys/npsas/ (accessed October 15, 2009).
————various years. *Digest of Educational Statistics*.
————Integrated Post-Secondary Data System. http://nces.ed.gov/ipeds/
U.S. Department of Labor, Bureau of Labor Statistics. Occupational Employment
    Statistics. http://www.bls.gov/oes/ (accessed May 20, 2008).
————"Employees on nonfarm payrolls by major industry sector 1960 to date"
    ftb//ftp.bls.gov/suppl/empsit.ceseeb1.txt (accessed May 21, 2010).
————. "Superseded Historical SIC Measures for Manufacturing, Durable
    Manufacturing, and Nondurable Manufacturing Sectors, 1949–2003." http://
    www.bls.gov/pc/home.html#data (accessed August 21, 2007).
————. *Occupational Employment in Selected Non-Manufacturing Industries*. 1981.
    Bulletin 2088.
————. *Occupational Employment in Mining, Construction, Finance, and Services*.
    1984. Bulletin 2186.
U.S. Department of the Census. "Historical Income Tables—Families." http://
    www.census.gov/hhes/www/income/fo7ar.html (accessed February 6,
    2008).
Vedder, Richard. 2004. *Going Broke by Degree: Why College Costs Too Much*.
    Washington, D.C.: The AEI Press.
Waldman, Don E., and Elizabeth J. Jensen. 2006. *Industrial Organization: Theory
    and Practice*, Boston: Pearson-Addison Wesley.
Wall Street Journal. 2009. "The CEO's Top Priorities," November 23, A22. http://
    online.wsj.com/article/SB10001424052748704204304574543633148686184.
    html (accessed January 7, 2010).
White House. 2009. http://www.whitehouse.gov/issues/Education/ (accessed
    January 7, 2010).
Wilshire, Bruce W. 1990. *The Moral Collapse of the University: Professionalism, Purity
    and Alienation*. Albany: State University Press of New York.
Wilson, W. J. 1987. *The Truly Disadvantaged: The Inner City, the Underclass, and
    Public Policy*. Chicago: University of Chicago Press.
Winston, Gordon C. 1999. "Subsidies, Hierarchy, and Peers: The Awkward
    Economics of Higher Education." *Journal of Economic Perspectives* 13 (Winter):
    13–36.
————. 2000. "The Positional Arms Race in Higher Education." Williams Project
    on the Economics of Higher Education, Discussion Paper 54 (April).
Zemsky, Robert. 2009. "Will Higher Education Ever Change as It Should?"
    Chronicle of Higher Education (August 7): A24–25.
————, William Wenger, and William Massy. 2005. *Remaking the American
    University; Market-Smart and Mission Centered*. New Brunswick, N.J.: Rutgers
    University Press.

Index